# GASLIGHT MELODRAMA

# Also available from Continuum International

Will Brooker
*Batman Unmasked*

Sue Harper
*Women in British Cinema*

Chris Jones and Genevieve Jolliffe
*The Guerrilla Film Makers Handbook, Second Edition*

Geoffrey Macnab
*Searching for Stars: Stardom and
Screen Acting in British Cinema*

Robert Murphy
*British Cinema and the Second World War*

Ulrike Sieglor (ed.)
*Heroines without Heroes: Reconstructing Female
and National Identities in European Cinema 1945–51*

Ginette Vincendeau
*Stars and Stardom in French Cinema*

# GASLIGHT MELODRAMA

## From Victorian London to 1940s Hollywood

Guy Barefoot

Continuum
NEW YORK   LONDON

2001

The Continuum International Publishing Group Inc
370 Lexington Avenue, New York, NY 10017

The Continuum International Publishing Group Ltd
The Tower Building, 11 York Road, London SE1 7NX

Printed in the United States of America

**Library of Congress Cataloging-in-Publication Data**

Barefoot, Guy, 1957–
     Gaslight melodrama : from Victorian London to 1940s Hollywood /
Guy Barefoot.
          p.   cm.
     Includes bibliographical references and index.
     ISBN  0-8264-5333-3 (alk. paper)— ISBN  0-8264-5334-1 (pbk. : alk.
paper)
     1. Melodrama in motion pictures.  2. Historical films—History and
criticism.  3. Gas-lighting.   I. Title.
     PN1995.9.M45 B37   2001
     791.43'653—dc21                                                      2001028475


**British Library Cataloging-in-Publication Data**
A Catalogue record for this book is available from the British Library.

     ISBN  0-8264-5333-3 hb
     ISBN  0-8264-5334-1 pb

To
Caroline, Christine,
Fere, Frank,
George,
Georgina, Ian,
John, Julian,
and Nick

# CONTENTS

# LIST OF ILLUSTRATIONS

# Acknowledgments

I AM GRATEFUL for the financial assistance of the British Academy, whose grant enabled me to visit Archives in the United States, and of Middlesex University, for helping fund the book's illustrations. My thanks to the staff of the Margaret Herrick Library, the Academy of Motion Picture Arts and Sciences; the Department of Special Collections, Theater Arts Library, UCLA; the UCLA Film and Television Archive; the Doheny Library, University of Southern California; the Library of Congress, Washington, D.C. (both the Humanities and Sciences as well as the Motion Picture, Broadcasting, and Recorded Sound Divisions); the National Archives at College Park, Maryland; the New York Public Library at the Lincoln Center for the Performing Arts; and to Charles Silver at the Museum of Modern Art, New York.

In Britain I have had help from staff at the British Library; the Newspaper Library at Colindale; the Mass Observation Archive at the University of Sussex; the Theatre Museum; and the London Gas Museum. At the British Film Institute I have had help from staff at the National Film and Television Archive; at the Department of Special Collections and (on many, many occasions) from staff at the BFI Library. My thanks to the members of the Gaslight and Victoria internet lists who helped me with my queries, and, of course, to Mr. Spamgle IV for the Monty Python information. Other individuals who are due thanks include Sara Barefoot, Christine Gledhill (whose enthusiastic teaching led me to the study of melodrama), Andrew Higson (for his detailed responses to this project when it was a Ph.D. thesis), Judith Palmer, and Paul Ward.

Finally, my thanks to Jane Greenwood, who originally commissioned this book, and to David Barker at Continuum for his editorial help.

Acknowledgment for the illustrations used in this book is made to Fotomas Index (Figure 1), Stills, Posters, and Designs at the BFI (Figures 2, 3, 4, 5, 6, 8, 9, 10 and 11), and MGM (courtesy of the Kobal Collection) (Figure 7).

# 1 Introduction: *Gaslight*, Gaslight, and Gaslight Melodrama

IN THE 1944 MGM film, *Gaslight,* a woman sees the gaslights dim when her husband is away from home. The fact that her perceptions are not confirmed, combined with her apparent tendency to lose or absentmindedly conceal objects, causes her to fear that she is also losing her sanity. By the end of the film it has become clear, to her and the audience, that her husband has been systematically attempting to drive her insane. Ten years previously he murdered her aunt but was disturbed before he could lay his hands on the object of his murder, a set of valuable jewels. Convinced that the jewels are still in the house, he has married his murder victim's niece, returned to the scene of his crime, and moved all the old furniture up into the attic, which he has had boarded up. He leaves the marital home only to return (by way of the empty house next door) to the attic, where he continues his search. The dimming of the light noticed by the woman is explained by her husband's lighting the gas on the floor above, while the 'lost' objects have been concealed by the husband as a ruse to make it seem that his wife is mad and should be committed to an asylum.

This particular scenario can be related to a wider trend. In the period between the late 1930s and the early 1950s a series of 'gaslight melodramas' set in the late-Victorian or Edwardian era were produced in the United States and Britain. In the following pages I will investigate the relationship between the melodramatic narratives of these films and their period settings. More generally, I will be studying films in the context of a broader pattern spanning literature, the theater, design, art-works, furnishings, and collectibles, and the responses to these different objects, productions and processes. I will trace a set of cultural discourses that meet in a specific cycle of films but which extend beyond those particular films and beyond film in general, looking at how individual films drew upon shifting, twentieth-century, Anglo-American attitudes to, and images of, an era on the edge of modernity.

Why gaslight melodrama?

Gaslight has an importance within the Hollywood film *Gaslight* as an element of the period furnishings, as a motivation for the film's 'expressionist' lighting, as a means of heightening suspense, in terms of a convoluted and melodramatic narrative, and a woman's subjective experience. Gaslighting was emphasized both within the film (from the opening to the closing credits, both shown over a shot of a domestic gaslamp) and in the film's promotional material (posters for 'MGM's melodrama' gave prominent space to a streetlamp lit by gas, and exhibitors were advised by MGM publicists to construct mock-gaslights to promote the film [see *Motion Picture Herald*, 6 May and 10 June 1944]), and of course in the film's title, which evoked the not so distant past and the Victorian theater, which had itself been lit by gas.

Gaslight features prominently in a number of other films of the 1940s, and provided reviewers with a means of identifying a marked trend within Hollywood. In *The Lodger* (also released in 1944) gaslighting is again featured beneath the credits, in the form of a pair of streetlights, and contributes to the *mise-en-scène* of the film as a whole. One reviewer praised *The Lodger* by writing of the producer that 'Robert Bassler has provided plenty of production values in carrying out with authenticity the London of the gaslight era' (*Variety*, 5 January 1944). The following year another reviewer identified *Experiment Perilous* as having 'a *Gaslight* theme' (*Los Angeles Times*, 21 June) and brought *Hangover Square* (an 'eerie murder melodrama of the London gaslight era' [*Variety*, 17 January]). There was an announcement *Morning Telegram* of 2 March that

> In keeping with the current cycle of mystery and horror pictures placed in the gaslight era of the turn of the century, M-G-M studios have now resuscitated Oscar Wilde's 'Picture of Dorian Gray,' putting it on exhibition yesterday at the Capital Theatre with all the fanfare and flourishes usually accorded important events at the cinema. All dressed up with extravagant sets and some pretty fine acting, it is right in line with the prevalent notion in Hollywood that eerie things and peculiar plots can be much better shown in costume than in modern dress.

The following years saw the release of *The Spiral Staircase* ('with a setting sometime back in the gaslight era': *New York World-Telegram*,

6 February 1946), *Ivy* (described in the London *Evening Standard*, 26 September 1947, as taking place in 'London by gaslight'), *Moss Rose* ('a new gaslight thriller': *New Yorker*, 12 July 1947) and *So Evil My Love* ('a true story of gaslit crime and passion': *Look*, 20 July 1948).

'Robert Siodmak, the director of *The Suspect*, once made a film called *Phantom Lady*, which has remained in my mind as a model picture of city night life,' noted Helen Fletcher in a review published in *Time & Tide* (12 May 1945):

> You'd think that, remembering *Phantom Lady*, his company would decree that in *The Suspect* tobacconist Laughton would murder his shrewish first wife to marry enchanting Ella Raines in the New York of today or at least in pre-war New York? But no, there's no world of today save the world of London by gaslight . . .

The particular combination of gaslight, crime, and melodrama evident in these and other films has not been restricted to either the United States or the cinema. *So Evil My Love* was produced for a Hollywood studio (Paramount) but filmed in Britain. *Fanny by Gaslight* (1944), another film made in Britain (in this case for the British studio, Gainsborough), was based on a novel of the same name, written by Michael Sadleir and first published in 1941. The same year also saw the publication of Howard Haycraft's *Murder for Pleasure: The Life and Times of the Detective Story*, in which Haycraft discussed the Sherlock Holmes stories in a chapter titled 'Profile by Gaslight.' The phrase 'profile by gaslight' was subsequently used for the title of a book, published in 1944, devoted to the investigator created by Sir Arthur Conan Doyle, in which Haycraft's discussion was reprinted, and which, in the words of the introduction, looked back to 'that nostalgic gas-lit London of the late nineteenth century which saw the realization of a snug and peaceful world that never would be any the worse and never could be any better' (Smith, 1944: no page number given).

The use of 'gaslight settings,' especially in conjunction with crime narratives, was noted in other films and books of the 1940s, and also in the theater. Gaslit settings were featured in both films concerned with crime and its investigation, such as *The Adventures of Sherlock Holmes* (1940), *The Verdict* (1946), *Room to Let* (1949), and in films such as *Dr. Jekyll and Mr. Hyde* (1941) and *The Picture of Dorian Gray* (1945), that added an element of the supernatural to their portrait of late-Victorian London. William Dinner and William Morum's stage play *The Late Edwina Black* was described by one reviewer as 'a neat and highly ingenious murder thriller in the "Gaslight" tradition' (*Reynolds News*, 17 July 1949); another theater reviewer, discussing *Pink String and Sealing Wax*, wrote that 'crime in costume remains the vogue. Your modern Othello would throw off a deer-stalker and Inverness cape before observing "Put out the gas-light"' (*Observer*, 5 September 1943). The latter play led the review-er for *The Times* to write that 'this particular gas-light, however, does not achieve the lurid glint which has shone in other exercises of this particular *genre*' (2 September 1943). Both *Pink String and Sealing Wax* and *The Late Edwina Black* were subsequently made into films, released in 1945 and 1951 respectively.

Not all these films, plays, and books reached a large audience, but *Gaslight* itself was, in its different forms, extraordinarily popu-lar throughout and beyond the 1940s. The MGM film version was based on Patrick Hamilton's play, *Gas Light: A Victorian Thriller*, and followed on from an earlier, British film adaptation of the same play. The play had opened at the Richmond Theatre at the end of 1938. In 1939 it transferred to London's West End, where it had a successful run. The same year it became one of the earliest stage pro-ductions broadcast on British television. It was then made into a film, starring Anton Walbrook and Diane Wynyard and directed by Thorold Dickinson for British National, which was released in Britain in May 1940. After being performed in Los Angeles, in December 1941 the play opened in New York under the title *Angel Street*. It was to prove to be one of the major successes of the Broadway stage during World War II, running for 1,295 perform-ances. It was still running on Broadway when the MGM film was released in May 1944. 'Nothing, apparently, can kill *Angel Street*, although one war, one movie and the ravages of time upon actors have tried to do so,' wrote the reporter for the *New York Daily News* (9 June 1944)—perhaps unaware that the play had been filmed not once but twice (though the British film was not publicly shown in the United States until 1952, when it was released under the title of the American stage version, *Angel Street*).

As well as the Broadway production, the play toured through-out the United States during the 1940s. It returned to Broadway in 1948 and to the West End in 1950. It was translated into French, Spanish, and German, and performed by a variety of theater groups from amateur companies (with whom the play became an established favorite) to the American Negro Repertory Production Company. Following on from the British television production of 1940, American television versions were broadcast in 1948, 1950, 1953, 1954, and 1958. Further British television versions were transmitted in 1947 and 1957 (for further details of stage and American television productions, see Leonard, 1981: 598–603). Jack Benny parodied the story, first on radio, then on television, with Barbara Stanwyck now playing the suffering wife. *Autolight*, Benny's television parody, was made in 1953, but its broadcast was delayed due to a legal dispute, in which it was argued that the television sketch constituted an infringement of copyright; in 1958 the Supreme Court decided that this was indeed the case, though *Autolight* was eventually broadcast in 1959 following Benny's payment of a fee to the playwright and the film company. Eventually, having been performed and parodied on the stage, the radio, the cinema screen, and the television screen, in the 1960s *Gaslight* was rewritten, by William Drummond, as a novel, appearing in the United States as *A Paperback Library Gothic* in 1966, and in a version published by Arrow books in Britain in 1967.

'Millions thrilled to the play "Angel Street" in New York and London,' it was claimed on the back of the American paperback edition of Drummond's novel. 'Millions of movie fans thrilled to Ingrid Bergman and Charles Boyer in the film version called GASLIGHT. Now an even more chilling experience awaits you in this taut masterpiece of Gothic terror and suspense.' 'Taut masterpiece' is a generous description of the novelization, but it is undeniable that, in its different forms, *Gaslight* has been highly popular and enduring. It is also true that, in their different forms, gaslight settings were prevalent throughout the 1940s. However, the popularity of *Gaslight*, and even praise for *Gaslight*, did not mean that it was seen as anything more than entertainment. Writing of the Broadway production of Patrick Hamilton's play, Burns Mantle announced (*New York Daily News*, 6 December 1941):

I have just seen the theatre come alive for the first time this season. But don't get me wrong. I mean the THEATRE. Not the important theatre. Or the theatre of social significance. No, no—not the intellectual theatre. Or the pseudo-intellectual theatre. Just the good old emotional hokum theatre in which your interest is definitely challenged around about 9:15 and held taut until 11 o'clock.

While even an enthusiast saw the combination of gaslight and melodrama as no more than 'emotional hokum' (taut, but no masterpiece), others saw different variations of that combination as old-fashioned and outmoded. '*Dr. Jekyll and Mr. Hyde* is unfortunately a dated play. It springs from the gaslight days, and scriptwriter John Lee Mahin has done little to modernize its tone,' complained one reviewer of the 1941 film version of Robert Louis Stevenson's story (*Brooklyn Daily Eagle*, 13 August 1941). The American release of the film adaptation of *Pink String and Sealing Wax* prompted the reviewer for the *New York Times* to write that, 'having dug back into England's gaslit past for what undoubtedly was meant to be a sharp view of Victorian life, the British film makers who fashioned *Pink String and Sealing Wax* have come up with a movie memento as archaic as a bustle' (4 October 1950). The verdict of *Variety* on *Uncle Silas*, another British film, was that the 'best hope for this is to exhibit it as a comic interpretation of a past era. As such it might draw here' (22 October 1947). Even the headline carried by the *Washington-Times-Herald* (17 February 1942)—'*Angel Street* at the National Electric Entertainment'—carried with it the implication that 'gaslit entertainment' might normally be expected to be less dynamic, less electrifying.

There is a scene in *The Lady Eve* (1940), the screwball comedy directed by Preston Sturges, in which a pair of confidence tricksters (played by Charles Coburn and Barbara Stanwyck) posing as nobility discuss the tricks they have played, and intend to continue to play, on a American millionaire (played by Henry Fonda). The scene contains the following exchange:

| | |
|---|---|
| SIR ALFRED: | . . . I took the further precaution of telling him the plot of 'Cecilia, or the Coachman's Daughter . . . a gaslight melodrama.' |
| THE LADY EVE! | (awe-struck): No! |
| SIR ALFRED : | Yes, I have to protect myself, too, you know. I have a shouting interest around here. I fed him full of hand some young coachmen, elderly Earls, young wives, and two little girls who looked exactly alike. |
| THE LADY EVE: | You mean he swallowed that? |
| SIR ALFRED : | Like a wolf . . .[1] |

'Gaslight melodrama' could signify a past lacking sophistication, an aristocratic world that even in the nineteenth century existed only on the stage or in the novel, and that in the twentieth century had become so transparently implausible that it could only deceive a character such as Henry Fonda's gullible Charles Pike. Melodrama itself has been looked down upon for its lack of sophistication, as a form of debased theater, one that deals in stereotypes, overblown emotions, unreal coincidences, moral schematization, and sentimentality. Why bother with such hokum?

These attitudes persist—it is still common to use 'melodramatic' as a derogatory term—yet in the past few decades they have been increasingly challenged. Thomas Elsaesser's article, 'Tales of Sound and Fury: Some Observations on the Family Melodrama,' first published in 1972, was one key work in this process. Another was *The Melodramatic Imagination: Balzac, Henry James, Melodrama, and the Mode of Excess*, a study, originally published in 1976, in which Peter Brooks argued that melodrama, far from being mere hokum, was central 'to an understanding of an important and abiding mode in the modern imagination' (1985: ix). Brooks discussed the nineteenth-century stage and the novel, and when Louis James announced that over the previous decade melodrama had moved on from being a term of critical abuse and was even acquiring a certain (and perhaps not entirely welcome) respectability (1980: 3), his primary point of reference was theater and literary studies. However, these developments had a vital influence within film studies. Christine Gledhill's introduction to the anthology, *Home is Where the Heart Is: Studies in Melodrama and the Woman's Film*, in particular, drew upon the work of Brooks in her identification of melodrama as a 'Nineteenth-Century Paradigm,' which laid down the 'institutional and aesthetic foundations from which cinema would draw' (1987: 19–24).

As Steve Neale noted, 'far from signalling the culmination of work in these areas, the publication of *Home is Where the Heart Is* coincided with and further helped to promote and to focus a great deal of additional publication and research' on melodrama and the woman's film (1999: 164–65). Among those publications was a further anthology based on papers delivered at the conference on melodrama that took place in London in 1992, an anthology that, the editors argued, pointed to 'melodrama's key role in modernity as a mediator of social and political change through diverse and personalized forms of popular culture' (Bratton, Cook, and Gledhill, 1994: 8).

While writers such as Brooks and Gledhill have made broad claims for melodrama, another tendency has been to focus on particular forms which melodrama has taken. The two tendencies can be found in Elsaesser's 'Tales of Sound and Fury,' in which he examines both 'the melodramatic imagination' over time and in different forms, and what he called 'the Hollywood family melodrama' of the 1950s, focusing in particular on the films of one director, Douglas Sirk, and on one of his films, *Written on the Wind* (1956) (see Elsaesser, 1987: 43). Initially it was the concern with the melodramas made in the 1950s by Sirk, as well as other directors such as Vincente Minnelli and Nicholas Ray, that was predominant within film studies, though over time interest has spread to the melodramas produced during other periods of Hollywood's history, to other forms of Hollywood melodrama, and to cinemas other than Hollywood. That initial concern was also, as Paul Willemen put it, with a group of family melodramas made 'by, for, and about Eisenhower America' (1972–73: 130). But if the significance of Hollywood melodrama lay in the way in which it was rooted in contemporary American society, where would that leave a melodrama such as *Gaslight*, dressed as it was in the costumes of the nineteenth century?

Nineteenth-century theatrical practices have indeed been increasingly acknowledged as having a central influence on Hollywood melodrama, but in their own ways nineteenth-century melodramas had often been by, for, and about their time. For David Grimstead 'the worst clichés of melodrama in the nineteenth century—the heroine tied to the railway tracks or the family about to be tossed into the snow for lack of mortgage money—were telling symbols for the latent fears in a society characterized by rapid technological change and widespread home ownership on time payments' (1971: 84). For Gledhill, links with the nineteenth century should not mislead one into understanding melodrama as an archaic form, since 'Americanization and Hollywood in particular facilitated the modernization of melodrama' (1992: 131). Yet the very notion of a Hollywood gaslight melodrama might suggest an archaism. Melodrama in general may have had a key role in modernity (a role once shared by gaslighting) but it might seem plausible to see *Gaslight* as one melodrama that remained stuck in the nineteenth century, perhaps even in the outmoded and implausible world of a gaslight melodrama such as 'Cecilia, or the Coachman's Daughter.'

In fact, the story of a man's attempt to make it appear that his wife is insane has been seen as having a vital relevance beyond the Victorian and a significance beyond the ability to grip an audience for a little under two hours. According to Adrienne Rich (1980: 90)

> Women have been driven mad, 'gaslighted,' for centuries by the refutation of our experience and our instincts in a culture that validates only male experience. The truth of our bodies and our minds has been mystified to us. We therefore have a primary duty to each other; not to undermine each other's sense of reality for the sake of expediency; not to gaslight each other.

The long-lasting popularity of *Gaslight* might therefore be explained by its continued resonance as well as by the efficiency of its narrative in the creation of suspense. That narrative has had a relevance across time that has appealed to different ethnic groups, nationalities, and eras. As an example of melodrama that Grimstead (1971) called the echo of the historically voiceless—'At last I can tell this to someone!' says the heroine at the end of the MGM film—its narrative of domestic tyranny and a woman's perception denied and then affirmed has a relevance by no means limited to the time of its settings or of its initial performances.

'Gaslighting' has come to be understood in even broader terms. In *Gaslighting: The Double Whammy, Interrogation, and Other Methods of Covert Control in Psychotherapy and Psychoanalysis*, Theo Dorpat observes that several 'British authors employ the term gaslighting or gaslight phenomenon to describe those situations in which an individual attempts to make others feel that a second individual is insane so that the latter will be taken to a mental hospital. Later studies in England and the United States considerably broadened the boundaries of the gaslighting concept' (1996: 32). For Dorpat gaslighting exists as a term to refer to 'the most commonly used and effective type of verbal communication individuals have for manipulating and controlling other people.' He notes that other writers had persuasively argued 'that gaslighting phenomena are both ubiquitous and inevitable. They play a significant role in human relationships, exert an important influence in the marriage relationship, and exercise a sometimes overlooked impact on the course of psychotherapy' (33).

In 1995 Maureen Dowd wondered whether then Republican leader Newt Gingrich had seen *Gaslight*. She explained her speculation by suggesting that Gingrich was the subject of a 'gaslight strategy' orchestrated by the White House with a view to making people doubt his sanity. '"Newt will not end up playing Ingrid Bergman. And somehow I can't see Clinton as Charles Boyer,"' was the reported counter from a Gingrich spokesperson. Anyway, Dowd concluded, 'the Gaslight strategy is misplaced. In the movie, the husband tried to make the wife unstrung because she wasn't unstrung. You can't Gaslight someone who is already a little lit' (*New York Times*, 26 November). Clinton and Gingrich, along with Dorpat's use of the word *gaslight*, takes us some distance from Hamilton's play, its film adaptations, similar films, and the time when they were first made and seen, as well as from the explicitly feminist concerns raised by Rich. However, such references draw upon the narrative of Hamilton's play and its later versions, and are a sign of the resonance of that narrative beyond an evening's entertainment.[2]

Another writer has addressed both those concerns while also attempting to examine what she at one point calls the 'gaslight films' of the 1940s in their historical context. According to Tania Modleski (1984: 21):

> In the forties, a new movie genre derived from Gothic novels appeared around the time that hard-boiled detective fiction was being transformed by the medium into what movie critics currently call '*film noir.*' Not surprisingly, *film noir* has received much critical scrutiny both here and abroad, while the so-called 'gaslight' genre has been virtually ignored. According to many critics, *film noir* possesses the greatest sociological importance (in addition to its aesthetic importance) because it reveals male paranoid fears, developed during the war years, about the independence of women on the homefront. Hence the necessity in these movies of destroying or taming the aggressive, mercenary, sexually dynamic 'femme fatale' whose presence is indispensable to the genre. Beginning with Alfred Hitchcock's 1940 movie version of *Rebecca* and continuing through and beyond George Cukor's *Gaslight* in 1944, the gaslight films may be seen to reflect women's fears about losing their unprecedented freedoms and being forced back into their homes after the men returned from fighting to take over their jobs and assume control over their families.

These comments introduce another set of issues. They raise questions about the relationship between the shadowy interiors of

*Gaslight* and the darkness of *film noir*, and the significance of gender in the nature of this relationship. They raise the issue of whether we should see films such as *Gaslight* as part of a female Gothic tradition, and thus for the purposes of the present discussion of the relationship between the Gothic, the melodramatic, and films that address a female audience. They also raise the issue of the relationship between cinema and its social context.

Raising these issues also raises a number of problems. There are problems with attempting to understand films as a direct reflection of audience fears, and more specifically, with understanding Hollywood films as a reflection of female fears, in particular with understanding *Rebecca*—a film released in 1940 before the United States had even entered World War II—as a reflection of women's fears of losing their jobs after the war was over. There are also questions to be asked about how we might understand terms such as *Gothic* and *film noir* and where *Gaslight* and other examples of what Modleski calls 'the gaslight genre' but which I refer to as the gaslight melodrama, might be placed in relation to such terms. And if one goes back to those films, and understands them as being about the 1940s rather than 1880s, 1890s, or 1900s, questions remain as to the significance of their period settings.

This book is an attempt to investigate that significance. My concern is with a cycle of films, with the examination of those films in relation to the period in which they were produced and exhibited, as well as a particular examination of their use of period settings, and the connotations that those particular settings had in the 1940s, from outmoded implausibility through sentimental appeal to patriarchal threat and more.

Like Modleski, I am interested in investigating films that drew upon a tradition that might be called Gothic, which appeared during and immediately after World War II, but which have tended to remain in the shadow of the 'hard-boiled' narratives of *film noir*. In the third chapter of this book I will investigate some of the complexities of what is meant by a Gothic tradition, and at different stages I will be discussing some of the complexities of the relationship between the critical constructions that are *film noir* and the gaslight melodrama. In undertaking this investigation I will be concerned with some of the films cited by Modleski and other writers who have done much to make up for the neglect that Modleski identified, under an assortment of different labels, from Mary Ann

Doane's 'paranoid woman's film' to Diane Waldman's 'Gothic romance film' (see Doane, 1988, and Waldman, 1983). However, though my own work overlaps and has drawn upon such studies, it differs from these on a number of counts.

My interest in films set in the late-Victorian or Edwardian era means that my own research has not been focused on *Rebecca* or other non-period films, nor will I be examining a 'Gothic romance' such as *Dragonwyck* (1946), which is set earlier in the nineteenth century. At the same time, my interest in the combination of turn-of-the-century settings and narratives of crime and sensation means that I will be examining a film such as *Hangover Square* which displays a good many of the symptoms of 'male paranoid fears' ('femme fatale' included) that others have detected as central to *film noir*. My intention here is to examine films in relation to their time in the sense that I want to look at the use of the past in a range of media including film. In particular, I want to investigate the often-conflicting attitudes evoked by the legacy of Victorianism and Victoriana traceable in Hollywood films, in films made in Britain, and in a wider cultural context. *Gaslight* has been seen as a critique of Victorian values (see chapter four), though this approach has tended to be formulated in response to the British rather than the American film version, and also to other British films of the 1940s. Yet, *Gaslight* and gaslit settings can and have been linked to a revival of interest in Victoriana (see chapter five). My concern with period settings, if partly directed towards films set just after the Victorian era, will lead me to examine the relationship between conflicting attitudes to the past as revealed in a series of films, and to investigate from where those attitudes came.

*Gaslight Melodrama* builds upon a doctoral thesis in which I focused on ten films. Concerned with setting up clear parameters to my research, my thesis was directed toward the examination of Hollywood crime melodramas with turn-of-the-century English or American settings, released between 1944 and 1950, in relation to theories of melodrama, the Hollywood studio system, and the films' cultural context. The essence of my understanding of 'crime melodrama' was that it signified a narrative that featured a crime, the investigation of that crime, the establishment and reward of innocence, and the identification and punishment of the guilty. My understanding of a Hollywood crime melodrama was that it included films made for one or other of the Hollywood studios, whether in the United States or elsewhere—hence, that it included *So Evil My Love*, a film made in Britain for Paramount. I identified the particular way in which *The Lodger* and *Gaslight* (both released in the first half of 1944) combined crime melodrama and late-Victorian settings to subsequently serve as a template in the formation and understanding of a cycle of Hollywood films set in the English or American past, arguing that the box-office success of these two films was influential in the production of three further titles—*Experiment Perilous*, *Hangover Square*, and *The Suspect*—released between December 1944 and February 1945, and that the pattern remained strong enough to produce further examples of the cycle in 1946 (*Spiral Staircase*), 1947 (*Ivy* and *Moss Rose*), 1948 (*So Evil My Love*), and, at the tail end, 1950 (*House by the River*). There are variations in the narratives and settings of these films, but their examination revealed a strong pattern of resemblance among them, while an examination of the discourses surrounding the films (from studio memos to newspaper reviews) indicated a marked contemporary understanding of these films in terms of melodramatic narratives and 'gaslight' settings, hence my own identification of the films as gaslight melodramas.

Some criteria of inclusion and exclusion are necessary in any research project, but this attempt to set up clear boundaries now seems limiting in more senses than one. Film cycles and genres have a significance in terms of what films are made and how those films are received, but they are not discrete categories. The material that I have examined has convinced me that in the 1940s the combination of gaslight settings and melodramatic narratives was a clearly recognized and significant phenomenon, one that certainly had more contemporary recognition than *film noir*, though such material has also brought home the degree to which gaslight melodramas could be presented and recognized under other generic categories.

'CRIME, MYSTERY OR ROMANTIC DRAMA—WHICH IS YOUR CHOICE? Perfect crime/gripping mystery/eternal love interest—which one of the three will produce the best box-office results at your theater? Concentrate on one, two or all three angles in ads and theater displays.' These questions, found in the American pressbook for MGM's *Gaslight* and directed at exhibitors of that film, point to how film genres in general are more fluid than they have often been characterized, and how *Gaslight* in particular can be seen as a blending of different genres.[3]

In addition, the significance of the combination of gaslight settings and melodramatic narratives was not restricted to ten films. To
begin with, there were other Hollywood films, such as *The Verdict*
(1946), a story of murder and investigation in 1890s London, which
merited consideration but which had been largely omitted in my
original study. Secondly, a number of other generically similar films
were made in Britain around this time. The MGM *Gaslight* came
out the same year that Gainsborough's *Fanny by Gaslight* was
released in Britain, and had been preceded by a film version of
Patrick Hamilton's play, produced at British National in 1940, while
the postwar period saw the release of *Pink String and Sealing Wax*
(1945), *The Mark of Cain* (1947), *Madeleine* (1949), *Room to Let*
(1949), and, moving into the early 1950s, *The Late Edwina Black*
(1951). My discussion here will concentrate on American rather
than British films, but in many ways what I am investigating is an
Anglo-American phenomenon, so it seems sensible, and illuminating, to refer to gaslight melodramas filmed in Britain (for American
and British companies) as well films made in Hollywood.

A few low-budget Hollywood productions of the 1940s—*The
Mystery of Marie Roget* (1942), *Bluebeard* (1944), and *Catman of
Paris* (1946)—used nineteenth-century Paris as the scene of crime
and its investigation, as did the more expensive (but generically
rather different) *Phantom of the Opera* (1943). The same city features in the British-made *The Face at the Window* (1939), *Latin
Quarter* (1945), and *So Long at the Fair* (1950), while sequences set
in Paris or other French locations occur in *Fanny by Gaslight*, *The
Verdict*, *The Mark of Cain*, and *So Evil My Love*. In investigating an
Anglo-American phenomenon my main concern remains with films
with British (which usually means English and often London) and
American settings. However, it is necessary to note the significance
of Paris in the generic world of this cycle of films, and also to be
aware of how a few other films placed a similar narrative pattern in
other locations: early twentieth-century Italy in the case of *A Man
about the House* (GB, 1947) and early twentieth-century Cairo in
*Temptation* (US, 1946), for example.

Some of the films listed above veer towards the horror genre and
suggest supernatural explanations or implications, which differenti-
ates them from crime narratives. At least two other films from the
1940s that invoke the supernatural—*Dr. Jekyll and Mr. Hyde*
(1941) and *The Picture of Dorian Gray* (1945)—are located in

essentially the same gaslit London presented in films such as *Moss Rose*, *The Lodger,* and *Gaslight,* and have therefore been included in this investigation. What this also suggested was a need to examine a broader timeframe. Examining the British film version of *Gaslight* as the well as the American version means going at least as far back as the beginning of the 1940s, and this longer span suggests the need to consider other Hollywood films, notably *Ladies in Retirement* (1941), *The Adventures of Sherlock Holmes* (1940), and *The Hound of the Baskervilles* (1939), as part of the same trend.

It would be possible to look further back. The latter two films were certainly not the first to feature Sherlock Holmes, while the 1941 version of *Dr. Jekyll and Mr. Hyde* had been preceded by a 1932 film version of the same story, a number of versions made in 1920, and several more prior to that date. *The Lodger* was the third film version of Marie Belloc Lowndes's novel of the same name, and in featuring Jack-the-Ripper it followed in the footsteps of two German films, *Waxworks* (1925) and *Pandora's Box* (1928). *The Threepenny Opera* (1931) was another German film that had presented a version of criminality in Victorian London, as did the first part of *To New Shores* (1937), while the British *The Face at the Window* was one of a series of melodramas of nineteenth-century crime starring Tod Slaughter, the first of which, *Maria Marten*, was released in 1935.

Some of these and other films from the 1930s and earlier will feature in the following chapters, though this study will be restricted to films and other material, made in the United States or Britain. Thus, in chapter four I will be examining how versions of Victorian repression are presented (and varied) in different film adaptations of Robert Louis Stevenson's *The Strange Case of Dr. Jekyll and Mr. Hyde*, with particular emphasis on the 1941 film but also with reference to the 1932 film and 1920 version starring John Barrymore. However, my research has led me to conclude that the combination of narratives of crime or sensation and late-nineteenth-/early-twentieth-century settings only became a significant element of film production in both Britain and the United States at the end of the 1930s and the beginning of the 1940s. It became a particularly identifiable trend in the middle years of the decade, though by choosing to examine the British as well as the American film version of *Gaslight*, as well as other films such as the 1941 version of *Dr. Jekyll and Mr. Hyde*, this has moved toward being a study of films made during the 1940s (as well as of the material upon which those films drew).

Of course, trends rarely fit neatly into decades. Patrick Hamilton's play *Gas Light* was first performed in the 1930s; *House by the River* was shot in 1949 but released in March 1950. In what follows I will discuss certain films made in the 1930s, and though I do not examine in any depth any film released later than 1950, it is worth noting that the British-made period crime film *The Late Edwina Black* was released in 1951, as was Hollywood's *Kind Lady*, while in 1952 MGM returned to serial murder in gaslit London with *The Hour of 13*—the same year that saw the belated American release of the British film version of *Gaslight*. Moving a little further on in time, at the beginning of 1954 20th Century-Fox released *The Man in the Attic*, a remarkably close remake of the version of *The Lodger* that the same company had released almost exactly ten years before. Yet if this indicates generic continuity, it also points to broader changes within Hollywood. *The Man in the Attic* was a semi-independent production, made by 'Panoramic Productions' for 20th Century-Fox, a move away from the vertically integrated system of production, distribution, and exhibition that gave rise to films such as the 1944 version of *The Lodger*. And while the 1944 film helped to bring a spate of gaslight melodramas, the 1954 film had no such effect.

Beyond the films already cited, reference will be made to a number of other titles which are relevant to the phenomenon I am examining but which cannot properly be described as gaslight melodramas. For example, in examining shifting attitudes toward the Victorian era it is appropriate to refer to *Victoria the Great* (1937)— not a film that emphasizes crime or sensation. But part of the point here is that it is impossible to examine genres only in terms of a group of films which conform to clear-cut generic conventions. This book could be seen as being concerned with two different tendencies within filmmaking—the crime film and the period film—and how particular films provide a meeting point for those tendencies.

*Gaslight Melodrama* has a broad, but overlapping, chronological structure. In chapter two I investigate the significance of gaslights and gaslighting in the nineteenth-century imagination, comparing and contrasting that significance with the role that gaslight has had in the cinema, along with the particular connotations it brought to crime narratives. I pursue related concerns in chapter three, in which I examine the sources of the gaslight melodramas of the 1940s, looking at the specific, generally twentieth-century, material from which they were directly adapted, as well as going back to the previous century to look at the tradition of narratives of urban crime to which they can be linked. Of a particular concern here is the relationship between nineteenth-century accounts of 'darkest London' and the representation of that city in American and British films of the 1940s. A further, related concern is with the notion of a Gothic tradition re-emerging in the films of this decade.

In chapter four I look at the twentieth-century reaction against the Victorian era, examining when such a reaction emerged, the forms it took, and how it developed, as well as the extent to which it is identifiable within the cinema. I am concerned here with questions of the relationship between intellectual trends and mass culture, and between modernity and the cinema. I am particularly concerned with screen (and to some extent stage) versions of two rather different Victorian novels: *East Lynne* and *The Strange Case of Dr. Jekyll and Mr. Hyde*. The primary focus is with Hollywood films and other American discourses, but the chapter also contains an examination of a reaction against Victorianism that took place in both Britain and the United States, and I refer to a number of British-made films that have been identified with this reaction.

In chapter five I look at how, from at least the 1930s onward, anti-Victorianism came to be combined with (and complicated by) a revival of interest in Victoriana. Again, my concern here is with film and its cultural context. I discuss how certain films appeal to the charm of the past as well as the cultural context that these films draw upon. I am particularly interested in signs of a revival of interest in Victoriana which becomes identifiable by the 1940s, though, just as I am concerned in chapter four with the complexities of a reaction against the Victorian, so in chapter five I address the ambivalences contained with this revival.

Some of these complexities and ambivalences are highlighted through a discussion of the MGM version of *Gaslight*. This focus on an individual film is extended in the following chapter, which is largely devoted to the textual analysis of two further gaslight melodramas—*The Suspect* and *House by the River*—though here again the MGM *Gaslight* will also be considered. I will examine the ways in which these (but also other) films function as melodramas, and the relationship between their period *mise-en-scène*, their melodramatic narratives, and the paradigm of classical Hollywood cinema. My overall conclusion will be set out in chapter seven, in which I will suggest the place of this particular study within film studies.

# 2 INDUSTRIAL LIGHT AND MAGIC: IMAGES OF GASLIGHT FROM THE NINETEENTH TO THE TWENTIETH CENTURY

ON 24 OCTOBER 1946, a memo was sent listing a series of changes that had been decided upon at a 20th Century-Fox script conference on the film *Moss Rose*. The changes, proposed by production chief Darryl Zanuck, began:

> Page 1, Line 1. Instead of the opening now in the script, the following was suggested: We come in on a long shot of a street. Gas lights of the period; wet pavement; fog.[1]

A slightly different opening had been added by the time the film was completed in 1947. The opening credits of the released film are shown over a montage of shots of a fast-moving train; the following shot is of the central character, Belle Adair (Peggy Cummins), in a darkened train carriage, partially illuminated by the lights of the surroundings as they flash past. This brief sequence is used to frame and introduce the main story, which begins as Zanuck had suggested, in a damp, foggy, and gaslit London street. The train is only returned to at the very end of the film, in a sequence which reveals that Belle Adair has left not only London but England—the main narrative of the film is set in London and Devon (the Old World), while the brief framing sequences, still set in the past, are located in Canada (the New World).

The energy of the *Moss Rose* credit sequence gives way to a more measured pace in the shots of Belle in the carriage, while the lights shinning into the train carriage in turn offer a contrast with the flickering gaslamps and foggy light which feature in the sequence that follows. There is movement in the street scene—both of the camera (which slowly pans) and within the frame (a hansom cab moves leisurely from left to right)—but the slow pace of this shot offers a marked contrast with the rapid montage of the credit sequence. In keeping with this shift, the background music moves from a rapid tempo toward the slower and somewhat eerie tone that accompanies the street scene.

The 'gas lights of the period' that feature at the beginning of *Moss Rose* function, along with other aspects of the *mise-en-scène*, as shorthand for turn-of-the-century London, a world that is presented in contrast to a more modern dynamism. In reviews, *Moss Rose* was identified as a 'gaslight thriller' (*New Yorker*, 12 July 1947), but also as a 'leisurely whodunit' (*Newsweek*, 14 July 1947), and the addition of the fast-paced credit sequence might be seen as an attempt to preempt complaints such as that raised in the *L.A. Examiner* (31 May 1947) that the film 'moves too slowly.'

Related to this was a general recognition that *Moss Rose* fell into a particular sub-division of the crime genre. In publicity for the film there was an attempt to emphasize how it differed from other— American, 'hard-boiled,' neon-lit—crime narratives. 'It was producer Gene Markey's belief that the English murderer has always been a much more subtle character than his American counterpart,' was how the pressbook put it. The notion of a generic subdivision was taken up in the review of *Moss Rose* that appeared in *PM* (3 July 1947), where it was suggested that all 'movie murder mysteries' had become so standardized that they could be fitted in one of two categories: 'type A, solved by Raymond Chandler's private eyes, in Los Angeles and environs; type B, solved by Inspectors of Scotland Yard, in London at the turn of the century.' The key generic elements of the latter type were identified as 'some fog, a hansom cab, a gas lamp flickering upon the ominous gleam of damp pavements. . . .'

The image of streetlights on wet pavement is one that has come to be particularly associated with Hollywood in the 1940s, though it is an image that tends to be linked to films set in contemporary America. Charles Higham and Joel Greenberg evoked 'the specific ambience of *film noir*' through the following description (1968: 19):

> A dark street in the early morning hours, splashed with a sudden downpour. Lamps form haloes in the murk. In a walk-up room, filled with the intermittent flashing of a neon sign from across the street, a man is waiting to murder or be murdered. . . .

Many other writers have discussed *film noir* with reference to lighting, from J. A. Place and L. S. Peterson's identification of the *noir* photographic style in terms of 'antitraditional lighting and camera' (1976: 327), to Martin Meisel's account of how the opening image of *Farewell, My Lovely* (1944)

> shows from above a group in shadow seated round a circle of light on a small table lit by a desk lamp. The camera moves in until the background is blank, and then, in the center of the white screen, under the name of the director, a light appears in a round metal shade which (seen from an angle) appears oval, like an egg or an eye. . . . As the story begins with voices questioning, with only the light to look at, the camera pulls back and we see from face level the waiting group around the lamp and the table, like a Mannerist scene or a Wright of Derby. . . .

When the bulb in the reflector reappears at the end of the film 'it becomes retrospectively clear that what we have seen, apparently from below, is not the direct, uncompromising stare of the third degree, but rather a reflection of the desk lamp in the white enamel tabletop that fills the screen' (1994: 75–77).

Such lights may reveal, or throw light upon a subject, but they can also exist as part of a framework of concealment. For Place and Peterson, 'the low-key *noir* style opposes light and dark, hiding faces, rooms, urban landscapes—and, by extension, motivations and true character—in shadow and darkness which carry connotations of the mysterious and the unknown' (327). The qualities of revelation and concealment are closely tied in with the status that *film noir* has as part of the crime genre, with its concern with investigation and mystery, though the streetlights, neon signs, and angled interior lamps that feature within such films also exist as signifiers of the contemporary urban environment that they present.

In line with Higham and Greenberg's description, *Moss Rose* opens with a setting that is half-lit, nocturnal, aqueous, and the setting for murder. Water was used by Hollywood cinematographers as a reflector of light; wet pavements could play a similar role to white enamel tabletops. In addition, the openings of both *Moss Rose* and *Farewell, My Lovely* indicate a continuum linking different forms of dramatic lighting. Meisel's discussion of the latter film comes at the end of an examination of light, dark, and seeing in which he looks at nineteenth-century stage melodrama, and notes how the rise of melodrama was closely tied to the theater's capacity to create and manage light: by way of the Argand light, then gas, limelight, electric arc, and finally the incandescent light. Imperfectly gaslit settings can serve a similar function as that described by Place and Peterson; they can carry connotations of the mysterious and the unknown. However, gaslight has also acquired other connotations that separate it from neon or electric light.

Compare the following extracts, both taken from crime novels:

> We went down a new alley . . . ribbons of light spoked across this one, glimmering through the interstices of an unfurled bamboo blind stretched across an entryway. . . . The bars of light made cicatrices across us. . . . For a second I stood alone, livid weals striping me from head to foot.

> In Pawlet Court on the western boundary of the Middle Temple the gas lamps were glowing into light. Hubert St. John Langton, Head of Chambers, watched from his window as he had every evening when he was working in Chambers, for the last forty years. It was the time of the year, the time of the day, that he loved best. Now the small court, one of the loveliest in the Middle Temple, took on the soft refulgent glow of an early autumn evening, the boughs of the great horse chestnut seeming to solidify as he watched, the rectangles of the light in the Georgian windows enhancing the atmosphere of ordered, almost domestic, eighteenth-century calm. Beneath him the cobbles between the pavements of York stone glistened as if they had been polished. Drysdale Laud moved up beside him. For a moment they stood in silence, then Langton turned away.

> He said: 'That's what I'm going to miss most, the lighting of the lamps. But it's not quite the same now they're automatic. I used to like waiting for the lamplighter to come into the Court. When that stopped, it seemed as if the whole era had gone for ever.'

The first is taken from Cornell Woolrich's *Black Path of Fear* (1944), and is quoted by David Bordwell as an example of how crime literature anticipated the look of *film noir* (Bordwell, Staiger, Thompson, 1985: 77—Bordwell acknowledges John Baxter as his source). The second is from a crime novel that was published more recently—P. D. James's *A Certain Justice* (1997: 20)—but that looks back to the past and conforms to detective story conventions that predate the 1940s.

This contrast could be taken as epitomizing two different traditions within crime fiction, the one fought out in the mean streets of the modern American city, the other English, cloistered and steeped in the past (even when contemporary in setting). The promotion for *Moss Rose*, with its notion of a more subtle English murder, appealed to just such a contrast, as did the reviewer who distinguished murder mysteries types A and B, and as also Raymond Chandler did when, in his essay 'The Simple Art of Murder,' he praised Dashiel Hammett's use of 'the American language,' and his breaking away from the predominance of the 'English formula' in crime writing (1980: 174 and 187).

The complications here derive partly in the fact that *Moss Rose* and Hollywood's type B films are American films. Writing of the detective story, Chandler spoke of 'its heavy crust of English gentility and American pseudo-gentility' (185). *Moss Rose* fits more comfortably within the latter rather than the former category, though on occasions cinematographer Joseph MacDonald gave the film's studio recreation of London something of same feel he was to convey in his work for such American-located films as *Panic in the Streets* (1950), *Pickup on South Street* (1953), and *The Street with No Name* (1948). However, what also complicates the opposition between gaslight and electric light is that the connotations of the former are by no means limited to nostalgia, or indeed to the mysterious and the unknown. Such complications form the subject of this chapter, in which I will examine what lies behind the gaslit opening of *Moss Rose*, an examination that will go back to the nineteenth century emergence of gaslight.

## Gaslight and the Nineteenth Century

A SENSE OF the range of nineteenth century, and to a lesser extent twentieth-century, discourses on the subject of gaslight can be gained by looking through the 'Convolute' of Walter Benjamin's *Arcade Project* devoted to 'Modes of Lighting' (Benjamin, 1999: 562–70). Some of the material found there was used by Benjamin in 'The Paris of the Second Empire in Baudelaire'; in that essay, looking back from the 1930s to the nineteenth century, Benjamin stressed the role of gaslight in the process of commodification and modernization, singling it out as a key instance of a technology that had come to be a relic of an earlier phase in industrial culture, and linking gaslight to the origins of the detective story. His interest in Baudelaire and nineteenth-century Paris as an earlier phase of industrial culture led him back to Baudelaire's essay, 'The Painter of Modern Life' (first published in 1845), and from that to the Edgar

Allan Poe story of 1840, 'The Man of the Crowd' (discussed also by Baudelaire), in which the narrator watches a London street scene and comments that 'as the night deepened, so deepened to me the interest of the scene; for not only did the general character of the crowd materially alter . . . but the rays of the gaslamps, feeble at first in their struggle with the dying day, had now at length gained ascendancy, and threw over everything a fitful and garish lustre' (see Benjamin, 1997: 50; Baudelaire, 1964: 7; Poe, 1908: 104–5).

Benjamin went on to write (1997: 50–51):

> The appearance of the street as an *intérieur* in which the phantasmagoria of the *flâneur* is concentrated is hard to separate from the gaslight. The first gas-lamps burned in the arcades. The attempt to use them under the open sky was made in Baudelaire's childhood; candelabra were placed on the Place Vendome. Under Napoleon III the number of gas lanterns increased rapidly. This increased safety in the city made the crowds feel at home in the open streets even at night, and removed the starry sky from the ambience of the big city more reliably than was done by its tall buildings. . . .

> Later, when the disappearance of the arcades made strolling go out of style and gaslight was no longer considered fashionable, it seemed to a last *flâneur* who sadly strolled through the empty Colbert Arcade that the flickering of the gas-lamps indicated only the fear of the flame that it would not be paid at the end of the month. That is when Stevenson made his plaint about the disappearance of the gas lanterns.

The references in the second paragraph are to *Les odeurs de Paris* (1913) by Louis Veuillot, and to Robert Louis Stevenson's essay, 'A Plea for Gas Lamps' (first published in 1881). Contrasting the disturbing quality ascribed to gas lamps in 'The Man of the Crowd' and the complaints about gaslight that Poe made in his essay 'The Philosophy of Furniture' (1840), with Stevenson's regret for the passing of gaslamps and the gaslighter, prompted Benjamin to write: 'There is some indication that only latterly was such an idyllic view of gaslight taken as Stevenson's, who wrote its obituary' (52).

Stevenson's 'obituary' was written when gaslighting had been in public use for nearly three-quarters of a century. Gas was first used to light Pall Mall in 1807, the Gas Light and Coke Company was formed in London in 1812, and gaslighting had become common throughout most of the British capital by 1816 (see Chandler and Lacey, 1949)—though as late as 1888 the 'Whitechapel Board of Works were debating the extension of gas lamps into the dimly lit alleys and culs-de-sacs of Spitalfields on the eve of the Ripper's first attack' (Fishman, 1988: 209). Gas was introduced to Paris at a later date, and its spread was initially less rapid; among the (literary) passages that make up Benjamin's *Arcades Project* is the following account of the introduction of gaslighting to the French capital: 'in January 1817, the Passage des Panoramas was illuminated. . . . The first attempt by businesses were not at all satisfactory; the public seemed resistant to this kind of lighting, which was suspected of being dangerous and of polluting breathable air' (Du Camp, in Benjamin, 1999: 563–64). Benjamin noted that electric streetlights were introduced at the Louvre in 1857 (1999: 562); however, electricity only became a serious competitor to gaslight in the 1880s, with the invention of the incandescent light bulb. In fact, the gradual abandonment of gaslighting did not follow directly on from this. Technological improvements, in particular the invention of the Welsbach lamp, led to a far brighter form of lighting by gas, to a competition between companies promoting different forms of lighting, and in some instances to the reintroduction of gaslighting. An advice manual published in 1901 could still argue that 'no artificial light is more satisfactory than gas, because no other requires so little attention and is so absolutely and continuously available' (*The Book of the Home*, quoted in O'Dea, 1958: 157). Even as late as 1930 an article in the trade publication *Gas World* could, under the heading 'Superiority of Gas for Public Lighting,' claim that gas provided a more effective form of streetlighting than electricity (reproduced in Barty-King, 1984: 157). In Britain during the 1930s gaslighting remained as common a form of streetlighting as electricity, and as late as 1938, the year when Patrick Hamilton's play, *Gas Light*, had its premiere at Richmond Theatre, new designs for gas streetlighting were still being produced, though after this date the use of gas for lighting declined sharply (see Barty-King: 196). Gaslight as a generic description thus emerges at a point when gas still existed as a form of municipal lighting but was moving toward marginalization (though that process of marginalization was an extended one, stretching from the time of Robert Louis Stevenson to that of P. D. James).

Suspicion of gas as a dangerous and a polluting form of light was not limited to Paris, or to the period when gaslight was first introduced.

Initial fears about fire being carried in pipes beneath the street were followed by concerns that the use of gas for lighting would lead to explosions, fires, and the release of noxious fumes. Such fears were fuelled by incidents such as the destruction by fire of a gaslit pagoda in St. James's Park in 1814. The naked gas flame did indeed present a fire risk, one to which theaters were particularly susceptible— according to Terence Rees at least two theaters a year were burnt down between 1866 and 1885, though the continued use of oil lamps was also a factor here (see O'Dea: 125). There was also a history of serious accidents in which the dresses of performers were set alight by naked gas jets (see Booth, 1991: 84), and gaslight also added significantly to the heat of theaters. Further objections to the use of gas (though not to gas alone) can be found in a curious pamphlet written by the novelist Wilkie Collins; in 'The Use of Gas in Theatres, or, The Air and the Audience: Considerations on the Atmospheric Influences of Theatres,' the author of *The Woman in White* and other sensation novels complained of the suffocating air, and of 'the emanations from gas and from the not universally-washed public that sits in its light' (1986: 23).

Tighter regulations and late nineteenth-century technological developments led to a safer as well as a brighter form of gaslighting, but traces of earlier fears about gas were retained into the twentieth century, though these fears were not necessarily linked to the use of gas for lighting. The gasworks remains a key image of industrialization, and as such has played a part in the representation of the age of industry in works ranging from *Gasmasks* (1924), the play devised by Sergei Tretyakov and staged, in a gasworks, by Sergei Eisenstein prior to his career as a film director, to the explosion at the gasworks that is reported to have precipitated the madman's outburst with which the 1941 version of *Dr. Jekyll and Mr. Hyde* opens.

As well as the gasworks being a physical symbol of industrialization, the spread of gaslight facilitated industrialization because it allowed factories to stay open for longer hours (a century later, Peter Baxter has noted, the use of electric lighting within the emerging film studios made a similar contribution to the exploitation of the workforce previously employed only until dusk, and thus to profits of the major Hollywood film companies [1975: 99]). For Wolfgang Schirelbasch gaslight was central to 'the industrialization of light in the nineteenth century,' and the concerns that it brought were not limited to fears of explosions, fires, and the release of obnoxious fumes. Gaslight produced a light that was brighter, more regular, and more capable of regulation. What this also meant was that it could be seen as part of a process of regulating the populace, not just the gas supply. Connection to a centralized gas supplier thus brought with it anxieties about a loss of autonomy. Earlier forms of lighting, such as candles and oil lamps, were individual and intimate. Gaslighting, like the railways, connected people to a network in a way that fundamentally altered how they saw themselves in relation to society at large (1988: 28–29). The melodrama of *Gaslight* is to some extent based on this inter-dependence, through the way in which the raising and the lowering of the gaslight in one place causes the light in another to dim or grow brighter (though it is also based on the notion of isolation within the city).

The link between gaslight and regulation could be the subject of approval. In 1821 it was noted in *The Times* that 'at length St. James's park is to be lighted with gas. This will put an end to the disgracefully immoral scenes that nightly occur, to the disgust of the respectable passenger' (quoted in O'Dea: 73). Gaslight was seen by some as part of a process of municipal improvement, and, as Benjamin noted, a move toward a safer city. But there are complexities here, as elsewhere. If gaslight was seen as industrial and modern, it was also understood as linked to the past—in Schirelbasch's words, it was 'still bound to the flame' (153). And while the writer for *The Times* saw it as a weapon in the battle against immorality, others would go on to link the glare of gaslight (the bright lights of the city) with immorality.

In 1836 the *Temperance Penny Magazine* gave the following description of the gin-palaces on Radcliffe Highway in the East End of London (quoted in Harrison, 1973: 170):

> at one place I saw a revolving light with many burners playing most beautifully over the door of the painted charnel-house: at another, about fifty or sixty jets, in one lantern, were throwing out their capricious and fitful, but brilliant gleams, as if from the brackets of a shrub. And over the door of a third house were no less than THREE enormous lamps, with corresponding lights, illuminating the whole street at a considerable distance. They were in full glare on this Sunday evening; and through the doors of these infernal dens of drunkenness and mischief, crowds of miserable wretches were pouring in, that they might drink and die.

Gaslights and gin-palaces were often linked together. The gas flame could suggest improvement and beauty or immorality and hell (or some combination of these). Visiting London in 1839, the Frenchwoman Flora Tristan wrote that 'it is especially at night that London should be seen; then, in the magic light of millions of gaslamps, London is superb' (1982: 17), noted that 'beer and gas are the main products consumed in London,' reported on the inferno of the gasworks (72–75), and spoke also of the gin-palaces in the vicinity of Waterloo Road, where 'you are dazzled by the light of a thousand gas lamps' and where 'prostitutes parade in all their finery' (85).

Gaslighting was quicker to develop as a form of exterior lighting than it was in the home. It was 'used for effect and display as much as for utility,' notes Raymond Williams (1973: 228). The utilitarian purpose served by streetlighting was supplemented by the exhibitions of light adopted in shops, hotels, gin palaces, and theaters. Even the installation of gas streetlights could, in effect, help turn the nighttime street scene into a stage, and shops into small theaters. One writer has speculated that the 'luminous yellow' of the gas jet may have encouraged the use of make-up, on account of the way in which it made faces unfamiliar in its light and placed every pedestrian and shopper 'on the stage' (Keogh, 1984: 21–22). According to Michael Booth, 'in combination with plate glass, gaslight afforded greatly enhanced opportunities for the display of goods in shop windows. . . . Peering through a brilliantly lit rectangle of glass into a wonderland of attractive goods for sale was like looking into a peepshow or at a stage flooded with light behind the proscenium' (1981: 4).

The installation of gas in the domestic environment was a slower process. There were practical disincentives here, but also aesthetic considerations and perhaps unwelcome associations. While Poe had described the 'fitful and garish' light of streets lit by gas in 'The Man of the Crowd,' in 'The Philosophy of Furniture' he wrote that gas 'is totally inadmissible within doors. Its harsh and unsteady lights offends. No one having both brains and eyes will use it' (1986: 416). This dislike of interior gaslighting was echoed in 1866 by a German writer who stated that gaslight was 'still almost completely excluded from living premises . . . and tolerated at most in corridors and kitchens' (quoted in Schirelbasch: 160). In 1878, an American writing a guide to English manners, pronounced that 'gas, whether it be in town or country, is not only thought unwholesome, but not "good form"' (quoted in Ford, 1981: 191). Were there cultural or national variations here? According to one commentator, gaslight was 'the first specifically bourgeois technology . . . at least in England, modern conveniences, such as gaslight (or bathrooms), came to be seen by upper-class homeowners as vulgar, and the comfort associated with these mechanical devices as nouveau-riche. In this context one comes across derogatory references to luxury. In America there was no such opposition, and photographs of interiors show gasoliers in the palatial drawing rooms of the wealthy, as well as the modest parlours and kitchens of the middle class' (Rybczyski, 1980: 143. For support of this in respect to the American situation, see the photographs reproduced in Myers, 1990).

The 1878 reference to the use of gas in town or country indicates a shift in which gaslight was initially an almost exclusively urban form of lighting, one that was most evident in public places, and which, when it was introduced into the home, tended to be established among people living in close proximity. This association remains predominant; just as *film noir* exists as a primarily urban form of crime drama, the reference to gaslight in the context of crime narratives tends to imply an urban setting. 'Cities given, the problem was to light them,' was how Stevenson opened his 'A Plea for Gas Lamps' (1899: 275). However, the particular bond between gaslight and the city was complicated, especially in the early twentieth century, when gaslight took root in certain rural locations, at least in the United States, where the isolated domestic gas machine provided light for a single building or a small group of buildings. By the 1930s even this practice had become less common, and was virtually killed off by the establishment of the Rural Electrification Administration in 1935 (see Worthington, 1986). In films, gaslighting is almost always used in urban settings; in a film such as *National Velvet* (1944) a nighttime, gaslit scene suggests the corruption of the city as opposed to the innocence of the country. The isolated gas streetlight seen in *Night of the Hunter* (1955) is evocative of the latter-day rural American adoption of gaslighting, though the isolation of that single gaslight can be related to the status of *Night of the Hunter* as an atypical film, one that consciously looks back to the past and sets itself apart from contemporary trends.

Walter Benjamin wrote of gaslighting mainly in reference to Paris, as in his comment that 'the first gaslights burned in the Arcades.' Paris has been associated with light from the Enlightenment onward, and in the mid-nineteenth century Charles Dickens wrote that 'London is shabby by daylight and shabbier by gaslight. No Englishman knows what gaslight is, until he sees the rue de Rivoli and the Palais Royal after dark' (quoted in Collins, 1987: 115–16). In the second half of the nineteenth century the French painter Manet, concerned as he was with portraying contemporary urban life, was probably the first to accord the gaslamp the status of an artistic subject (see, for instance, Manet's 'The Bar at the Folies-Bergère'—for Émile Zola, Manet's art 'could only have been developed in Paris; it has the slender grace of our women, made pale by gaslight' (quoted in Reff, 1987: 142); for a picture, or rather pictures, of how streetlighting came to be taken up as an artistic subject, see Jansen, 1974 and 1992). Examples of the continuation of this tradition can be found in a number Seurat's paintings and illustrations by Toulouse-Lautrec (a tradition to which films such as *French Can-Can* [1955] look back). Yet a particular association between London and gaslight emerged during the nineteenth century, and lingered on to be adopted in a range of twentieth-century works, from the poetry of T. S. Eliot to the films of 20th Century-Fox.

Edgar Allan Poe provided one picture of London by gaslight in 'The Man of the Crowd,' though Poe's city lacks any specific landmarks. The London described by Dickens is a more precisely delineated imaginary city. And while Dickens had delighted in the gaslights of Paris, he also left numerous descriptions of gaslit London, in both his fiction and his journalism, though the emphasis in these descriptions tends to be as much on the dark as the light. In *Sketches by Boz* (first published in 1839), in his description of a Drury Lane gin shop, he emphasizes the contrast between the gaslights the surrounding darkness, writing (1995: 217–18):

> You turn the corner, what a change! All is light and brilliancy. The hum of many voices, issues from that splendid gin-shop which forms the commencement of the two streets opposite, and the gay building with the fantastically ornamented parapet, the illuminated clock, the plate-glass windows surrounded by stucco rosettes, and its profusion of gas-lights in richly-gilt burners, is perfectly dazzling when contrasted with the darkness and dirt we have just left.

Elsewhere in *Sketches by Boz* Dickens wrote (74):

the streets of London, to be held at the very height of their glory, should be seen on a dark, murky winter's night, when there is just enough damp gently stealing down to make the pavement greasy, without cleansing it of any of its impurities; and when the heavy lazy mist, which hangs over every object, makes the gas-lamps look brighter, and the brightly lighted shops more splendid, from the contrast they present to the darkness around.

A darker picture is given of a later night walk, of which he wrote that 'the river had an awful look, the buildings on the bank were muffled in black shrouds, and the reflected lights seemed to originate deep in the water, as if the specters of suicides were holding them to show where they went down' (1997: 74), and again in *Bleak House* (1852–53), where he described the lamplighter at dawn, striking 'off the little heads of fire that have aspired to lessen the darkness' (quoted in Ford: 188). Such descriptions look toward the image of London presented in Gustave Doré's and Blanchard Jerrold's *London* (1872), in which the city appears to be divided into daylight and nighttime halves (a division also evident in George Augustus Sala's 1859 *Gaslight and Daylight*); in Doré's illustrations of the London poor, gaslights feature prominently, though the prevailing tone is one of darkness (see Figure 1. See also Raymond Williams's suggestion that the perception of 'darkest London,' and of the separation of East from West London, was a consequence of bright lights of the West End [1973: 229]).

Dickens was a key, if inevitably transformed, source for later representations of Victorian London. Doré's illustrations have also been significant in this context, as have reports compiled by Henry Mayhew (see, for instance, Mayhew's description of the 'intense white,' though here self-generating gaslamps used in a Lambeth market [1851: 9]). At a later date, Conan Doyle provided a significant source for the development of an image of late-Victorian and Edwardian London; Raymond Williams has written that 'Conan Doyle's London has acquired, with time, a romantic atmosphere which some look back to with a nostalgia as evident as any rural retrospect: the fog, the gaslight, the hansom cabs, the street urchins, and through them all, this sharp eccentric mind . . .' (227). Of course, a London of fog and gaslight was not created by Doyle alone. The concern with contemporary urban life displayed by the French impressionists and post-impressionists had worked its influence across the Channel by the end of the nineteenth century.

Figure 1.
Gustave Doré,
'Bluegate Fields'
from *London*
(1872).

Gaslight features prominently in 'Piccadilly by Night' (1885–88) and other urban (though not necessarily London-based) paintings by Atkinson Grimshaw. When London came to be taken as a suitable subject for art and poetry, the lighting of the city became part of that concern (see, for example, Oscar Wilde's 'Impression du Matin,' 1997: 129). There is a continuum linking this concern with the work of twentieth-century, modernist writers such as T. S. Eliot, in whose poetry gaslight features significantly.

Gaslight could fulfill an ambivalent function here. The close of the first of Eliot's 'Preludes,' ending as it does with the line, 'And then the lighting of the lamps' (1974: 23), perhaps reveals a poet's concern with delineating the contemporary urban environment (and in Eliot's 'Rhapsody on a Windy Night' (26–28) it is the streetlight that provides the commentary), but it also suggests a nostalgia reminiscent of Stevenson's obituary for the lamplighter, though this suggestion may in part be a product of the time that has passed since the writing of Eliot's poem, time which has seen gaslighting all but disappear from the urban scene.

The emergence of a nostalgia for gaslight and the changing perception of the light given off by gaslamps cannot be separated from the spread of electricity as an alternative and ultimately dominant form of lighting. In the first half of the nineteenth century commentators could stress the brightness of gaslight. Schirelbasch writes that brightness was the outstanding feature noted of gaslight: it was '"dazzling white," "as bright as day," or "an artificial sun"' (40). An alternative was to stress its glare, as did Edgar Allan Poe. In 1821 one British writer looked back to a time when 'the light afforded by the street lamps hardly enabled the passenger to distinguish a watchman from a thief, or the pavement from the gutter. The case is now different; for the gas-lamps afford a light little inferior to daylight' (Colin Mackenzie, quoted in Chandler, 1949: 2). There is some evidence of a shift by the middle of the century; in 1850 an experiment with electric lighting in St. Petersberg drew the response that 'the light of the gas lamps appeared red and sooty, while the electric light was dazzling white' (quoted in Schirelbasch: 115), while in a French medical textbook (quoted in Schirelbasch: 118) published in 1880, it was noted:

> as soon as we look away from the broad thoroughfare into one of the side streets, where a miserable, dim gaslight is flickering, the eye-strain begins. Here darkness reigns supreme, or rather, a weak reddish glow, that is hardly enough to prevent collisions in the entrance or the stairs, in a word, the most wretched light prevails.

Technological improvements in the second half of the nineteenth century may have done something to counter this perception of gaslight as a 'wretched light,' but the increasing availability of electric light did lead to a different understanding of gaslight. It could be associated with the old-fashioned and the antiquated, hence the 'gaslight melodrama' referred to in *The Lady Eve* (see chapter one). In 1944 a compilation film that included extracts from an assortment of early films presented in a mocking manner was given the title of *Gaslight Follies*—gaslight, while still used in places, had clearly come to be seen as the now outmoded light of an earlier era.

It could also be viewed in an increasingly nostalgic light. 'The word *electricity* now sounds the note of danger,' wrote Robert Louis Stevenson in 'A Plea for Gas Lamps' (1899: 281):

In Paris, at the mouth of the Passages des Princes, in the place before the Opera portico, and in the Rue Drouot at the *Figaro* office, a new sort of urban star now shines out nightly, horrible, unearthly, obnoxious to the human eye; a lamp for a nightmare! Such a light as this should shine only on murders and public crime, or along the corridors of lunatic asylums, a horror to heighten horror. To look at it only once is to fall in love with gas, which gives a warm domestic radiance fit to eat by.

As Walter Benjamin pointed out, and as other accounts should have made clear, Stevenson's description contrasts with a different tradition, in which the light of gas is seen as inappropriate indoors, or in which it is gaslight that is associated with nightmares. The latter understanding was maintained in the twentieth century. There is a long tradition of gaslight being associated with mystery; Asa Briggs notes that '"natural gas" had itself been spoken of at first as a "spirit" and was "more or less of a mystery." It is also remembered as adding a touch of mystery to London'—in which context he cites *Fanny by Gaslight* (1990: 401). 'A city is characterized by its lights and it is to its lights, acting on its continual mist, that London owes much of the mystery of its beauty,' wrote Arthur Symond in 1909 (1984: 60). But if mystery could be connected with beauty it could also be linked to horror. Writing on a wartime revival of interest in tales of horror, Edmund Wilson commented that he had supposed that the ghost story had been killed by electric light (*The New Yorker*, 27 May 1944). Gaslight becomes associated with the crime but also the horror genre (on the internet, the 'gaslight reading list' is devoted to the discussion of stories written between 1800 and 1919 that can be classified under 'mystery, adventure, and The Weird'),[2] an association that, ironically enough, becomes exemplified in various versions of Stevenson's *The Strange Case of Dr. Jekyll and Mr. Hyde*.

While one effect of the passage of time was to bestow a romantic charm upon gaslight, another effect was to give that same light a sinister edge. Compare, for instance, the description that Benjamin offers of the brilliance of the Paris arcades in the Second Empire with the following account, taken from Émile Zola's novel of 1868, *Thérèse Raquin*:

At night the arcade is lit with three gas jets in heavy square lanterns. These gas jets hang from the glass roof, on to which they cast up patches of lurid light, while they send down palely luminous circles that dance fitfully and now and then seem to disappear altogether. Then the arcade takes on a sinister look of a real cutthroat alley; great shadows creep along the paving-stones and damp draughts blow in from the street until it seems like an underground gallery dimly lit by three funeral lamps (1962: 32).

Stevenson's more nostalgic account of gaslight is premised part-ly on the nature (and warmth) of that light but to a great degree on the figure of the lamplighter, whom he invests with a mythical sig-nificance that contrasts with the 'sedate electrician somewhere in a back office' (p. 280). There is a line here that runs also through Stevenson's 'The Lamplighter' (one of the poems included in his *A Child's Garden of Verses*, 1885), *The Lamplighter* by 'Miss Cummins'—a evangelical story, reprinted numerous times through-out the second half of the nineteenth century and the first half of the twentieth, of an orphan befriended by an elderly gaslighter—and that carries on up to P. D. James's *A Certain Justice*. With his grad-ual disappearance, the once familiar, urban figure of the lamplighter acquired a romantic status, as did gaslight itself—as when Rebecca West looked back to her childhood in *The Fountain Overflows* (1957), writing of (interior) gaslighting: 'It was more poetic than electric light, and I am sorry that so many children of today never see it' (1984: 143).

The association linking gaslight with the past, and the way in which it was viewed with nostalgia, worked its way into the cinema. The warm glow of the gaslighting is singled out as a key motif by David Bordwell and Kristin Thompson in their account of how *Meet Me in St. Louis* (1944) 'seeks to uphold what are conceived as char-acteristically American values of family unity and home life' (Bordwell and Thompson, 1997: 420). Variations can be found within film's romantic presentation of gaslight. In Hollywood's *The Plough and the Stars* (1936) the flame of the gaslamp offers a soft echo of the flames of the Republican torches (before the lamp is cal-lously knocked down by the armored cars of the British), while in the British *Champagne Charlie* (1944) hundreds of gas flames con-tribute to the affectionate recreation of the atmosphere of the Victorian Music Hall. However, nostalgia is a complex emotion (one that has been understood in terms of sickness as well as affection), and nostalgia alone cannot account for the resonance retained by gaslight in the twentieth century. *Champagne Charlie*, for instance, also draws upon the link between gaslight and the stage, an association that had a fundamental significance in the nineteenth century.

## From Stage to Screen

GASLIGHT HAD BECOME almost synonymous with the stage by 1838, when Henry Hetherington published the periodical, *Actors by Gaslight; or, Boz in the Boxes*; this link was still evident at the very end of the nineteenth century, when Theodore Dreiser, in his novel *Sister Carrie* (1900), referred to a stage performer dressed in a military costume as a 'gaslight soldier' (1998: 359). And though the word *limelight* has remained a more common synonym for the stage, in the nineteenth century the link between gaslight and the theater, and in particular gaslight and melodrama, had been made stronger by Augustin Daly's *Under the Gaslight; or Life and Love in These Times: An Original Drama of American Life in Four Acts* (1867), one of the key stage melodramas of the time. The play also indicates how gaslight had become a defining feature of urban life (American as well as European)—gaslight as 'these times' rather than the later understanding of gaslight to mean past times. However, the key factor here was clearly that, as Nicholas Vardac notes, 'the principal means for lighting the stage in the years prior to the motion picture depended upon gas' (1949: 8).

Gaslighting was installed in the Covent Garden and the Olympic Theatres in London in 1815. Initially introduced in foyers and exteriors, in 1817 its use was extended to the stage and the auditorium. Most other London theaters followed suit in the years that followed. Gaslight gave a light that was significantly brighter than earlier forms of stage lighting (wax candles and oil lamps), and it could be controlled with relative ease—lights could be dimmed, extinguished, or relit, initially by hand, later by a pilot light, turning lighting effects into an element of the drama.

Gaslight in the nineteenth-century theater—as elsewhere—was not universally accepted. Some theaters were slow to adopt it; it was not introduced to Sadler's Wells until 1857, though in general it was the theaters outside the main urban centers that delayed its installation. There were initial complaints that it provided a too brilliant form of stage lighting, and for a period some theaters continued to use oil lights. 'Everything upon the stage and in the audience part is a glare of undistinguished lights painful to eye,' complained one commentator (quoted in O'Dea: 126). There were also the problems and fears of heat and atmosphere already mentioned.

Once it had firmly established itself, gaslight was challenged by other forms of lighting. Carbon arc lights had been used in the theater as early as 1846, when they were introduced into the Paris Opera. These, however, were noisy, they could not be dimmed, and produced a harsh, white light. Limelight was first introduced in 1857, while at the Paris Opera electric spotlights were first used in 1860. In 1881 the Savoy became the first London theater to be lit entirely by electricity. The new form of lighting could be used in unexpected ways; according to Michael Booth, 'the late Victorians and Edwardians were fascinated by the application of electric light to an already long-standing romantic stage fairyland, and from *Iolanthe* (1881) onward tiny electric lights powered by batteries sparkled in the hair, among floral bouquets, and upon the costumes of female dancers and supers' (1991: 92). By the beginning of the twentieth century the gas flame had largely made way for incandescent lighting.

Just as there were those who objected to the replacement of gas for streetlighting, the progressive abandonment of gaslighting in the theater met some resistance. Henry Irving in particular, who had been exploiting the full range of theatrical lighting, including darkening the auditorium during scene changes, continued to take his own gas jets and apparatus with him and to use them in theaters where gaslighting had been replaced. 'We used gas footlights and gas limes there until we left the theater for good in 1902,' wrote Ellen Terry of her work with Irving. 'The thick softness of gaslight, with the lovely specks and motes in it, so like *natural* light, gave illusion to many a scene which is now revealed in all its naked trashiness by electricity' (quoted in O'Dea: 160).

Vardac also refers to the softness of gaslight. In his account of staging in the melodramatic theater, the turn to electricity that took place toward the end of the nineteenth century is identified as having the effect of showing up the painted backdrops still in use in theaters, their artificiality having previously been masked by 'the soft lights and mysterious shadows of gas lighting. . . . Footlights, overhead light borders, vertical wing-and-tormentor borders provided arbitrary and distorted lighting which may have been tolerable with oil or gaslight sources but which, with the bright, directional rays of the electric bulb, served to expose and destroy the illusion of two-dimensional scenery.' Vardac goes on to say that by the time these problems had been ironed out, the popular stage had lost its place to popular cinema, where electricity gave 'a thorough and three-dimensional realism' (8–9).[3]

Peter Baxter, in his account of the history and ideology of film lighting, has criticized Vardac's assumption that developments in film lighting constituted an advance in pure representation, arguing that what happened was rather that one set of codes replaced another (Baxter, 1975: 105). The introduction of electric light had, as Vardac suggested, highlighted problems within the conventions of stage realism as it was then understood. In the theater, there were two responses to this, 'one intended to re-establish stage realism under the new light, the other set out to abolish physical illusionism altogether, to replace representation by revelation' (85). Early narrative films, such as *The Great Train Robbery* (1903), conformed to the model of featureless illumination dominant within the theater, a model which tended to wash away the facial features of the actors. But the absence of subtle shading initially did not tend to be seen as a defect. This perception began to change around 1914, as backlighting—rather than make-up, gesture, or position—began to take over the function of separating major characters from their surroundings. 'What we understand as the growing naturalism of the cinema, as well as of the stage, was the suppression of one constellation of conventions which technological changes had more or less suddenly made visible, and the imposition of another, made possible by the new technology,' argues Baxter (96), who suggested that these new conventions had become the dominant mode of film lighting by 1920. However, the subsequent absence of any major reversal of their preeminent position since that date was not attributable to the correctness of this mode, nor to the overwhelming influence of a few great cameramen, but rather to 'the determinants which have made the film an extension of realist narrative art and the product of a large, potentially highly profitable industry' (106).

Whether or not film's development did become limited to an extension of realist narrative, Hollywood lighting after 1920 was not totally homogenous. One variation was the way in which soft lighting effects emerged in the late teens and the 1920s as an alternative to a hard-edged look. 'It is acknowledged by cinematographers in general that the need of absolutely sharp definition is a thing of the past,' wrote Joseph Dubray in 1928. 'The dramatic quality of present day cinematography demands a certain softness of contours throughout the whole image' (quoted by David Bordwell, in Bordwell, Staiger, Thompson, 1985: 342). However, the intensified standardization that came with the introduction of direct sound worked against the variety of soft effects employed in films such as *Sparrows* (1926) and *Sunrise* (1927); the style became less varied, and more integrated within realist narrative conventions, as it also became more pervasive, and thus a modified soft style became the norm for the sound film (see Kristin Thompson's 'Major Technological Changes of the 1920s' in Bordwell, Staiger, Thompson, 1985: 287–93).

It has also been suggested that there were subsequent reactions against the dominant lighting conventions of the Hollywood sound film. J. A. Place and L. S. Peterson, for instance, have argued that it was in reaction to dominant 'high-key' lighting conventions that the harsher, 'low-key' lighting style of *film noir* emerged in the 1940s (1976: 327). However, this contrast has itself been questioned. It has been noted that Place and Peterson base their analysis on a small sample of films. All the stylistic features they describe (which include features such as unbalanced compositions as well as low-key lighting) can be found in films never classified as *noir*, and relatively few can be identified in a title accepted as *film noir* such as *The Big Sleep* (1946). More generally, *film noir* was 'a more stylistically heterogeneous category than critics have recognized' (see Narremore, 1998:167–68).

What one can identify are successive ways in which perceived contrasts between different forms of light (at times in conjunction with other aspects of film form) are linked to wider cultural divides. Ellen Terry's opposition between the 'thick softness' of gaslight and the 'naked trashiness' of electricity, and Nicholas Vardac's opposition between 'the soft lights and mysterious shadows of gas lighting' and the 'bright, directional rays of the electric bulb,' seem premised on an opposition between the nineteenth and twentieth centuries, and while Vardac's paradoxical attribution of a three-dimensional realism to the flat surface of the cinema screen was made in the context of an examination of the *connections* between the two media, his account also offers a contrast between the theatrical stage and the cinema screen.

There is a line leading from Vardac's reference to electricity's 'bright, directional rays' to Richard Hoggart's description of most mass-entertainments as 'full of a corrupt brightness' (Hoggart, 1958: 282). For Hoggart, that 'corrupt brightness' was inextricably linked with the process of 'Americanization'; for other writers, the status of *film noir* as 'a self-contained reflection of American cultural preoccupations in film form' (Silver and Ward, 1980: 1) is tied in with both its origins in hard-boiled crime writing (as opposed to the English detective tradition) and a style of lighting which can be described as harsh or hard. Looking beyond *film noir*, Thomas Elsaesser's discussion of Hollywood melodrama—and thus to some extent the critical interest in Hollywood melodrama as a whole—opens with a quote from Douglas Sirk in which the director referred to his use of 'deep-focus lenses which have the effect of giving a *harshness* to the objects and a kind of enameled, *hard* surface to the colours' (my italics) (1987: 43). What Sirk explained as a means of bringing out the 'inner violence' of the characters, was specifically linked by Elsaesser to the modern American home.

Gaslight, which had once itself seemed to epitomize the bright lights of the city, and which had provoked complaints that it was 'intense but hard' (see Schirelbasch: 153), could serve here to present a contrast with the brightness or hardness of electricity or neon. To some extent this came to be its function within the crime genre. Thus the description of *Moss Rose* as a 'gaslight thriller' served to distinguish the film from other crime thrillers perceived as more characterized by a stark modernity.

Paradoxically, this distinction was facilitated by developments within film lighting. Lighting effects had been used on the nineteenth-century stage, though more through a use of limelight than gas, and often for the primary purpose of spectacle—unless special effects were called for, actors and scenery tended to be subjected to the general and undifferentiating glare of which commentators complained. For film-makers, the increasing use of lighting effects and selective lighting in part had a novelty value (one that was stressed in promotional material—see Bordwell, Staiger, Thompson, 1985, illustration 17.29), in part served as a means of modeling faces, figures, and objects, and in part functioned to foster clarity and the impression of depth. But a new emphasis on effects lighting also involved a shift toward a light that had a narrative function, and that emanated from a specific source within the story. While gaslight disappeared as the actual means of dramatic illumination, it could return in crime films as well as other genres, as a dramatic (or melodramatic) subject.[4]

Films made in the initial decades of the twentieth century could still present gaslighting as an aspect of the contemporary scene—as was the case, for instance, in the gaslit dosshouse scene in Charlie Chaplin's *The Kid* (1921), though here the fact that gaslighting fixtures are shown in the context of poverty is suggestive of their developing marginalization. More generally, gaslights have served within film as part of the iconography of the not too distant past—a past on the edge of modernity. In this context they can evoke nostalgia, as Bordwell and Thompson note of *Meet Me in St. Louis* (1944), but there are complexities within that nostalgia, and associations that went beyond the nostalgic (as Andrew Britton, 1977, has noted of *Meet Me in St. Louis*). Other films of the 1940s retained traces of the diverse ways in which gaslight had featured in the nineteenth-century imagination.

In *Citizen Kane* (1941), for instance, Charles Foster Kane's 'Declaration of Principles' are introduced in a scene in which Kane (Orson Welles) announces: 'I've changed the front page a little, Mr. Bernstein. That's not enough, no. There's something I've got to get into this paper besides pictures and print. I've got to make the New York 'Inquirer' as important to New York as the gas in that light.' Gaslight features here as part of the film's period *mise-en-scène*, and Kane's reference to it is in keeping with a turn-of-the-century understanding of gaslight as a vital part of urban life. But Kane's words are undercut by a narrative development in which his 'Principles' are torn to shreds, figuratively and literally, and also by a mid-twentieth-century understanding of gaslight as anything but vital to urban life.

Period *mise-en-scène* is more evident in *The Magnificent Ambersons* (1942). In particular, in the ball sequence at the beginning of Welles's second film, gaslights figure as part of rich furnishings of the Amberson mansion, their ornate fittings and slightly flickering lights contributing to an atmosphere of luminous and nostalgic charm. Here gaslighting features not as a key aspect of urban technology but as a part of world set against the changes of modernity—the world pointed to in Eugene Morgan's (played by Joseph Cotten) comment that 'the times that are gone, they aren't old, they're dead. There aren't any times but new times.' *The Magnificent Ambersons* is characterized by regret for the passing of the old rather than a celebration of the new (as such, it is in the tradition of Stevenson's 'A Plea for Gaslamps'), but here also the 'magnificence' of the title is undercut and tinged with irony, just as the opening, gaslit brilliance gives way to a darker tone, countered only by the bland fill light of the final scene added at the studio's insistence.

In other films gaslight retains its function as an aspect of the period *mise-en-scène*, while bringing with it other connotations. The period furnishings of *The Lodger* (1944) and *Hangover Square* (1945), for instance, are combined with the conventions of the crime or horror film, and use light to suggest mystery, disorientation, and threat. Both films make as much use of low-key lighting as any con-temporaneously-set *film noir*. Indeed, if there is one Hollywood moment which comes closest to the Cornell Woolrich description, quoted at the beginning of this chapter, of bars of light making cic-atrices of the human figure, it is the shot in *The Lodger* of the char-acter, known as Slade but by now identified as Jack-the-Ripper (Laird Cregar), crawling along a catwalk high in a gaslit music hall, his face made grotesque by the light as he moves into extreme close-up.

*The Lodger* uses a variety of light sources, the (electric?) torch-es of the policemen which cut across the screen as well as the gas fit-tings of street, theater, and lodgings (see Figure 2). In *Hangover Square* the focus is more clearly upon the fittings and flame of gaslight. In the shots of gas lamps that appear throughout the film there is a repeated emphasis on the flame. In a scene set in Scotland Yard, for instance, a gasolier hangs prominently above the charac-ters, its four flames made even more evident by the clear glass bowls that surround them; a further gas lamp can be seen on one of the side walls. Fire plays a key role in the film, which begins and ends with acts of arson; in between, a bonfire night celebration allows the murderer to dispose of his victim's body. The flames of the gas lamps provide an echo of this theme of fire as danger, while also carrying traces of other connotations acquired over time (nostalgia, urban life, theatricality, and so on). John Brahm, director of both *The Lodger* and *Hangover Square*, seems to have been particularly fond of emphasizing lighting and the sources of lighting; the most strik-ing moment of his earlier *The Undying Monster* (1942) is a shot apparently taken from within a fireplace. Gaslight settings evidently gave him scope to indulge this taste; his *The Brasher Doubloon* (1947), based on Raymond Chandler's *The High Window*, is less visually distinctive.

Figure 2. *The Lodger* (1944).

## Toward the Modern City

THE HOLLYWOOD FILM industry, which has mostly attempted to conceal the industrial aspects of production, did not tend to stress the industrial significance of gaslight. Thus my interest in this chapter in what lies behind the gaslit opening of *Moss Rose* has led onto a discussion of developments and concerns that are either missing or hidden as much as revealed by this and other films. Indeed, in discussing *Moss Rose*, it is necessary to point out that this film's narrative of the urban streets gives way to a second half in which the setting is an English country house. This move can be linked to developments within the English detective story. A genre that emerged in the nineteenth-century city (through Poe, Dickens, and Doyle, among others) developed into a form of fiction at the heart of which was the enclosed, seemingly timeless environment of the English village and the country house (what W. H. Auden (1980) called 'the guilty vicarage'). As the setting of *Moss Rose* moves from the city to the country, the 'gaslights of the period' give way to candlelight and oil lamps, and the different connotations brought by these forms of lighting.

*Moss Rose* is a film of a certain interest, though in a number of ways it is interesting for what it might have been rather than what it is. One way in which this operates is at an authorial level. The film was a long-standing project of Howard Hawks, and had Hawks, rather than Irving Rapper, directed the film it might have been something more than the 'leisurely whodunit' of which the *Newsweek* reviewer wrote. Longtime Hawks collaborator Jules Furthman was one of several writers employed on the project. Indeed, it appears that Hawks himself made an uncredited contribution to the script (see McCarthy, 1997: 352 and Mast: 1982, 397). The relevance of all this is that it suggests another (unrealized) film behind the actual 20th Century-Fox production. In a comparable way, the nineteenth-century legacy of gaslighting was drawn upon by the 20th Century-Fox production, though in many ways Hollywood's gaslight melodramas smoothed over the more complex aspects of gaslight's history.

For Hollywood, a key function of gaslighting was that it provided a means of differentiation. In terms of the crime genre, it assisted in the type A or type B distinctions of which another *Moss Rose* reviewer wrote—the distinction between the contemporary and the turn-of-the-century crime narrative. However, such distinctions could not be absolute. At one stage *Moss Rose* was to have opened with a title which introduced the film as taking place in 'London, shortly after the turn of the century—the gaslit renaissance of styles, manners and morals that shyly succeeded the hidebound Victorian era.'[5] While that title was never used, the film's gaslit setting did retain an element of signifying a point of change, a move from the Victorian to the modern.

Three years later the same studio that made *Moss Rose* produced *Night and the City*, another crime film set, and in this instance made, in London. In the course of this chapter I have referred to the emergence of a particular association linking London and gaslight; in the chapter that follows I will examine further the image of a dark, nineteenth-century London. However *Night and the City*, as well as being produced for 20th Century-Fox, has a modern-day setting and shifts the emphasis away from London being a city only just emerging from the past, giving it instead the characteristics that have come to define *film noir*. The film thus plays against certain expectations. Yet this is also to say that its London setting brings with it some of the type B features evident in *Moss Rose*. There is even a scene in *Night and the City* featuring a nightclub which is lit by candles and gas, a sign of the film's generic confusion and of the blurred boundaries separating the gaslight melodrama from the contemporary crime drama.

# 3 GOTHIC SOURCES/LONDON DISCOURSES: THE DARK METROPOLIS ON PAGE AND SCREEN

WHEN A TRADE dispute in 1947 led the American film industry to threaten a boycott of British cinemas, an editorial in *The Times* (17 October) pretended to suggest that 'there is, in fact, only one Hollywood product for which no amount of ingenuity can ever provide a substitute, only one loss which we must steel ourselves to writing off as irrecoverable, and that is the Hollywood version of life in Great Britain.'

Comments such as this had appeared periodically in the British press. Two years previously Richard Winnington had written in the *News Chronicle* (3 March 1945) that Hollywood was currently producing 'film after film about Great Britain, mostly from books by British authors,' and a new 20th Century-Fox film was but the latest, monstrous example of this trend.

> *Hangover Square* (Tivoli, Sunday. Directed by John Brahm) is *based* on the book by Patrick Hamilton, which he describes as a story of darkest Earls Court in 1939. This is a brilliant, ruthless piece of writing, eminently filmable. The hero, George Harvey Bone, is a schizophrenic, a decayed, dipsomaniac motorcar salesman from a third-rate public school. The heroine, like her Fascist lover, is vicious, empty, resentful. They deceive Mr. Bone, and are killed by him in the end. The book evokes with hatred and truth the atmosphere of a breeding ground of Fascist thugs. This is no morbidly sensational thriller. It is a study in decay wrought with something like the fierce artistry of a Zola.
>
> I mention all this to show the measure of contempt in which the producers hold the author, and what is even more important, you and me.
>
> For the scene is shifted to Chelsea—are these some of the *Gaslight* sets?—and the time to 1903. The schizophrenic becomes a brilliant composer (it's always safer to make a homicidal maniac an artist) engaging the usual hideous one-move-

ment concerto. The late Laird Cregar lumbers around with a Karloffian glare in the spacious mists which happily blur the architectural monstrosities. And a pure love interest is introduced between George Sanders and Faye Marlowe to offset Linda Darnell's hardness and ring the box-office bell.

Winnington, while not quite accurate in his synopsis of Hamilton's novel (in which George Harvey Bone never reaches the heights of selling motor-cars), nor doing justice to Bernard Herrmann's delirious score, was quite correct in stating that the 20th Century-Fox production was neither a faithful adaptations of that novel nor an accurate portrayal of London life. But why did the studio switch the novel's setting not just from Earls Court to Chelsea but from 1939 to 1903? Why was *Hangover Square*, along with a number of other adaptations from around the same time, transformed from a novel set in a contemporary or near-contemporary world into a film set in another era? And if 20th Century-Fox drew upon Hamilton's novel in what could be described as a selective manner, what other sources were significant? Winnington mentioned *Gaslight* (also based on Hamilton's work), though the sets he saw were more likely to have been previously used in *The Lodger* (made for 20th Century-Fox the previous year by the same director-producer-writer team, and also starring Cregar and Sanders). But what was significant here beyond any such specific influences? What particular significance does London have in this—Hollywood's imaginary London, but also that image of dark London developed in the nineteenth century that can be seen as leading into Hamilton's 'darkest Earls Court,' but perhaps also to Hollywood's dark and misty metropolis—and perhaps again to those films that have come to be known under the title *film noir*? Might *Hangover Square* be seen as belonging to a Gothic tradition, an urban variation on the tale of terror?

These questions are asked as part of my concern with the relationship between films and their source material. In particular, I am interested in the part that period settings play in this relationship, and will be investigating this with regard to specific examples, through an examination of the decision making process at 20th Century-Fox, later through the example of *Fanny by Gaslight*, but also with reference to broader patterns of influence. In effect, this chapter can be divided into three related stages. In the first stage the emphasis will be on the process of adaptation that led to the sort of changes introduced in the filming of *Hangover Square* but in other examples to the modernization of nineteenth-century fiction. The second stage focuses on the relationship between the image of London found in certain films of the 1940s and nineteenth-century accounts of the dark city. In the third stage the discussion is taken further back, to the notion of a Gothic tradition that can be traced back from the 1940s to the 1790s; the intention here is to identify signs of such a tradition, but also to examine critical usage of the Gothic tradition, and how such a tradition has been constructed or even invented.

## Nineteenth-Century London at 20th Century-Fox

THE MAJORITY OF the films listed in the filmography to this book were adaptations from either literature or the theater (or both, in a case such as *Kind Lady*, whose immediate source was Edward Chodorov's play, which was in its turn based on a Hugh Walpole story), the exceptions being *Bluebeard*, *The Case of Charles Peace*, *Catman of Paris*, and *Madeleine*. The literary adaptation has been one of the ways through which period settings have featured within films, and literary or theatrical source material can have a similar function here to that of period decor. Andrew Higson has argued that in British heritage films of the 1980s and early 1990s, source material became one of the 'properties on display,' along with stately homes, landscapes, interiors, and furnishings (1996: 233). This understanding of source material as a treasured property can be extended even back to the 1940s, and to Hollywood as well as British cinema. A British trend can be traced back to (and beyond) films such as *Henry V* (1945) and compared with American costume dramas such as *The Age of Innocence* (1993) (see Higson, 1996: 235–36), while the latter film drew upon earlier Hollywood productions, notably *The Heiress* (1949), based on Henry James's *Washington Square* (1880)—which also reached the screen by way of a stage version.

However, source material has served different purposes within the film industry. 'If British cinema has been markedly literary, as the American cinema—similarly indebted to the novel—has generally not been, this is due as much to the *kind* of adaptation as the number,' notes Brian MacFarland, who observes also that 'the term "property developer" has [for certain critics] taken on sinister connotations, suggesting one who engages in the brutal transformation of a fondly remembered site into something rich and strange—and inferior' (1986: 120). Even within Hollywood distinctions can be made between those films based on sources which provided a literary prestige to be exploited (though this did not prevent the kind of brutal transformation to which MacFarland refers), and those where the source material provided little more than a starting point. The literary source material of MGM's *The Picture of Dorian Gray* provided one, though not the only one, of the film's selling points; in the film's pressbook three potential promotional angles were suggested—mystery ('the idea is not to disclose what's actually in the picture'), horror ('sensationalize the picture'), and 'selling Oscar Wilde as a famous author and "The Picture of Dorian Gray" as his most popular literary work.' The following year, another studio, Warner Bros., brought to the screen another story written in the late nineteenth century, Israel Zangwill's *The Big Bow Mystery* (1892). But Warner Bros. devised a new title—*The Verdict*—and in its pressbook described the film simply as a 'new mystery film.' What Zangwill's less prestigious story provided was a location (late nineteenth-century London) and an idea (the story is a 'locked room mystery') rather than literary reputation.

*The Big Bow Mystery* had in fact been filmed previously, in 1928 as *The Perfect Crime* and in 1934 as *The Crime Doctor*. Both these earlier versions had retained the basic locked room premise, but modernized the story and moved the setting to America. Bearing this modernization in mind, rather than seeing the gaslit and fog-strewn setting of the 1946 version as the necessary consequence of the film's source material, it is more plausible to see this setting as having been inspired by the release in the previous couple of years of films such as *Gaslight* and *Hangover Square*.

Different trends within the crime genre—on the one hand an emphasis on contemporary iconography, on the other hand the use of, and even the transformation into, period settings—can be further brought out if one looks at the numerous Sherlock Holmes films made in the first half of the twentieth century. Conan Doyle's Sherlock Holmes stories were first published in the years between 1887 and 1927, though most are set in the nineteenth century. They have, indeed, acquired a particular association with the 1890s, an association strong enough for it to be possible to put that statement the other way round, and to say that 1890s London has come to be particularly associated with the figure of Sherlock Holmes. This process was well established by the 1940s; the notion of Holmes and Watson being figures separated from the contemporary (specifically from contemporary conflict) can be identified in the 1944 anthology of writing on Sherlock Holmes, *Profile by Gaslight*, and in particular in Vincent Starrett's poem '221B,' which was included in that anthology (Smith, 1944: 290) and contains the lines:

> *Here, though the world explode, these two survive,*
> *And it is always eighteen ninety five.*

The two 20th Century-Fox films, *Hound of the Baskervilles* (1939) and *The Adventures of Sherlock Holmes* (1940), had a significant influence on this process, in that they placed Holmes and Watson (played here by Basil Rathbone and Nigel Bruce) in a clearly Victorian milieu, circa 1895 (*The Adventures of Sherlock Holmes* opens with a quotation signed Sherlock Holmes, dated 9 May 1894). However, the Victorian settings of the 20th Century-Fox films were, at the time, something of a break with tradition. The majority of the Sherlock Holmes films made in the first half of the twentieth century were given a *contemporary* setting. This was the case with the fifteen two-reel Stoll films produced in the 1920s and the five films from the 1930s starring Arthur Wontner as Holmes. Updated settings were also featured in *Sherlock Holmes* (1931) (which found Clive Brook as Holmes up against Chicago-style gangsters), *The Speckled Band* (1931) (of which *Variety* commented that the studio had turned Holmes's 'quarters in Baker Street into an ultra-modern office, complete with stenogs [sic] and dictaphones' [25 March 1931]) and *A Study in Scarlet* (1933) (see Haydock, 1978, for details of these and other film versions).

Modernization was also evident when Sherlock Holmes was portrayed on the stage, though here there was also evidence of a curious combination of old and new. The actor William Gillette, who had to a large degree made the part his own, made his farewell stage appearance as Sherlock Holmes in 1929, in a performance in which most of the cast appeared in modern dress. However, it was noted in the *New York Times* (26 November 1929) that the settings were period and Gillette himself appeared in period costume.

Following on from the two films they made at 20th Century-Fox, Rathbone and Bruce made a further twelve Sherlock Holmes films at Universal between 1942 and 1946, films which again placed the characters in contemporary settings. It has been suggested that the significance of this updating for Universal was that it eliminated expensive sets and costumes (Haralovitch, 1979: 55). This was no doubt an important consideration, but what was also important in the context of the crime genre was the premium placed on the contemporary (on guns, cars, 'stenogs and dictaphones,' and the paraphernalia of modernity). However, the presence of a different strand of crime narrative within the cinema (the tradition, largely neglected within film studies, of the gentleman amateur investigator), combined with the particular and developing Victorian connotations of the Sherlock Holmes stories, existed as an alternative pressure, and led to a variation on the combination of old and new found in the Gillette's final appearance as Holmes. Hence this report on the Universal films, also in the *New York Times* (28 May 1944):

> An attempt to 'modernize' the detective and his Boswell in two previous films in which Holmes was called upon to solve problems of the current war, in Canadian and Washington locales, proved disappointing, according to Mr. Rathbone. From now on the stories were to be kept 'timeless'—a kind of present-day proposition so far as modern conveniences such as telephones and automobiles are concerned, but with dialogue and characteristics strictly of the Victorian era, it is explained.

On the other hand, an early script written for the 1939 version of *The Hound of the Baskervilles* elicited the following comment from Darryl Zanuck:

> One of the tasks this job entails is to modernize the stilted dialogue in the original without, however, robbing it of its traditional Sherlock Holmes flavor. Little effort has been made to do this in this preparatory version.[1]

These differing drives—on the one hand toward modernization, on the other hand back to past—can also be detected in different versions of *The Lodger*. The 1944, 20th Century-Fox film is clearly signaled as being set in late-Victorian London, the time of the Jack-the-Ripper murders which it purports to portray. The 1954 remake *The Man in the Attic* retained this late-Victorian setting (along with a good part of the dialogue of the earlier film). Marie Belloc Lowndes's 1913 novel on which the film was based was itself derived from the Jack-the-Ripper murders, although it in fact makes no direct reference to the murders committed in 1888 and has a setting that appears to belong to the twentieth rather than nineteenth century (though this is never made explicit). The two British film versions that came out in 1926 and 1932 both followed the novel in featuring a murderer named 'The Avenger' as opposed to Jack-the-Ripper. They also used contemporary as opposed to period settings. That is, in the case of the 1944 version, as in the case of *The Verdict*, a Victorian setting was imposed upon, rather than simply derived from, the film's source material.

This was even more clearly the case with another film based on a Marie Belloc Lowndes novel—*Ivy* (1947), which was produced at Universal at a time when the studio was aiming for a more prestigious product, and which was adapted from Lowndes's *The Story of Ivy*. Originally published in 1927, the Lowndes novel had a 1920s setting. A discussion of promotional possibilities for *Ivy* led to the following memo:

> There's a good story in the fact that the book, *Ivy* is a modern story but we switched the time back to 1909 to enable us to get added dramatic effect. This is very rarely done, the switch usually being in the opposite direction. However, we might be able to find one or two other instances.[2]

Leaving aside the question of whether an Edwardian setting did add drama to the narrative, the speculation that it might be possible to discover other instances of such changes was correct. *Hangover Square* and *The Suspect*, two films set in London at the beginning of the century, were both based on novels set in London in the 1930s; *Experiment Perilous*, a novel set in 1940s New York was made into a film which still used a New York setting but which shifted that setting back to the beginning of the century (with a flashback sequence going still further back in time); *Some Must Watch*, an Ethel Lina White crime novel set on the Welsh-English border in the 1930s, became *The Spiral Staircase*, the action of which takes place in New England in the 1900s. After the release of *Ivy* the trend was continued with adaptations of *The House by the River*, a novel written by A. P. Herbert with a Thames-side, post-World War I setting, which became a film directed by Fritz Lang set in late-Victorian America, and of *X vs. Rex*, a Philip MacDonald novel set in 1930s London, which retained its London setting when filmed as *Hour of 13* but was moved back to the late-Victorian era.

One explanation for this trend is that by the 1940s period settings had re-acquired an appeal, at least in the eyes of filmmakers, though 'gaslit London' existed as but one alternative in the paradigm. When MacDonald's *X vs. Rex* was originally filmed by MGM—in 1934 as *The Mystery of Mr. X*—the novel's contemporary, London setting had been retained. In deciding to remake the story of a jewel thief who assists the authorities in catching a serial killer specializing in the murder of policemen, MGM did not immediately choose a period setting and for some time seemed disinclined to opt for one in London. A series of different script versions, the first of which was written in 1945, moved the setting from contemporary London to Rio de Janeiro to Buenos Aires to New York to Cape Town before returning to London, a script dated 1 January 1951 announcing that 'the action takes place in London during the gaslight period of the 80s.' This is the setting that was essentially retained in the completed film, a later script version's differing only in specifying 'the gaslight era at the turn of the century,' while the pressbook referred to the film's 'background of 1890 London.'[3]

In the 1940s, Hollywood Majors from MGM to Warner Bros. placed crime narratives in gaslit, nineteenth-century settings, though it is ironically appropriate that this trend should have been particularly marked at 20th Century-Fox. The name has perhaps inevitably provoked comments such as Darryl Zanuck biographer Mel Gustow's statement that 'with justification, partly because of Zanuck's costume epics, in the late thirties his studio was referred to as "Sixteenth Century-Fox"' (1971: 69–70). A variation on this story is provided by George F. Custen, who suggests that it 'was said (though not within Zanuck's hearing) that the man credited with creating the cinematic hard-boiled style at Warner Brothers now headed a studio that should be renamed Nineteenth Century-Fox.' In fact, most films made at 20th Century-Fox while Zanuck was in charge were set in the twentieth century. However, a number of such films exhibited what Custen calls 'a nostalgia of place'—titles such as *Chad Hanna* (1940) were set in American locations that seemed to exist in isolation from modernity. In addition, a significant number of other 20th Century-Fox films had an explicit period setting—according to Custen's calculations, almost a quarter of the films made at the studio under Zanuck were set between 1865 and 1920 (200). Many of these were set in nineteenth-century America. Having left Warner Bros., Zanuck had set up his own production company, 20th Century; the first film released by this new company was *The Bowery* (1933), set in New York in the 1890s. When 20th Century and Fox merged in 1934 the new company continued to use late nineteenth-century American settings, often as a backdrop for musicals, but also for films such as *In Old Chicago* (1938)—the studio's most expensive film of the decade, and also the one that took the most at the box-office (see Solomon, 1988, and Finler, 1992). But on other occasions the films produced at both 20th Century and 20th Century-Fox returned to the non-American past. Thus Shirley Temple, the leading star at 20th Century-Fox in the 1930s, often found herself in nineteenth-century dress, whether in a context that was American (*Dimples*(1936)), British (*The Little Princess* (1939)), or British Imperial (*Wee Willie Winkie* (1937)).

The studio continued this practice in the 1940s. On 12 December 1944, *Hollywood Reporter* announced: "20th [Century]-Fox Going in Heavily for Period Pix." The article mentioned ten titles, purchased (*Forever Amber, Captain from Castile*), in production (*Dragonwyck, Sitting Bull, Centennial Summer, Miss Pilgrim's Progress, Times Have Changed*), or completed (*A Royal Scandal, Nob Hill* and *Hangover Square*).

Initial scripts for *Hangover Square* had moved the setting only very slightly further back from the novel's 1939 to 1937—on 16 December 1943 the film had been described in *Hollywood Reporter* as 'a *modern* story dealing with a schizophrenic whose disordered mind shuttles between love and murder' (my italics). The small time shift had the effect of removing any sense of the approaching war along with the novel's references to fascism within Britain; what these scripts also did was to make the story conform more clearly to the conventions of the crime genre. Hamilton's novel does end in murder but it contains none of the investigative machinery common to crime fiction; in contrast, in all of the *Hangover Square* film scripts a prominent role is given to characters who function as investigators, detectives, writers of detectives stories, or psychiatrists (collapsed in the completed film in the figure of a psychiatrist employed by Scotland Yard who writes articles about methods of murder).

The setting was moved further back in time following comments made by Zanuck after a script conference. Zanuck's demands were as follows:

> The story should be laid in London in 1910 [this later became 1903]. It is essential that we put it back to 1910 in order to get

the flavor of mystery that goes with the period. Today when you think of crime you think of the FBI and scientific systems etc., and all the mystery has gone out of it.

To this he added that the script was 'over-written from the stand-point of set,' needed to be confined to the $850,000 budget, and that there was 'no reason why we cannot use all of the streets and sets as they are from *The Lodger*.'[4]

Two explanations for the film's period setting are present here, one based on associations linking London, crime, and the past, under the umbrella of 'mystery,' the other based on the practical and economic question of the availability of the sets from *The Lodger*.

'Mystery' is a term that has been used in a variety of different fictional contexts. For the purpose of this discussion it is significant for its use in the eighteenth-century Gothic novel (*The Mysteries of Udolpho*), nineteenth-century urban narratives and gaslit settings (*The Mysteries of London*), and through how, particularly in the United States, it has come to signify 'crime fiction,' especially though not exclusively the traditional detective story mainly associated with England and usually based around a murder and its investigation (*The Mystery of the Hansom Cab* among many others). Zanuck's yearning for the mystery of the past did not preclude 20th Century-Fox from also releasing *The House on 92nd Street* in 1945, a film that did involve crime, the FBI, and 'scientific systems' in a contemporary American setting, just as it had not prevented Zanuck, when he had been in charge of production at Warner Bros., from producing gangster films such as *The Public Enemy* (1931). His comments do not imply a rejection of a 'scientific systems' approach to crime narratives but are based on the notion of two strands of crime fiction, one associated with present-day America, the other with an England of the past.

These strands were not distinct from each other, and those involved in the production of one form of crime narrative could also be responsible for the other. Thus John Brahm went on to direct, and Robert Bassler (producer of *The Lodger* and *Hangover Square*) to produce, *The Brasher Doubloon* (1947), an adaptation of one of Raymond Chandler's 'hard-boiled' novels of contemporary American crime, while Barré Lyndon scripted both *Hangover Square* and *The House on 92nd Street*, all of these films being made under the overall supervision of Darryl Zanuck. In addition, films such as *The Lodger* and *Hangover Square* were set on the edge of modernity, and used this to contrast modern methods of detection with a more traditional approach, in a manner that can be traced back to the Sherlock Holmes stories or perhaps to the writings of Edgar Allan Poe. Thus in *The Lodger* emphasis is placed on the use of finger-printing as a new method of detection, while in *Hangover Square* John Harvey Bone, having absent-mindedly committed one murder, goes off to see a Scotland Yard employee, someone whom he describes as 'very brilliant in new ideas about the mind.' But it was clearly perceived to be important to differentiate forms of crime narrative, here and in other instances such as *Moss Rose*, and this perception appears to have been a key element in the decision to rewrite *Hangover Square* with a period setting.

The practical and economic considerations were important also, but in relation to these associations between England and the past. The sets from *The Lodger* would not have been the only ones available on the studio lot, nor would they have been unadaptable to a different period. In fact, the cost of period settings could be an incentive for the updating of a setting, as appears to have been in case with Universal's Sherlock Holmes films. One can infer from this that the economic value of re-using sets rested primarily in the desire to accentuate the connections between *The Lodger* and *Hangover Square*, and so to repeat the box-office success of the earlier film.

In addition, if the source material for *Hangover Square* did set up an association with the film's gaslight setting it was not through the novel itself but through the name of its author. Thus the reviewer who referred to *Hangover Square* as 'another of Patrick Hamilton's gaslit psychological thrillers' was drawing upon the association between Hamilton and gaslit settings that had been established through his play, *Gas Light*, and its adaptation for the screen (*New York Herald Tribune*, 8 February 1945), associations that may also have been in Richard Winnington's mind when he wrote his attack on the adaptation of *Hangover Square*.

## Londonania

HOLLYWOOD'S ROLE AS 'property developer' represented one facet of the importance of source material. But what did these films draw upon beyond their immediate sources, how did any such material work its way onto the screen, and what transformations accompanied this process?

In a discussion of what he called 'the elusive cinematic city,' Colin McArthur has argued that Hollywood's economic and aesthetic hegemony over world cinema has meant that when cities either within or outside the United States appear on cinema screens throughout the world they tend to 'project the needs, fears, fantasies and representations of particular American ideologies,' rather than the self-definition of other places and peoples. He went on to note, however, that such cinematic cities can also draw upon discourses that predate Hollywood and are not traceable to American sources alone.

Examining representations of London on film, McArthur cites a dance number—entitled 'Limehouse Blues'—in the film *Ziegfeld Follies* (1946), which 'shows a bleak, fog-ridden Thames-scape populated primarily by Chinese but also by stalwart 'bobbies,' Bill Sykes-type ruffians, pawky and cheerful pearly kings and queens, and bizarre down-and-outs.' He suggests that this sequence is informed by 'a composite discourse derived from travellers' accounts of London, the novels of Charles Dickens (particularly *Bleak House*), the Sherlock Holmes stories of Sir Arthur Conan Doyle, and press accounts of the Jack-the-Ripper murders.' According to McArthur, this 'construction of London (or diverse aspects of it) is evident in many Hollywood-based or Hollywood-financed movies,' including MGM's *Gaslight*, 20th Century-Fox's *Hangover Square* and Warner Bros.'s *The Verdict*, leading McArthur to suggest that 'the "London discourse" shaping the above films may have found the harsh black and white of the classic *film noir* a more congenial form of expression [as opposed to the color of *Ziegfeld Follies*], hence the clustering of these titles around the 1940s' (1997: 34–35).

Travelers' accounts, Dickens's novels, Conan Doyle's stories, and newspaper reports of Jack-the-Ripper represent only the tip of a nineteenth-century iceberg. A good idea of the range of lesser known 'low-life' material circulating in London during the nineteenth and early twentieth century can be found in two articles published in the *Indiana University Bookman*: Donald Gray's 'Picturesque London' and Martha Vicinus's 'Dark London.' Both authors divide the material they describe into five categories. Gray (1977: 41–42) identifies:

> 1) Collections of views of London; 2) Pictorial or verbal sketches of contemporary London scenes, events, characters; 3) Illustrated collections of London street cries; 4) Antiquarian sketches, mostly verbal; 5) Histories of particular localities.

Vicinus divides her material under the headings: 'Fast Life Guides,' 'Night Life Guides,' 'Ragged London,' 'Criminal London,' and 'Reforming London.' Under 'Fast Life Guides' she lists material dating mainly from the first half of the nineteenth century that follows on from an eighteenth-century tradition of pornographic introductions to city life—'fiction purporting to be written by "men of pleasure" or prostitutes,' guides to London brothels, gambling dens and supper rooms, and an assortment of 'short-lived journals specializing in gossip, innuendo, and facetious tales.' The 'Night Life Guides' include fiction emphasizing London's night life, from music halls to expensive brothels and gambling dens, as well as short journalistic but fictionalized accounts of visits to 'famous, but socially remote, night spots, such as the East End's theatres.' The 'Ragged London' material includes accounts of the London poor with particular emphasis on children and child labor, as well as fiction by Edwin Pugh, Arthur Morrison, and others. The material categorized under the title 'Criminal London' dates mainly from the second half of the nineteenth century, in particular from the period between 1870 to 1900, though it also includes material from up to 1935; it 'includes accounts of outright criminal behavior and police activity,' a quantity of popular ephemera—penny and two-penny broadsides and pamphlets describing famous murders, trials and rapes—a 'small quantity of detective fiction and fictionalized autobiographies,' plus books, pamphlets and broadsheets on subjects such as the trial and execution of Charles Peace, the poisoning of Charles Bravo, 'the Whitechapel mystery,' and publications such as *Police News*. The 'Reforming London' material includes mission work-accounts, a few books on prisoners and prison-reform, and a more substantial body of material on prostitution, agitation against 'the white slave trade,' and schemes for the reform of prostitutes (Vicinus, 1977a: 63–92).

What links are there between such books, pamphlets, and papers and films of the 1940s? The clearest line of connection would seem to be that running from the material listed by Vicinus under the heading 'Criminal London.' In the 1940s, along with films directly or indirectly based on the stories of Conan Doyle, titles such as *The Lodger, Room to Let* (both based on the Jack-the-Ripper murders), *The Case of Charles Peace,* and *So Evil My Love* (adapted from a fictionalized account based on the death of Charles Bravo), provided evidence of a continued preoccupation with criminality in Victorian London, while the legacy of nineteenth-century fast life guides and literature on prostitution remained at a more submerged level. Another line of connection can be traced back from the 1944 screen adaptation of Michael Sadleir's 1941 novel, *Fanny by Gaslight*.

As well as being a writer of both fiction and non-fiction, Sadleir was a publisher (of his friend and drinking companion Patrick Hamilton, among others), a bibliographer, and a collector. He amassed substantial collections in a number of fields, specializing in Gothic and Victorian novels as well as what he called 'Londonania.' What Gray and Vicinus describe in their articles is a collection 'based on Michael Sadleir's collection of low-life material, purchased by the Lilly Library in the United States in 1971' (Vicinus, 1977b: 2). On Sadleir's own account, he made use of this material in his fiction: he stated that he had 'from the first looked forward to using predominantly non-fictional Londonania as decor for fiction. That process began with the writing of *Fanny by Gaslight* and *Forlorn Street*' (1951: xxii and xxiii).

In some ways this use is most evident in *Forlorn Street* (1946), a novel which continued the preoccupation with prostitution evident in *Fanny by Gaslight*, but placed more emphasis on the 'down-market' side of the trade, and which was supplemented with quotations from, and references to, W. T. Stead's account of child prostitution published in the *Pall Mall Gazette*, the *Illustrated Police Gazette*, Gustave Doré, Henry Mayhew, and other Victorian sources that can be traced back to the collection described by Gray and Vicinus. Indeed, for one reviewer of *Forlorn Street*, the author was 'so interested in documenting and describing this fantastically evil London that the book is more often like a report on social conditions than it is like a novel' (*San Francisco Chronicle*, 1 November 1946, quoted in Stokes, 1980: 3–4), though, as Vicinus notes of the material Sadleir collected, 'however attractive or fearful it may be to reader and author, it is an interpreted world that we see in print, and not an objective account of darkest London' (1977a: 67). But this image of London also resurfaces, in its re-interpreted form, in Sadleir's earlier novel, *Fanny by Gaslight* and, re-interpreted again, in the film adaptation of that novel made at Gainsborough (see Figure 3)—a film promoted in its pressbook as a story mainly based on Sadleir's 'collection of unique Victorian data.'

Re-interpretation needs to be stressed. As Vicinus indicates, Sadleir collected a wide range of material on London, but there are

Figure 3. *Fanny by Gaslight* (1944).

generalizations that can be made about his collection: it was often material that had ephemeral status, much of it was what might be called 'street literature,' while Vicinus notes that, at least with respect to the fast life guides, the readership must have been largely male. The siphoning of this material into a private collection represented a shift in status, as the ephemeral became collectible (see chapter five for a further consideration of this), and a shift also from the public to the private. The reformulation of the material in that collection in the form of a popular, twentieth-century novel constituted another shift, back from the exclusive and the private toward a wider audience, and also involved the remolding of that material so that it became, in Sadleir's words, 'decor' for a romance. The adaptation of that novel into one of a cycle of costume melodramas identified as appealing primarily to a female audience (see Harper on the female audience for this and other Gainsborough films of the period, 1994: 121) represented a further shift. The status of this ephemera changed again with the purchase of the collection by an American academic institution, as it became an 'irreplaceable file of primary sources for the study of London

life, popular culture, and entertainment in nineteenth-century England'
(Vicinus, 1977b: 2).

Like *Forlorn Street*, Sadleir's *Fanny by Gaslight* is concerned
with detailing the various aspects of Victorian prostitution and
pornography, in this case through a narrative in which the heroine
(the illegitimate daughter of a politician) is brought up in house situated above a brothel, and later, though seemingly never becoming
a prostitute herself, is employed in a high-class brothel (where she
meets, as one does, another politician, with whom she proceeds to
have an affair). There are a number of different narrators within
Sadleir's novel. Sections are presented as being the story of Fanny
told by herself, though written by Gerald Warbeck, a book-publisher
who discovers her in the 1930s. A further section is narrated by
Harry Somerfield, the man with whom Fanny has an affair in the
1870s, while each of these period narratives are framed by the opening and closing sections, which are located in the 1930s and narrated in the third person, but essentially through the eyes of Warbeck.
Thus the heroine's story is framed by a male narrative.

In bringing this story to the screen, Gainsborough appears to have
been intent on building on the box-office success of *The Man in Grey*
(1943). Sadleir's novel was modified to fit in with the successful formula of the earlier film, the actors Phyllis Calvert, Stewart Granger
and James Mason providing variations on the parts they had played
in the earlier film, while the Regency London of *The Man in Grey*
became the Victorian London of *Fanny by Gaslight*. However, while
*The Man in Grey* had framed its period narrative with opening and
closing scenes set during World War II, no such device was used in the
film version of *Fanny by Gaslight*, though in one scene Somerfield
does look to the future, and (in tune with a wartime emphasis on com-
munal values) to a world without class distinctions.

Reviewers concentrated rather on the film's 'escapism,' on specu-
lating on its appeal to women, and on comparisons between film and
novel. For the *News Chronicle* reviewer (6 May 1944) the film was
'period romantic, away from the war, and has been labeled by experts
as a "women's film"'; in the *New Statesman* (6 May 1944) it was
noted that 'in general the seamier episodes have been toned down.' A
further pressure for change can be identified here: censorship. Sadleir
had used the clandestine or semi-clandestine material (produced both
before and after the Obscene Publications Act of 1857) he had collected as the basis for a novel about prostitution, illegitimacy, and

extra-marital sex. In a number of ways film censorship was relaxed in Britain during World War II, as is demonstrated by the fact that *Fanny by Gaslight* was released, with the British Board of Film Censors objecting to no more than a single (unidentified) word of dialogue. However, if the film did retain some aspects of Sadleir's novel, its 'toning down' of that material can be explained partly by the fact that censorship tends to be directly operated mainly by filmmakers and production companies rather than those officially appointed as censors; in the case of *Fanny by Gaslight,* material likely to raise objections from the British censors appears to have been removed before the proposed film was submitted for approval.

In fact, the completed film did run into censorship problems, but in the United States rather than Britain. Submitted to the Production Code Administration (PCA), the body whose approval was necessary if it was to be released in major cinemas in the United States, it was initially refused their certificate of approval. Objections were made to the fact that particular scenes were set in a brothel, to Fanny's illegitimacy, to her and Somerfield living together outside of marriage, as well as to individual passages of dialogue. After an initial period when it was suggested that some of these issues were so central to the film's narrative that it would simply have to be rejected, followed by a period when it was argued that certain scenes would have to be reshot, *Fanny by Gaslight* was eventually given Code approval without any reshooting, though short eighteen minutes of film. But the film was not released in the United States until 1948, and when it was, as well as having lost a certain amount of footage, it was under a different title: *Man of Evil.*

The title change can be partly explained by the fact that, though James Mason's role as the villain in the film was a secondary one, by this date he had acquired a box-office appeal in the United States (which Phyllis Calvert, who played Fanny, had not), and partly on account of the American connotations of the word 'fanny,' the PCA having initially objected to the original title, relenting only on the condition that the distributors would 'submit all advertising and exploitation material to the Advertising Advisory Council and to avoid any use therein of such expressions as "his Fanny," "her Fanny," etc., even though it could be said that the use of such phrases referred to the leading characters in the film.'[5]

These different versions of Victorian London—*Man of Evil,* Gainsborough's *Fanny by Gaslight,* Sadleir's *Fanny by Gaslight,* and

the material that Sadleir collected and made use of in his novel—
point to the persistence of a certain mythology of the dark metropolis as well as to the ways in which that mythology became progressively reformulated, and ultimately reshaped to fit the demands
of the Hollywood studio system. Examining this process brings out
some of the same issues observable in relation to *Hangover Square*.
Thus it is notable how both *Hangover Square* and the censorship
problems of *Fanny by Gaslight* could be understood in Britain at the
end of World War II in terms of Anglo-American conflict—and how
around the same time a similar understanding also colored reports
that MGM had attempted to have all prints of the British film version of *Gaslight* destroyed so that their version should be unchal-
lenged (see C. A. Lejeune's review of the American version, *The
Observer*, 16 July 1944). More generally, one can note how films
drew upon discourses from the previous century, though this process
tended to be indirect rather than direct, and a question of transformation rather than simple continuity.

## Descent and Invention

THE FILM VERSION of *Fanny by Gaslight* opens with a sunlit London
scene in which two rather well-spoken girls are shown playing a
game of catch to the background sound of the street-cries of a cock-
le seller. When one of the girls throws the ball down some steps, she
dares her friend—Fanny—to collect it. Fanny (played at this point
by Ann Stevens) does so, and then, dared again, goes through the
door at the bottom of the steps, despite (or because of) the fact that
it is made clear that what is beyond the door is forbidden territory.
The scene moves from a daylight exterior to a half-lit interior—from
'picturesque London' to 'dark London.' Fanny walks on down a
flight of stairs, glancing at a suggestive painting on the wall, starting
when she sees what turns out to be the statue of a woman, but continuing on toward a partially curtained-off part of the room.

Viewers in the United States did not see what Fanny saw beyond
the curtain, for the forbidden place that Fanny had entered was the
brothel underlying her apparently respectable Victorian home, and
beyond the curtain she was to meet a couple of prostitutes. As the PCA
made clear to Eagle-Lion films, who were to distribute the film in
America, 'scenes in houses of prostitution, no matter how delicately
handled in presentation, are objectionable.' Joseph Breen, director in
charge of the PCA, later wrote to William Burnside, of Eagle-Lion:

It will be necessary to change the character of the bawdy house. You will recall that we agree that it might easily be changed to that of a gambling establishment. This would be acceptable.

You will have in mind our thought regarding the deletion of the shot of the little girl talking with the 'ladies,' early in the picture, and our further thought that if this scene were deleted and a new scene shot, affirmatively establishing it that the house was a gambling house, we might avoid the necessity of making other changes in subsequent scenes.[6]

The brothel never became a gambling house, but by the time *Fanny by Gaslight* had become *Man of Evil* the sequence of the little girl talking to the ladies had been removed. The shot of the girl approaching the curtain remained.

Scenes in which a girl or young woman looks beyond a curtain are a characteristic feature of the Gothic novel. Perhaps the most famous example appears in Ann Radcliffe's *The Mysteries of Udolpho* (1794), when the curiosity of the heroine, Emily, induces her to investigate what lies beyond a veiled recess in the castle of Udolpho—and having done so, to drop senseless to the floor (1980: 348). Here the reader does discover what Emily thought she saw (a human body partly eaten by worms), what she actually saw (a wax figure designed to convey an image of human mortality), though only after a gap of a few hundred pages (662).

Not being a Gothic narrative, *Fanny by Gaslight* does not deal in such horrors, and while it might be interesting to speculate whether those audiences denied a sight of young Fanny and two prostitutes experienced that sublime terror that Gothic novelists such as Radcliffe aimed to evoke through obscurity, the twenty second shot that shows Fanny approaching the curtain cannot really be said to offer a sufficient build-up for any such reaction. Yet, with its dark, slightly subterranean (forbidden and forbidding) interior and curious heroine, the opening sequence does offer a taste of the Gothic. Another film released the same year and also set in Victorian London—MGM's *Gaslight*—has come to be commonly discussed as a 'Gothic romance' (see, for instance, Fletcher, 1995), while *The Lodger*, also released in 1944, inspired one reviewer to write: 'It's a Gothic we all enjoy, and the latest edition of the *Globe* brings shivers with its details of yet another murder' (*New Statesman*, 12 February 1944). This suggests a further but related set of sources that these and other films drew upon, a Gothic tradition, more specifically an urban variation of the Gothic, one that can be traced back to the late-eighteenth-century Gothic novel, but that reached the cinema by way of a nineteenth-century transformation of such fiction.

An eighteenth-century Gothic novel such as *The Mysteries of Udolpho* was set in the past, outside Britain, and for the most part in an isolated location. But over time, Gothic settings have been subject to change, in terms of both historical period and geographical position. According to Christine Gledhill, the Gothic's importance to Victorian melodrama arguably lay in its return to an atavistic past,

> its medievalism providing a theatrically pictorial vocabulary—the castle, the towers and dungeons, the landscape and the elements—with which to construct a symbolic arena for the acts of figures in whom moral polarities could be invested without depending on either transcendent hierarchies or the constraints of realist discourse. In its turn the Victorian has provided for Hollywood—notably its 1940s cycle of gothic romances—exactly the same function: a past that could be recalled to reincarnate moral conflict contemporary society believed it had outgrown (1987: 32).

For Robert Mighall, the Gothic does not simply involve a return to the past; it is based upon a contrast between the past and a more enlightened modernity. It is founded on anachronism:

> novels which have historical settings, such as *The Castle of Otranto* (1764), *A Sicilian Romance* (1790), and *The Mysteries of Udolpho* (1794), feature heroes and heroines who are blessed with modern attitudes and sensibilities. They are the reader's counterparts, menaced by the Gothic past in the form of feudal despots and corrupt ecclesiastics. This emphasis on anachronism is reversed but still maintained when the context is modern and proximate; then the threat derives from isolated vestiges which survive into the present and threaten the values of modernity (1999: 276–77).

This combination of modernity and the past is central to the films and other works discussed here. For if the Victorian provided Hollywood with an atavistic past equivalent to that recalled in earlier Gothic novels and dramas, that past was again inhabited by anachronistically modern, enlightened Scotland Yard employees.

However, what is significant here is not just the combination of old and new, but how these were combined. In the anachronistic combination of period and modern used when William Gillette played the part of Sherlock Holmes in a 1929 stage production, it was the leading man (Gillette as Holmes) who was dressed in the costume of the past, while the supporting cast appeared in modern dress. If the Gothic is primarily a 'Whiggish' mode, premised on a belief in the value of progress and of escape from the corruption of the past, and if Hollywood films built on this premise, such films could also be informed by a certain nostalgia, part of the same process that shifted Sherlock Holmes from modern intelligence seeing through the fog of London to a figure restating past values in a confusingly modern world.

It is possible to map Gothic shifts more precisely. A survey of nearly sixty Gothic novels from the late eighteenth and early nineteenth century has led Franco Moretti to conclude that 'in general, Gothic stories were initially set in Italy and France; moved north, to Germany, around 1800; and then moved north again, to Scotland, after 1820'—a lone tale set in Renaissance London was very much the exception' (1998: 16). But while the 'original' Gothic fiction may have tended to avoid cities in general and London in particular, and while a form of what Robert Heilman called 'new Gothic' developed through Charlotte Brontë's novel *Jane Eyre* (1847) (see Heilman, 1958) and thence to Daphne Du Maurier's *Rebecca* (1938), to *Rebecca* (1940), the film directed by Alfred Hitchcock, and to other 'Gothic romance' films of the 1940s, the Victorian era also saw the emergence of what can be called the 'urban Gothic,' which provided another channel through which the Gothic reached the cinema screen.

The notion of the 'urban Gothic' has been invoked by Kathleen Spencer, who argued that it was a development of the 1880s (1987: 91). Writing of *Bleak House* (1852–53), Alan Pritchard has spoken of Charles Dickens's 'perception that the remote and isolated country mansion or castle is not so much the setting of ruin and darkness and mystery and horror, as the great modern city: the Gothic horrors are here and now' (quoted in Mighall, 1999: 69). However, a case can be made for placing the emergence of the urban Gothic at an earlier date. The growth of the nineteenth-century metropolis was accompanied by a growth of a publishing industry catering to this emerging market. The city became an increasingly prominent subject of literature and theater, and one way in which this exhibited itself was in the cycle of novels of urban mysteries initiated in France with Eugene Sue's *The Mysteries of Paris* (1842–43) and taken up in Britain by G. W. M. Reynolds's *The Mysteries of London* (1844–48), though also traceable back to Dickens's *Oliver Twist* (1837–39), from which sources it can be seen to have bled into the London discourse of which McArthur spoke and Sadleir collected, wrote about and used.

In his introduction to the re-issue of the Reynolds serial novel, Trefor Thomas has argued that such novels represent 'an urbanization of eighteenth-century Gothic, and a new consciousness of the city as inexplicable and impenetrable' (1996: ix). This urbanization represented a transformation—for Michael Sadleir (writing in his capacity of historian of the Gothic) in the 1830s and 1840s 'the Gothic novel crashed, and became the vulgar "blood,"' though the spirit of melodrama and terror persisted and persists unsubdued (1944: 199). Put another way, one can suggest that *The Mysteries of London* and its sequel *Mysteries of the Court of London* (1849–56) replaced the Gothic castle and surrounding forest with a city of underground chambers and passageways, and thus helped to bring home to the modern urban novel the violence and sensationalism that had tended to be located in the past and the foreign.

It may be that what allowed this process to take place was a perception of the city, while not distant in the sense of the locations of earlier Gothic fiction, as an unfamiliar and disorientating place. This concern with the exploration of the dark corners of London was continued throughout the Victorian era, in fiction but also in accounts such as Gustave Doré and Blanchard Jerrold's *London* (1872), William Booth's *In Darkest London and the Way Out* (1890), and a stream of other titles. But if, as Mighall notes of *Oliver Twist*, 'parts of London, despite their distance from the castles and monasteries of the Radcliffean landscape, are rendered as strange and remote in their own way as these more traditional Gothic locales' (1999: 43), the relocated Gothic cannot be described as a purely fantastical environment. Mighall argues that even the Gothic novels of Horace Walpole, Ann Radcliffe, Matthew Lewis, and Charles Maturin aspired to a historical and geographical 'authenticity' in the sense that their picture of sixteenth-, seventeenth- or eighteenth-century Spain, Italy, or southern France (only Walpole actually went back as far as the Middle Ages) accorded

with received Anglo-Saxon and Protestant wisdom about the still
feudal nature of the Catholic south. The nineteenth-century shift
from Italian castle to London rookery—or, as Mighall nicely puts it,
as drains replaced devils (1999: 62)—was a move that retained
many of the features of the Gothic, but also threw them into relief.
This is illustrated not just in the fiction of Reynolds and others but
also in more identifiably factual accounts, such as the report in the
*Quarterly Review* on the policy of street clearances then being
undertaken, where it was announced, of the destruction of a London
house that had been a 'notorious haunt of felons,' that 'many went
to see it previous to its demolition, when its mysteries (far surpass-
ing those of Udolfo [sic]) were exposed to the public gaze, with all
its sliding-panels, trap-doors and endless devices for concealment or
escape' (Anonymous, 1855: 430).

The Mysteries of Udolpho retained a significance as a point of
reference. In the 1860s, Elaine Showalter has noted, 'reviewers
appreciated the tremendous power sensation fiction obtained by
translating the fantasies of the Gothic imagination into Victorian
domestic realism' (1976: 2); when Henry James praised Wilkie
Collins's *The Woman in White* in 1865, he wrote that 'instead of the
terrors of *Udolpho* we were treated to the terrors of the cheerful
country-house and the busy London lodgings. And there is no doubt
that these were infinitely more terrible. Mrs. Radcliffe's mysteries
were romances pure and simple; while those of Mr. Wilkie Collins
were stern reality' (1974: 123). Both James and the *Quarterly
Review* reporter suggested a distinction between realism and the
Gothic, between London as it was in actuality and the landscapes
imagined in Gothic fiction. What they were documenting might
rather be seen as a further reformulation of the Gothic and its relationship between ancient and modern. While in the first half of the
century the Gothic novel was, according to Daniel S. Burt, 'largely
subsumed by other popular literary forms for a new working-class
readership who demanded more realistic and recognizable sensation' (1981: 142), that process evidently remained unfinished for the
perhaps more well-to-do readers of Wilkie Collins and other novels
of sensation.

How did this work its way into the cinema? Late-Victorian,
urban Gothic writers such as Robert Louis Stevenson, Oscar Wilde,
Sir Arthur Conan Doyle, and Bram Stoker provided a fund of material that in the twentieth century was to be made and repeatedly

remade into films in Hollywood and elsewhere. While the 1948 adaptation of *The Woman in White* emphasized the country-house setting rather the busy London lodgings, the 1941 version of *Dr. Jekyll and Mr. Hyde* (examined in more detail in the following chapter) followed on from a line of versions of Stevenson's book that perpetuated a tradition of London as a dark and Gothic city, a tradition into which *Hangover Square*, another tale of divided identity, was fitted. However, discussions of the Gothic in 1940s Hollywood have by no means been restricted to adaptations of nineteenth-century novels (the eighteenth-century Gothic remains virtually untouched by filmmakers), and have not tended to see the Gothic as an urban phenomenon. In particular, over the last twenty years a number of writers have developed the idea of a cycle of 'Gothic romance' films which emerged in Hollywood in the 1940s.

Diane Waldman, for instance, has referred to 'a cycle of films produced in Hollywood in the 1940s for a specifically feminine audience, and a direct descendent of the Gothic novel' (1990: 55–56). While McArthur linked *Gaslight*, *Hangover Square* and *The Verdict* to *film noir*, the 'female Gothic' (*Gaslight* included) has tended to be differentiated from a male orientated *film noir*, though some writers have also stressed connections between the two cycles. For Thomas Schatz the 'roots of *film noir* can be traced to the Gothic romances of the nineteenth century, the more recent popular fiction of Daphne Du Maurier (author of the best-selling *Rebecca* [1938]), and the frequently cited detective fiction of Hammett and Chandler' (1999: 233); he goes on to say that 'as the two cycles developed during the early 1940s, the female Gothic displayed a remarkable "family resemblance" to the hard-boiled detective in basic structure, thematic and gender-related concerns, and deployment of *noir* stylistics' (236).

According to Murray Smith, urban settings predominate and are at times foregrounded in *film noir*; settings also tend to be contemporary and American. The female Gothic, on the other hand, 'is sometimes set in the "present" but often in the Victorian era.' The action is often located in a rural mansion rather than the city streets, persistent motifs include sweeping staircases, candelabra, and four-poster beds, while 'the somewhat "fantastic" setting and milieu is perhaps the most powerful argument for naming the genre the female *Gothic*, since these iconographic factors clearly derive from the original Gothic novels of the late eighteenth century' (1988: 64).

Smith argues that the 'settings and social milieu of *film noir* and the female Gothic are quite distinct' (64), but his examination of the urban and contemporaneously set 'female Gothic' film *Deception* (1946) leads him to conclude that 'while *film noir* and the female Gothic oppose each other in some sense, in certain respects they are homologous' (67).

Questions need to be asked here that are relevant not just to studies of the Gothic romance film but also to my own investigation into the genealogy of *Hangover Square* and other gaslight melodramas. What is meant in this context by phrases such as 'a direct descendent of the Gothic novel,' and in what sense did the iconography of the 1940s gothic romance film 'derive from the original Gothic novels of the late eighteenth century'? What direct descent cannot be taken to mean is direct adaptation. The following titles are listed by Waldman (1983: 39) as belonging to the 1940s cycle of Gothic romance films (other writers have suggested only slight variations): *Rebecca* (1940), *Suspicion* (1941), *Shadow of a Doubt* (1943), *Gaslight* (1944), *Experiment Perilous* (1946), *Undercurrent* (1946), *Dragonwyck* (1946), *The Two Mrs. Carrolls* (1947), *Secret Beyond the Door* (1948), *A Woman's Vengeance* (1948), and *Sleep My Love* (1948). An examination of the source of these films in fact reveals that they were based on novels, stories, and plays written by a variety of authors from Daphne Du Maurier to Aldous Huxley, none of which date from earlier than the 1920s.

Just as *Hangover Square* was a 'modern story' which became a costume melodrama, *Experiment Perilous* was transformed in Hollywood from a novel located in contemporary New York to one mainly set at the turn-of-the-century. Other films seem to have acquired a Victorian setting in the writings of critics. Thus Murray Smith's reference to films sometimes set in the present but often in the Victorian era might be appropriate to an understanding of 1940s Gothic that would include titles such as *The Lodger* and *The Verdict*, perhaps even the 1903-set *Hangover Square*, which shared the iconography of *The Lodger* and was described by one reviewer as a crime story 'with all the usual props: flickering street lights on narrow alleys, shadowy rooms with Victorian furniture' (*New York Herald Tribune*, 8 February 1945). It doesn't really fit the films listed by Waldman. *Gaslight* is set in Victorian London, *Experiment Perilous* in turn-of-the-century New York (though with a flashback sequence going back to nineteenth-century Europe), while *Dragonwyck* opens in 1844 in a Connecticut that would be better described as feudal rather than Victorian; none of the remaining titles in Waldman's list are period films. They might be seen as examples of the new or modern Gothic rather than Victorian Gothic. The heroine in *Rebecca* does not inhabit a Victorian world, though she is confronted with the vestiges of the past that have lingered on in a modern world.

On the whole such films have also only come to be labeled Gothic at a relatively recent date. To the best of my knowledge, the word *Gothic* does not appear in any film publicity from the 1940s. It did, very occasionally, feature in film reviews, though with differing connotations. One example has already been quoted: *The Lodger* was seen to evoke 'a Gothic,' which seems to have been understood as a newspaper murder account. Two other instances can be cited: the source of *Jane Eyre* was described by Campbell Dixon as having 'all the ingredients of the conventional Gothic thriller successfully practiced even to this day by Miss Du Maurier and by A. J. Cronin in *Hatter's Castle*' (unidentified and undated source, British Film Institute Library microfiche), while *The New York Times* review of *Rebecca* includes the following comment— 'Rebecca's ghost and the bluebeard room in Manderley become very real horrors as Mr. Hitchcock and his players unfold their macabre tale, and the English countryside is demon-ridden for all the brightness of the sun through its trees and the Gothic serenity of its manor house' (29 March 1940). Thus the word 'Gothic' was in use at this time, and could be applied to a tradition that might link the Gothic romance film of the 1940s to the nineteenth-century Gothic of *Jane Eyre*, though such usage seems to have been infrequent. And while on the one hand it is interesting that horror, the macabre, and the Gothic should appear together here in a single sentence in the *Rebecca* review, it is significant also that the writer of this review sets up a *contrast* between the demonic (what we might call the Gothic) and the Gothic *serenity* of the house.

A search of the British Library catalogue for fictional titles published as 'a Gothic Romance' revealed a gap between *The Midnight Groan; or the Spectre of the Chapel; Involving an Exposure of the Horrible Secrets of the Nocturnal Assembly: A Gothic Romance* (1808) and *Madness at the Castle: A Gothic Romance* (1966). This points not to the disappearance of Gothic fiction for a century and a half, but to the way in which the Gothic re-emerged as a generic and promotional term in the 1960s. *Gaslight* does not appear to have been discussed in terms of the Gothic in the 1940s; in a sense it became a Gothic narrative, first in the 1960s when a novelization of the story was published as a 'paperback Gothic,' then again in the 1980s when it began to be discussed by critics as a Gothic romance film.

This can be one function of criticism, to identify previously unacknowledged or submerged traditions. Rosemary Jackson, for instance, has argued that the 'uneasy assimilation of gothic in many Victorian novels suggests that within the main, realistic text, there exists another non-realistic one, camouflaged and concealed, but constantly present' (1981: 124). What needs to be clarified is the relationship between identification and invention. Is the Gothic an invented tradition?

The historian Eric Hobsbawn has described an 'invented tradition' as

> a set of practices, normally governed by overtly or tacitly accepted rules and of a ritual or symbolic nature, which seek to inculcate certain values and norms of behavior by repetition, which automatically implies continuity with the past. In fact, where possible, they normally attempt to establish continuity with a suitable historic past. A striking example is the deliberate choice of a Gothic style for the nineteenth-century rebuilding of the British parliament, and the equally deliberate decision after World War II to rebuild the parliament chamber on exactly the same basic plan as before (1992: 1–2).

The reference here is to a variety of Gothic different from the novels of the 1790s or the films of the 1940s; whatever the relationship between a Gothic style of architecture and the Gothic as a mode of fiction, it would be misleading to take them to be identical. In addition, while Hobsbawn makes the point that invented traditions are used to serve the interests of dominant powers, the case for a female Gothic tradition has been that it has existed as an oppositional tradition, at times that it has been one that has been excluded from the literary canon. Yet his reference to the attempt to establish a continuity with the past does have a relevance to the notion of a Gothic tradition, which arguably has been successively re-invented with the purpose of constructing an ancestry.

The notion of an invented continuity with the past can be traced back to the origins of Gothic fiction, with Horace Walpole's *The Castle of Otranto* having been initially published in 1764 under the pretense that it was a rediscovered medieval manuscript. This appeal to a Gothic past has been repeated at later dates (as has the device of the supposed document from the past, recently given a late twentieth-century twist in *The Blair Witch Project* [1999]). According to Louis James, 'the term "Gothic" has been used indiscriminately to describe early Victorian penny-issue fiction ever since Montague Summers issued his *Gothic Bibliography* in 1940, and the practice is encouraged today by booksellers who find this raises the price of these novels on the American market' (1974: 72). Twenty years later, the mass market publishing industry began to bring out a series of novels which in many cases had been first published in the 1950s but were now repackaged and sold as paperback 'Gothics,' their covers announcing them to be 'in the Du Maurier tradition' or 'in the Gothic tradition of *Rebecca*' (see Russ, 1973: 666). That is, the label 'Gothic,' despite the fact that the word has been invoked to suggest a barbaric past, has on different occasions been applied to books with a view to adding to their value.

But constructing a Gothic ancestry can serve a critical as well as a commercial purpose. Within academic circles there has been a tendency to emphasize the continuity of a Gothic tradition and the degree to which its appeal has worked *across* history. Mary Ann Doane, for instance, while careful to emphasize that the 'female Gothic narrative is incarnated in cinematic texts in a relatively strictly delineated historical period—from *Rebecca* in 1940 to the late 1940s,' frames this statement with the comments that such films 'appropriate many of the elements of the gothic novel in its numerous variations from Horace Walpole and Ann Radcliffe to Daphne Du Maurier and beyond,' and that Gothic narratives continued on beyond this period, 'displaced to another medium,' the 1950s witnessing 'the beginnings of a flourishing trade in Gothic paperbacks which continues to this day' (1988: 124). This emphasis on continuity, which Doane accentuates by dating the emergence of the Gothic paperback in the 1950s when in the source she goes on to cite the development is placed in the 1960s (Russ: 667), can be set against other accounts which place more stress on the particular historical context. Thus Janice Radway has argued that the Gothic paperback phenomenon can be explained partly in terms of the dynamics of the publishing industry—the need to win back female readers alienated by the predominance of the Mickey Spillane school of paperbacks—and partly in terms of the changing situation and self-image of those readers, and has noted that 1972 marked 'the beginning of a decline in the modern Gothic's popularity,' as the trade in Gothic paperbacks began to make way for a different kind of fiction aimed at female readers, which removed the mystery plot and made the heroine-hero relationship more overtly erotic (1981: 143–45). The Gothic, then, is best seen not as a constant of the imagination but as a literary, dramatic, or cinematic mode that emerges and changes within specific historical contexts.

## From the Medieval to the Suburban

A FURTHER SHIFT within the Gothic noted by Robert Mighall was the nineteenth-century de-romanticization and suburbanization of the Gothic. As evidence of this he cites a description in Wilkie Collins's novel *Armadale* (1864–66) of 'a great overgrown dismal house, plastered with drab-colored stucco, and surrounded by a naked unfinished garden, without a shrub or flower in it,' located in a dreary 'new neighborhood, situated below the high ground of Hampstead, on the southern side.' According to Mighall, 'the sensations formerly conjured up by spectacles of mouldering antiquity are here evoked by newness, the desolation of the unfinished rather than the ruinous' (1999: 119).

A remarkably similar description can be found in a novel written some eighty years later: Joseph Shearing's *For Her to See* (1947). At the beginning of the Victorian-set novel the central character, Olivia Sacret, visits a friend, who lives in Clapham, at 'The Old Priory, Tintern Road.' The house is described as

> a building in the style of the Gothic revival, feebly copied, with castellated roof below the chimney pots, a tower with pinnacles, arched hooded windows, a Norman porch and wide steps with plaster dogs sitting at attention on the balustrades. . . .

As Olivia approaches she is characterized as smiling

> at the ostentatious house before her, that she knew to be a sham in all the pretensions it implied.

> There had never been a monastic establishment here; the name had been given vaguely, because of the supposed character of the architecture that had probably been chosen because of the name of the road by someone who could recall the ruins of Tintern, but not that it was an abbey. . . .

> The place was truly ugly, even the shrubs and trees were clipped, overcrowded or badly planted, so that they seemed unreal. . . . The house, of large ungainly proportions, was ill set, the stucco painted a drab yellow incongruous with the turreting, the Gothic intention, the chimney stacks, belching slow-rising smoke, were absurd, the monkey puzzle trees behind, crooked and twisted, the Venetian blinds at the windows another evidence of a lack of taste. . . . (1948: 10–11)

The Gothic appears to have multiple functions in the context of this novel. One function is to point to the novel's factual basis—to the actual events (the death of Charles Bravo in suspicious circumstances, reports of which formed part of the 'criminal London' section of Michael Sadleir's 'Londonania') that took place in 1876 at 'The Priory,' a Victorian Gothic house in Bedford Hill Road, Balham, a South London address similar if not quite identical to that given in *For Her to See*. In this sense this particular work of fiction does operate within the constraints of realist discourse; the castellated building described in the above passage is a feature of suburban London rather than of a fantastic landscape. 'The Old Priory' is also presented as a sham, a recent construction offering a feeble pretense of antiquity. The self-consciously artificial Gothic of *For Her to See* provides a further dimension to the notion of the Gothic as an invented, and successively re-invented, tradition. At the same time the Victorian environment described by the author is no longer the new and immediate reality it was in the previous century. It has come to take on the function served by the vestiges of medievalism in earlier Gothic novels, though this assumption is complicated by this Gothic romance's ironical and de-romanticizing perspective, a shift comparable to the movement from the medieval, Italian castle of Horace Walpole's *The Castle of Otranto* to the Victorian, Glaswegian 'castle' of A. J. Cronin's novel *Hatter's Castle* (published in 1931, filmed in 1941).

*For Her to See* provided another pathway into the cinema. It was, almost immediately, made into the film *So Evil My Love*, one of several films released in 1947 or 1948—the others being *Moss Rose*, *The Mark of Cain*, and *Blanche Fury*—adapted from novels published in the 1930s and 1940s under the name of Joseph Shearing. That name was in fact one of several pseudonyms used by a female author, others being Marjorie Bowen and George Preddy; the author's 'Joseph Shearing' novels tended to be based on reports of actual nineteenth-century murders. *For Her to See* was thus itself a recently constructed 'Victorian novel,' another example of how the immediate sources for British and American gaslight melodramas tended to be of near-contemporary origin. Yet the way in which the Shearing novels of the 1930s and 1940s drew upon the sensational novels of the 1860s, which were themselves a reformulation of the Gothic novels of the 1790s, indicates a longer ancestry. The problem with tracing such a line is that one can lose sight of the actual nature of the relationship between different media and across a century or two.

In *For Her to See* the Gothic is also tied in with an understanding of the Victorians as lacking taste, with Victorian architecture and design being associated with pretension and ugliness. That understanding, how it worked its way into the cinema and how the cinema contributed to it, will be more fully explored in the following chapter.

# 4 LADY ISABEL, DR. JEKYLL, AND OTHER VICTORIANS: TWENTIETH-CENTURY RECEPTION, REACTION, AND RECONSTRUCTION

IN ELLEN WOOD'S novel, *East Lynne*, Lady Isabel, wife of the respectable and prosperous lawyer Archibald Caryle, suspecting that she has lost her husband's affection and frustrated by the confinements of married life, abandons her husband, her children and her home to elope with Captain Francis Levison. Betrayed by Levison (who is eventually revealed to be guilty of murder as well as adultery and deception), she comes close to death, and it is the report of her death that prompts Archibald to marry Barbara Hare, the very woman of whom Lady Isabel had become obsessively jealous. In fact, the train crash in which Isabel had reputedly lost her life has deprived her only of her illegitimate child and her beauty. Isabel returns to East Lynne, disguised and (largely) unrecognized in tinted spectacles, to act as her children's governess, to watch over the death of her son William, and then, after a brief scene of recognition and forgiveness, to die herself.

First published in 1861, *East Lynne* had become a bestseller after an enthusiastic review in *The Times* (25 January 1862), and the novel had continued to sell in quantities throughout the remainder of the nineteenth century. First adapted for the theater in 1862, and subsequently in numerous different versions, it also became an extraordinarily popular stage melodrama, the play becoming such a reliable standby of provincial companies in Britain and the United States that the phrase, 'Next Week - *East Lynne*,' developed into a cliché of repertory practice.

*East Lynne* continued to be produced in the twentieth century, in adaptations for the stage, radio, cinema and more recently television. The first film version was released in 1902. It was followed by two versions which came out in 1908, and there were further adaptations in 1909 (when it was filmed as *Led Astray*), 1910, 1912,

1913 (when three versions were made), 1915, 1916, 1921, 1922 (in both an Australian version and as part of a British series with the memorable title, *Tense Moments with Great Authors*), 1925, and in 1931. 'If a census of opinion were taken as to which is the most popular drama ever written there is little doubt that *East Lynne* would be placed at the top of the poll with an enormous majority of votes. . . . Nor does the popularity of the play show any signs of abatement,' it was noted in *Bioscope* (7 September 1916) on the release of the 1916 version starring Theda Bara. This film was the first of three versions made for Fox Studios; it was followed by a 1925 film starring Alma Rubens, and a 1931, Oscar-nominated film with Ann Harding in the leading role. To tie-in with the latter film, *East Lynne* once again appeared in print, though this time in a novelization written by Arlene de Haas, complete with stills from the film.

However, the popularity of *East Lynne* came to be increasingly challenged by other responses. Following the screening of one British version, *Variety* reported (18 July 1913) that

> [a]n irreverent male unit of raucous voice seated with 26 other people in the new Cecil Spooner theatre in the north-eastern frontiers of the Bronx larfed [sic] out loud last Monday night when Sir Francis Levison won his first kiss from Lady Isabel at the American premiere of the English film importation of the dear old matinee standby of repertoire and stock, *East Lynne*.

The release of the 1921 version provoked the British trade journal *Kinematograph Weekly* (24 November 1921) to comment that 'to disinter the corpses of Victorian novels long since deceptively laid to rest, and to cause their anemic ghosts, imbued with a semblance of life, to hold the stage again is not a process that ought to commend itself to the modern producer. . . . It would have been better and kinder to have let *East Lynne* remain what it was, a half forgotten literary curiosity.' The 1931 version was found by another reviewer to be 'all very out-moded in this sophisticated world of ours' (*World*, 21 February 1931); elsewhere it was ambivalently noted that 'Fox has rescued the venerable antique from the scorn and disrepute it has recently endured' (*Picturegoer Weekly*, 26 September 1931).

The first screen burlesque—*East Lynne in Bugville*, which featured a pre-*Perils of Pauline* Pearl White—appeared in 1914. Further burlesques and parodies followed in 1917 (the Australian *An East Lynne Fiasco*), 1919 (Mack Sennett's *East Lynne with*

*Variations*), and 1931 (the British *East Lynne on the Western Front*). And if the continuing, twentieth-century popularity of *East Lynne* is indicated in the sheer number of times it was filmed up till the beginning of the 1930s, the fact that no film versions have appeared since that time suggests that Ellen Wood's story of Victorian motherhood and suffering had lost its appeal and significance for modern audiences. Even the absence of film parodies after *East Lynne on the Western Front* indicates that the play came to lose its central place in British and American culture—though in 1945 the (non-burlesque) version made in 1915 did resurface in the compilation film, *Gaslight Follies*, now accompanied by a soundtrack of caustic comments from radio comedians Milton Cross and Ethel Owen. Not that such help was needed, according to one reviewer (*Boston Sunday Post*, 11 November 1945), for 'the old-time stilted and over-emphatic pantomimic antics of the silent film days plus the lachrymatory plot, would be enough to send any present-day audience into hysterics of laughter' (though this does suggest that it was silent cinema that was being held up for ridicule as well as Victorian sentiment—and the reviewer did allow that 'perhaps a tear or two' would mingle with the mirth of the audience).

Versions of *East Lynne*, played straight or otherwise, did continue to appear in other media. '*East Lynne* was the premiere bill on this full hour show. And not the least inclination toward satire,' noted another *Variety* reporter (12 May 1937) of a version broadcast on radio. Evidently, by this time there was a certain expectation that performances would adopt a satirical approach, though when this approach was adopted it could itself provoke an unsympathetic reaction. 'Poking fun is the cheapest form of criticism, and when laughter and scorn are directed at sincere sentiment, honesty and virtue, then the laughter simply surrenders to the crudest form of mob thinking,' protested the reviewer for the *Christian Science Monitor* of a 1926 stage version, produced at Greenwich Village by Kenneth MacGowan, Robert Edmond Jones and Eugene O'Neill (quoted in *Show*, 1962, 2 (1): 15). Of another version played for laughs, produced on the British stage, the reviewer for the *Daily Telegraph* complained that 'behind it all was the hollowness of sophistication' (25 January 1934). Later British versions include the television adaptations of 1976 and 1982; the producer of the latter stated (in *The Listener*) his intention of restoring 'the book and its author to their former position of eminence' (Colin Shindler in *The Listener*, 23 and 30 December 1982).

*East Lynne* could seem to encapsulate a certain image of the Victorian era and Victorian values; reactions to *East Lynne* can be seen as a barometer of shifting attitudes to that era and those values. In Ellen Wood's novel, when Lady Isabel elopes with Captain Levinson, she becomes subject to the full wrath of Victorian morality, the consequences of actions becoming a dire warning for the novel's female readers (Wood, 1984: 289):

> The very hour of her departure she woke to what she had done: the guilt, whose aspect had been shunned in perspective, assumed at once its true, frightful colour, the blackness of darkness; and a lively remorse, a never-dying anguish, took possession of her soul for ever. Lady—wife—mother! should you ever be tempted to abandon your home, so will you awaken! Whatever trials may be the lot of your married life, though they may magnify themselves to your crushed spirit as beyond the endurance of woman to endure, *resolve* to bear them; fall down upon your knees and pray to be enabled to bear them; pray for patience; pray for strength to resist the demon that would urge you to escape; bear unto death, rather than forfeit your fair name and your good conscience; for be assured that the alternative, if you rush on to it, will be found far worse than death!

Such unrelenting morality could, as the *Kinematograph Weekly* reviewer suggested, seem out of place in the twentieth century (unless accorded classic status by the BBC), as could the novel's appeal to sentiment, along with the sentimentality and melodrama of the stage versions.

By the 1940s a reaction against Victorianism had become well established, in the cinema and elsewhere. While adaptations of *East Lynne* were no longer being made for the cinema, other films were being produced to give a different perspective on Victorian suffering. According to Jeffrey Richards, the British film version of *Gaslight* influenced

> a whole genre of British films of the Forties, set in upper middle-class Victorian households and dramatizing the myth of Victorian 'hypocrisy,' by contrasting the surface appearance of regularity, order and social hierarchy with the concealed reality of tyranny, intolerance and familial strain. *Pink String and Sealing Wax*,

*Hatter's Castle, So Evil My Love* and *Madeleine* all follow in the footsteps of *Gaslight* and represent a critique of nineteenth-century family structure and middle-class mores, which came to the fore in particular during World War II (1986: 71–72).

But *Gaslight* did not originate any such critique. For at least one writer the cause was rather found in the nineteenth century itself, the London *Evening Standard* reviewer commenting of *So Evil My Love* (27 May 1948):

> Sustained by countless novels and plays and eagerly seized on by the makers of films is the Great Victorian Myth. The Myth has almost succeeded in converting the younger generation to a belief that Victorian domestic life was full of thwarted motherhood, tyrannical husbands and fathers, and spiritual frustration in dark, rambling houses. The trouble all began, I suspect, from the day when that unhappy woman in *East Lynne* looked down at the body of her baby and cried piteously, 'Dead, and never called me mother!' Not a dry eye in the house! Clearly the thing to do was to torture the heroine, and if you put her in crinolines you could torture her much more severely.

Apart from what it says about the lineage of *So Evil My Love*, this points to complexities within *East Lynne*, and within twentieth-century attitudes toward the Victorian. For while Ellen Wood's novel and the subsequent stage versions which introduced the infamous cry, 'Dead, and never called me mother!' (a line nowhere to be found in the novel) could be seen to encapsulate Victorian morality, the very insistence on endurance and forbearance—the novel's appeal to women to 'pray for strength to resist the demon that would urge you to escape'—also implied an undercurrent of dissatisfaction within the Victorian home.

*East Lynne* was capable of being seen as the embodiment of Victorian values but also as a documentation of oppression and suffering. It can be seen as a deeply conservative work, yet it is also open to feminist readings (see, for instance, Kaplan, 1992) and rewritings (both literal and figurative). Describing the 1931 film version, one reviewer wrote that 'the plot follows the novel by Mrs. Henry Wood, which was written in 1861, when feminine rights were first being fought for in England and a stand was being made against the way women were treated in law and business' (*New York Daily News*, 21 February 1931). The origins of a critique of Victorianism can be traced back to the Victorian era itself, and even to those works that seem to be at the heart of Victorian values (and if the twentieth century saw numerous parodies of *East Lynne*, it is necessary to point out that a tradition of burlesque stage versions dates from close to Lady Isabel's first stage appearance). Yet Ann Harding's angry portrayal of Lady Isabel also represented a reinterpretation of *East Lynne* for the 1930s. As such, it was part of trend in which the more 'Victorian' aspects of the story were made more palatable for modern audiences.

Film versions of *East Lynne* perpetuated but also modified a tradition. In other screen adaptations the setting was modernized. The 1916 film, starring Theda Bara, moved the story to contemporary America; Lady Isabel and Francis Levison escape in an automobile. The 1921 version directed by Hugh Ballin also updated the story, as did the 1922 Australian version. Another American film released in 1931, *Ex-Flame* was billed as a 'modernized version of *East Lynne*,' though the *New York Times* reviewer wrote (24 January 1931) that it 'is really not that at all. In all essentials it is simply a restatement of that old melodrama in modern dress.' For this film Lady Isabel had became Lady Catherine, and Sir Archibald Carlyle was now Sir Caryle Austin. Lady Catherine (also known as Kitty) deserts her husband (but in this story takes her child with her) when he kisses his old tennis partner in the garden after a drink too many, takes up with a series of different men, loses custody of the child and then attempts to kidnap him; in the words of the reviewer, the film ends with 'a grand reunion, in which Sir Carlyle admits he has been a cad and a bounder.' A restatement perhaps, but one that recalled neither the language nor the attitude adopted by Ellen Wood's Sir Archibald Carlyle.

Beyond 1931, Hollywood continued to produce numerous other maternal melodramas. Examining this trend, Christian Viviani has identified two strands; one, narrating the sufferings of a weakly pathetic heroine, sometimes situated in the recent past and generally characterized by a European setting; the other having a more decisive and energetic heroine and an American setting. Viviani argues that while Europe was progressively eliminated from American films about maternal sacrifice after 1930, Americanized (and modernized) versions of such narratives came into their own in the 1930s (Viviani, 1987). In this sense there is a continuity and persistence with narratives which can be traced back to the Victorian era but also a transformation of those narratives and a move away from those features which identified them as Victorian. Evidently, the story of maternal sacrifice continued to maintain a hold on audiences, but the particular Victorian trappings of *East Lynne* came to be seen as a liability.

Such trappings were to return. 'For many years, although today it seems ludicrous, costume pictures were completely taboo, because of exhibitor insistence—foolishly listened to by distributors and producers—that costume pictures were not wanted by the public,' wrote David Selznick in a memo to Spyrous Skouras. 'When I scheduled the first *Little Women* [1934] for production, the heads of the RKO circuit (then affiliated with the RKO studios) actually suggested that I should modernize it! The gigantic success of *Little Women* opened up costume pictures, after years of exhibitor-inspired prohibition of them' (25 June 1956, in Behlmer, 1989: 414–15). But, leaving aside the particular question of how influential the Selznick-produced film was in a revival of costume films, a novel such as Louisa May Alcott's *Little Women* (1868) may have had an appeal for filmmakers and audiences of the 1930s because it seemed less firmly restricted to the codes of Victorian morality, and because it placed melodrama (as represented in the novel by the stories written by 'little woman' Jo) at a distance. In other instances, Victorian trappings resurfaced to bring with them an accentuation of the connotations of tyranny and oppression.

Jeffrey Richards has identified this tendency in the British version of *Gaslight* and other films such as *Pink String and Sealing Wax*. Going a little further back in time, he has also argued that the film melodramas of the 1930s starring Tod Slaughter 'constitute a critique of Victorian patriarchy' (Richards, 1998: 158). For Raphael Samuel the versions of *Great Expectations* (1946) and *Oliver Twist* (1948) directed by David Lean can be linked to 'a stigmatization of the Victorian which had been gathering strength since the turn of the century, and which reached some kind of apogee in Labour's election victory of 1945'—in these films, in marked contrast to later, 'sunnier' versions of Dickens, Victorian Britain is often seen as a dark, slum-infested country (Samuel, 1994: 419).[1] These accounts identify a British or English phenomenon, and if Samuel suggests that the Dickens adaptations can be seen 'as a kind of English counterpart to the Hollywood *film noir*' (421), there is an implication that while in Britain the Victorian provided an appropriately dark location for film melodrama, in the

United States such gloom tended to come in modern dress. Yet while Hollywood ceased to make any more versions of *East Lynne* after 1931, the stern Victorian patriarch had continued to appear in occasional Hollywood films, such as *The Barretts of Wimpole Street* (1934), while the 1940s saw Hollywood's own period counterpart to *film noir*, with dark views of Victorian Britain being evident in films from *Ladies in Retirement* to *So Evil My Love* (made in Britain but for a Hollywood studio).

While *East Lynne* was repeatedly filmed up to, but not beyond, 1931, another Victorian novel, Robert Louis Stevenson's *The Strange Case of Dr. Jekyll and Mr. Hyde*, was repeatedly filmed both before and after that date. MGM's 1941 *Dr. Jekyll and Mr. Hyde* is significant here for its representation of the repressions of Victorian society but also for its place in a long line of versions of the novel. A discussion of film versions of Stevenson's novel should thus provide a further insight into the shifting place occupied by the Victorian in the twentieth-century imagination. However, given the number of such films and my particular concern with the 1940s and the period leading up to that decade, after a brief run-through of the versions made in the period up to 1920, the focus of the next section of this chapter will be on *Dr. Jekyll and Mr. Hyde* as it was filmed in three versions, dating from 1920 (in the version starring John Barrymore, directed by John S. Robertson and produced by Adolph Zukor for Paramount—see Figure 4), 1932 (directed and produced by Rouben Mamoulian, again for Paramount, and starring Fredric March), and 1941 (starring Spencer Tracy, directed for MGM by Victor Fleming, who co-produced with Victor Saville—see Figure 5). What this focus will also enable is a closer attention to the individual films, and how they might be seen as part of a twentieth-century derogation of the Victorian. Having discussed these particular films, I will return to the broader picture, undertaking an examination of the notion of an American revolt against Victorianism in and beyond film, and comparing this notion with how such a revolt has been characterized in a British context.

## Jekyll and Hyde

STEVENSON'S *The Strange Case of Dr. Jekyll and Mr. Hyde* was originally published in 1886, and was first performed in a stage adaptation in New York in 1887. The first cinematic version of the novel appears to have been the film, known as either *Dr. Jekyll and Mr.*

Figure 4. *Dr. Jekyll and Mr. Hyde* (1920).

Figure 5. *Dr. Jekyll and Mr. Hyde* (1941)

*Hyde* or *The Modern Dr. Jekyll*, made for the Selig Polyscope Company in 1908. A Danish adaptation was released in 1910, a British version—*The Duality of Man*—appeared the same year; it was followed in 1912 by a further American version, by three 1913 versions, and a series of other adaptations and parodies which are too numerous to list in their entirety. 1920 alone saw the version starring John Barrymore, another starring Sheldon Lewis, a third version of the novel directed by F. W. Murnau under the title *Der Januskopf*, plus a couple of parodies, one called *When Quakel Did Hyde*, the other simply *Dr. Jekyll and Mr. Hyde*.

The versions starring Barrymore, March, and Tracy are all located in a Victorian setting. This might seem hardly worth commenting upon; Jekyll and Hyde have become inextricably associated with an imaginary late-Victorian London also inhabited by such characters as Sherlock Holmes, Dorian Gray, Count Dracula, and (moving from fiction toward fact) Jack-the-Ripper. In fact, the London of the Stevenson novel lacks any clear landmarks, and little information is provided by its author to establish the date at which the events described take place. The continued resonance of the novel may be partly attributable to this imprecision, which has helped to give the story a mythical dimension. Moreover, the passage of 'Jekyll and Hyde' into the language, as a term denoting a split personality, has led it to be understood as having a contemporary relevance, rather than being a condition limited to any one particular historical period. That the first confirmed (but no longer extant) film adaptation of Stevenson's novel should have been known as *The Modern Dr. Jekyll* might suggest either an updating of the story, or that, whatever era he inhabits, Jekyll is a modern figure (though one who contains the atavistic Hyde).

Jekyll's status as a modern scientist is made explicit at one point in the 1932 version, when he says to the less forward thinking Dr. Lanyon (Holmes Herbert):

> Look at that gas lamp. But for some man's curiosity we should not have had it, and London would still be lighted by linkboys. And wait, one day London will glow with incandescence! It will be so bright that even you will be moved by it.

The casting of Spencer Tracy in the 1941 version followed on from *Edison the Man* (1940), in which Tracy had portrayed another figure closely connected with scientific advance (in this case with electricity rather than gas). However, Jekyll's status as a scientist, his association with progressive ideas, both presented as a contrast to those who surround him (Jekyll may be modern, but his colleagues are not), and as lingering associations that are less than progressive (at one point Tracy's Jekyll finds it necessary to defend himself by proclaiming: 'I'm not a witchdoctor') his experiments are interpretable as either science or alchemy.

The 1941 version provoked one critic into writing that the film industry should 'render unto Victoria that which is Victorian and don't mix it up with Sigmund Freud who came after the good Queen and the excellent author' (*Dallas Morning News*, 19 October 1941). The particular reference here was to the dream sequences seen as Jekyll is transformed into Hyde, sequences which used imagery derived from Surrealism as a means of imagining the Jekyll/Hyde character's state of mind. It is probably true that such additions to the narrative say more about Hollywood in the 1940s than the concerns of Robert Louis Stevenson (or Freud); however, leaving aside the question of whether Freud might himself be described as a Victorian, true to the notion of the Gothic being based on anachronism, it is precisely this mixture of the Victorian and the modern that has tended to characterize adaptations of Stevenson's novel.

An understanding of the story as essentially modern, or simply a preference for a contemporary as opposed to a period *mise-en-scène*, could, here also, lead to that story being updated. While the John Barrymore version made in 1920 was set in the past, when Sheldon Lewis played Jekyll and Hyde the same year the action was moved to contemporary New York. The 1932 *Dr. Jekyll and Mr. Hyde* was, in fact, something of an exception compared to other horror films of the time, which tended not to use period settings, and while Sherlock Holmes, Dracula, and Jack-the-Ripper all provided the inspiration for films made in the early 1930s, neither *Sherlock Holmes* (1931), *Dracula* (1931), nor the British remake of *The Lodger* (1932) were set in the past. All later versions of *Dr. Jekyll and Mr. Hyde* (excluding comic variations such as *The Nutty Professor*) have located the story in a Victorian but still half mythical landscape. When Graham Greene reviewed another film, *The Face at the Window* (1939), he described it as taking its audience 'back into that vague Victorian period when anything might happen —when Jekyll was shrinking into Hyde and the ape committed its murders in the Rue Morgue' (*The Spectator*, 6 October 1939), an imaginary location that mixes London and Paris and fiction written in both halves of the nineteenth century. To some extent the 1941 *Dr. Jekyll and Mr. Hyde* is a further example of a film set in such an imaginary city. Yet this version is also remarkably specific in the point at which it opens. It is significant that the opening scene of the Spencer Tracy film is set in the week of Queen Victoria's Jubilee in 1887.

The 1920, John Barrymore version lacks any such specific markers. Its status as a composite version of the Victorian Gothic is enhanced by the fact that it is not simply based on Stevenson's story but also on Oscar Wilde's 1891 novel, *The Picture of Dorian Gray*. A scene in which Hyde visits an opium den appears to be taken directly from Wilde's novel, a number of the intertitles are direct quotes from Wilde's text, and in this version the father of Jekyll's fiancée, Sir George Carew (Brandon Hurst), who introduces the saintly Jekyll to hedonistic pleasures, has a role remarkably similar to that of Lord Henry Wotton in *The Picture of Dorian Gray*. In the 1940s the Wilde novel was to provide MGM, the studio responsible for the version of *Dr. Jekyll and Mr. Hyde* produced at the beginning of that decade, with another vehicle for imagining late-Victorian London. However, in the 1920 Barrymore film the emphasis on a hedonistic world from which Jekyll initially stays aloof can be contrasted with later versions which give more emphasis to *late-Victorian* propriety and hypocrisy. In this film the figure of Sir George Carew is closer to an image of the Regency rake than the Victorian patriarch, while the costumes of the film are at times suggestive of the early rather than the late-Victorian era.

A comparison of the portrayal of Jekyll's prospective father-in-law in 1920, 1932, and 1941 is especially illuminating in this context. There is no such figure in Stevenson's novel; the point of departure here appears rather to be Thomas Russell Sullivan's stage version, first performed in 1887, which established many of the features later taken up in Hollywood, notably the fact that Jekyll has acquired a fiancée and that toward the end of the narrative he murders her elderly father. In Stevenson's novel there is a figure named Sir Danvers Carew—a polite, elderly Member of Parliment who is murdered by Hyde for no apparent reason. In the Barrymore film Hyde murders Sir George Carew, a man who, as well as being the father of his fiancée, has a disreputable past, who doesn't believe that Jekyll can be as good as he looks, and who introduces the saintly doctor to both the music hall and to the idea of man's divided personality. For the 1932 film this character had been transformed into Brigadier-General Carew (Halliwell Hobbes), a blimpish figure constantly insisting on the need for punctuality, who expresses disapproval of the time Dr. Jekyll spends on his charity patients and is outraged at his prospective son-in-law's unconventional ideas and actions. Carew has become the archetypal disapproving Victorian patriarch, and when Hyde attacks him at the end of the film he can be seen as attacking Victorian patriarchy itself. This does not make the film an unambivalent critique of Victorian values—Victorian society is characterized as repressive and hypocritical but Hyde is identified as evil—though it does at least point to the fact that a forbidding image of the Victorian patriarch had worked its way into Hollywood typage.

In the 1941 film directed by Victor Fleming the equivalent character is now called Sir Charles Emery (Duncan Crisp). Here Hyde's prospective father-in-law is again representative of propriety and punctuality, though the character is a softened version of Halliwell Hobbes's Carew, initially expressing disapproval of Jekyll's defiance of convention but given to relaxing his stern demeanor, indicating approval when he is led to believe (erroneously) that Jekyll has taken an interest in slum improvements, and still affected by the memory of his own marriage.

What the versions directed by Mamoulian and the Fleming have in common is a *mise-en-scène* that is identifiably late Victorian. Discussing the 1932 film, S. S. Prawer notes that when Hyde changes back into Jekyll in the presence of Lanyon it is also in front of a portrait of Queen Victoria (1980: 100). This does indeed appear to be the case, though is only apparent if one pays very close attention to the screen (the portrait is placed in the half-lit background). The opening of the 1941 film brings the Victorian setting much more into the foreground.

The first words spoken in the latter film are delivered by a bishop (C. Aubrey Smith) giving the following sermon in a fashionable London church:

> . . . with security in our hearts, with right thinking in our minds, we arm ourselves with intolerance of all evil. So it is on this glorious Sabbath morning in this momentous year of eighteen hundred and eighty-seven we naturally turn our thoughts toward that way of life as exemplified by Victoria, our beloved Queen,

for this week begins Her Majesty's golden jubilee. . . . From her heart has come an ever-increasing flow of virtue and moral blessing. She came upon a world sadly mired in the ways of the flesh. But during her reign the forces of good have achieved noble and great victory over the forces of evil. And though we know not the time nor the season we know that in God's own time evil shall be wiped out by good. And may we not live for that day we can be assured that the character of this realm and its people has taken root in a new goodness . . . in the family hearth, the shops of industry, in the very Christian graciousness with which men and women . . . it is because of these things that . . . the world moves forward today.

However, this apparently clear statement of the values of morality, the family, capitalism, progress, and Christianity—values that are explicitly characterized as Victorian—becomes less clear as it continues. As he delivers his sermon the bishop begins to lose his assurance. The reason for this is an interruption from a member of the congregation. A man (later referred to as 'that outrageous individual' by Emery) is first seen rising from his seat, but being restrained by his companion, and apparently restraining, or struggling with, himself. He is then heard giving vent to a maniacal laugh and launching into a tirade that begins: 'Evil wiped out, eh! So you want to take all the fun out of life, eh, bishop! Good old Beelzebub . . .' This interruption is, of course, a foretaste of the subsequent appearance of Hyde. The 'outrageous individual' (played by Barton MacLaine) is later identified by Jekyll as having been taken over by his 'evil' self, just as Jekyll himself will later be taken over by Hyde. What is made explicit in this opening scene is the way in which this other self is in revolt against the key tenets of Victorianism.

It is not a revolt that is allowed to triumph. The man is led out, the remainder of his words drowned by those of the bishop, and then by the sound of the organ and the choir breaking into the next hymn. A policeman is called, though before he can be charged with being drunk and disorderly, Jekyll intervenes and (the policeman deferring to Jekyll when he hears who he is) has the individual taken to the hospital. Jekyll's intervention might seem to identify him as more sympathetic than others such as Emery who interpret the incident purely in terms of outrage, and indeed the man responsible for that outrage appeals to Jekyll as a fellow 'full-blooded young man,' correctly identifying an affinity between himself and the respectable doctor. However, Jekyll is also clearly identified as assisting in putting down the disturbance (the bishop later thanks him for doing just this)—church, law, medical science, and class interests are shown combining to suppress what is explicitly portrayed as a revolt against Victorian values.

There is another shift identifiable here, away from the saintly Jekyll portrayed by Barrymore and March, who are both shown spending their time helping needy patients in the charity hospital, and neglecting society dinners on account of this work. When this happens in the 1920 film, the after-dinner arrival of Barrymore's Jekyll at the house of his fiancée allows for a scene in which it is Sir George Carew who introduces the notion of a divided personality, following which he paraphrases Oscar Wilde by arguing that 'the only way to get rid of a temptation is to yield to it,' and then, as 'illustration' of his argument, takes Jekyll out to a music hall. In the 1941 film, Tracy's Jekyll is not shown engaged in charitable work—when he arrives late for dinner it is due to his scientific experiments rather than his philanthropic activities—and in this film it is Jekyll who introduces, at the dinner table, the idea of man having a 'good' and 'evil' side, thereby offending not just his prospective father-in-law (as is the case in the 1932 film) but a whole array of straight-laced representatives of Victorian respectability.

In the latter film Jekyll's opinions are clearly linked to a rejection of Victorian hypocrisy when one of the dinner guests interrupts him to say, 'But aren't you being a bit presumptuous in assuming that there's evil in all men?' to which Jekyll replies, 'Oh, but isn't that true? Wouldn't we all be hypocrites if we didn't admit that? After all, we've all had thoughts that we, er, didn't want published or shouted out loud, and we certainly have had desires that are not confined to a drawing room.' The latter part of this speech is accompanied by a pan along the dinner table, revealing a series of suitably disturbed and outraged faces. The shift away from the portrayal of Jekyll as a saint is accompanied by an increased emphasis on the dominance of prudery within Victorian society rather than simply over individual members of that society.

Asked to report on this scene for the producer Victor Saville, screenwriter John Balderstone wrote: 'We know what's bothering Jekyll at this point. It isn't his experiments, nor the man in the hospital. It's frustrated sex, sublimated and decent and reverent and pure love and all that. But, I repeat, frustrated sex.'[2] Balderstone's enthusiasm for stressing the sexual aspect of the narrative is also shown in his comment on what he called the 'Hyde-Tart relationship,' of which he wrote: 'Just one tiny thing that I'd like to see, and that is a riding whip or dog whip lying around, perhaps his hand closing on it once when the girl is there. To us there is an added value in this one track that suggests the relationship in Hydeish minds between sex and cruelty, and a flash of the whip would tell an awful lot. And I'd rather see a whip mark than bruised shoulders. The image created would be one of sexual perversion allied with cruelty, instead of mere brutality in general, and this would be very valuable for those who understood it.'[3] Two developments can be identified here. On the one hand there is an increasing emphasis on the story being one of sexual desire, repression, and sadism. On the other hand this emphasis is itself constrained by Hollywood censorship, so that it is only accessible 'for those who understood it.' For what Balderstone considered valuable was exactly the sort of understanding that was likely to concern the censors. Shown the same script, and discussing the same scene, Joseph Breen of the Production Code Administration had written: 'The dialogue that ends this scene, beginning "I'm hurting you because I like hurting you" and running to the fade-out, is *unacceptable*, by reason of containing a definite suggestion of sadism.'[4] No whip is shown in the completed film, and at no time does Hyde say 'I'm hurting you because I like hurting you,' though it is indicated that he has hurt and indeed whipped his mistress. That is, Balderstone's thoughts and what Mahin had had Hyde say in this instance remained as unpublished material, like the thoughts of which Tracy's Jekyll spoke at dinner.

The Barrymore, March, and Tracy portrayals of Jekyll and Hyde are all versions of a more general theme of advanced but eventually fatally flawed thinkers struggling against their more conservative colleagues. Such characters have, of course, been the basis of numerous films about mad scientists, most of which have no marked connection with twentieth-century notions of Victorianism. What is significant for the purposes of this discussion is the way in which this theme is associated in certain films with an idea of Victorian society and its norms. One can see this developing and becoming solidified in the three films discussed above, up to the point where the story is explicitly located at the high-point of Queen Victoria's reign, and thus dramatizes the subversion of the values underpinning that reign (without being subversive itself).

The Victorian world inhabited by Jekyll and Hyde would appear to have served a particular function for Hollywood, a function that was not limited to adaptations of Stevenson's novel. It provided a setting that could be characterized in terms of a surface propriety that concealed sex and sexual cruelty, the irony here being that what was being concealed could itself only be suggested behind the surface propriety demanded by the Production Code. 'The late-Victorian period, with its heavy draperies, plush sofas, gaslights, antiquated telephones, tight-lacing and the claustrophobic atmosphere in which erring husbands went secretly to prostitutes is an appropriate setting for an action in which it the secrecy demanded by petty bourgeois morality, that leads man to crime,' wrote Lotte Eisner of the Fritz Lang-directed *House by the River* (1976: 293). A stigmatized Victorianism, accompanied by the representation of rebellion against Victorian restraint, came to be incorporated into the conventions of Hollywood filmmaking as an 'appropriate setting,' but was itself contained and restrained by censorship and filmmaking codes that demanded the restoration of order.

## America

BROADER ARGUMENTS HAVE been made about the importance of a reaction against Victorianism within American culture, and the role that Hollywood played in this reaction. Titles such as Stanley Coben's *Rebellion against Victorianism: The Impetus for Cultural Change in 1920s America* and *Assault on Victorianism: The Rise of Popular Culture in America 1890–1945*—an anthology edited by John Ingham—reveal an understanding of Victorianism as having a specific significance within American culture, and reactions against the Victorian as having a specific significance within American popular culture. Victorianism has been described as 'a transatlantic culture' (Howe, 1975: 508) and it has even been argued that the United States was, at least in some respects, more Victorian than Britain—or, as Ann Douglas puts it, in her book on *The Feminization of American Culture*, that 'even England [sic], whose Queen was the source of the word "Victorian," was less entirely dominated by what we think of as the worst, the most sentimental, aspects of the Victorian spirit' (1979: 5). And if this spirit was located and perhaps particularly pronounced in the United States, so also, it has been argued, was the spirit of reaction. Thus Ingham has described the period between the 1890s and World War II as 'the story of the struggle for control of American popular culture between Victorianism, the dominant force of the late nineteenth century, and an amalgam of subcultures which attempted to extend their influence through the use of new forms of mass media during the first half of the twentieth century.' This assault on Victorianism apparently emerged in America in the 1890s, and confidence in Victorianism was seriously eroded in the first decade of the twentieth century, but 'it was in the twenties that the mighty edifice of Victorianism finally succumbed to change, though vestiges continued into the thirties and remain today.' In relating this argument to film, Ingham argues that some early film-makers, such as D. W. Griffith, 'attempted to use the movies as a way to promote Victorianism,' but the main tendency was for cinema to function as 'an extraordinary and pervasive and powerful organ of popular culture to challenge the hegemony of Victorian values' (Ingham, 1987: 5–6).

Ingham here draws upon the work of Larry May. In *Screening out the Past*, his account of the birth of mass culture and the motion picture industry, May has written of how the cinema came to embody tensions erupting within what he calls the Victorian culture of America. He argues that there were attempts to make the new medium into an extension of Victorianism—initially the tendency was to show heroes or heroines overcoming 'dangers such as drink, overspending, and sexual women, suggesting the conscience of the old culture still prevailed. Starting around 1913, this began to change, first with the comedy genre. Formerly, the viewers had laughed when the characters failed to meet Victorian standards; now they laughed at the Victorian standards themselves' (1983: 100). He goes on to describe how the films of key figures in the early history of Hollywood, such as Mack Sennett, Theda Bara, Mary Pickford, and Douglas Fairbanks, broke with Victorian convention, though in different ways and to varying degrees. He notes that 'almost every future mogul perceived that films portraying values different from those of Victorianism would draw bigger audiences' (175).

The 'irreverent male unit' referred to at the beginning of the chapter, who laughed at *East Lynne* from his seat in the Cecil Spooner Theatre in the Bronx, can thus be seen as part of a larger trend. While the 1913 version of *East Lynne* was not intended as a comedy, the reception of the film fits in with May's argument of a shift from the attempt to use film as an extension of Victorianism toward the ridiculing of Victorian values. Yet May's and other accounts of a reaction against Victorian standards leave questions about the justification for, and significance of, speaking of the Victorian in an American context, the basis upon which a reaction against the Victorian can be measured, and the particular role that the cinema played in any such reaction.

A variation on this narrative of conflict between Victorianism and more modern values, one which is again related to mass culture in general and the cinema in particular, has been provided by Donald Albrecht in his examination of the place of modern architecture in the films of the 1920s and 1930s. According to Albrecht, these decades saw the popularization of modernism. He writes that

> not only did architects themselves promulgate their work with unprecedented fervor in books, manifestoes, and exhibitions, but artists in other media soon began to adopt the characteristic features of the new style. Novelists and playwrights set high-toned comedies and dramas in ultra-modern penthouses. Fashion photographers shot layouts aboard sleek ocean lines. Comic book illustrators drew their super-human heroes flying through the air above futurist cities.

The simplicity of modernism made ideal decorative backdrops, 'but appreciation for the modern style went deeper than for just its graphic value. Many members of the generation born at the end of the nineteenth century welcomed it as an antidote to the Victorian clutter and fussiness of their parents' interiors.' Albrecht goes on to say that 'no vehicle provided as effective and widespread an exposure of architectural imagery as the medium of the movies' (1986: xi–xii).

For Albrecht there were a number of key stages in the emergence and proselytizing of modern architecture, from Alfred Loos's article 'Ornament and Crime' (1902), through to Le Corbusier's book *Towards an Architecture* (1923), and, in addition to the buildings designed by these and other architects, to the succession of exhibitions of design and architecture held in Paris in 1925, Stuttgart in 1927, New York in 1932, Chicago in 1933–34, up to the New York World's Fair of 1939–40, the latter promoted with the slogan 'Building the world of tomorrow.' He traces the use modern architecture in film back to *L'Inhumaine* (1924), and from that to *L'Argent* (1928) (both made in France) and other European avant-garde film of the 1920s. He goes on to identify the emergence of modernist design in a series of examples of Hollywood films from the 1930s, and to note that the modernist influence on Hollywood lasted through most of that decade, with three studios in particular—Paramount, RKO, and MGM—setting out to create a modern 'look' to their films.

Albrecht's account suggests that an examination of how the cinema was affected by a twentieth-century reaction against Victorian style, and perhaps also Victorian values, needs to do more than pay attention to those elements that appear in certain films. While *So Evil My Love, Dr. Jekyll and Mr. Hyde,* and other films of the 1940s may have perpetuated a dark and oppressive image of the Victorian era, in the 1920s the fact that the setting of a nineteenth-century novel by Émile Zola was given a modernist look in *L'Argent* might suggest that modernity had acquired an appeal that a more 'Victorian' *mise-en-scène* did not have. Those elements that did *not* appear in films are significant as well as those that did.

There are complexities here. On the one hand, the use of Victorian settings in the 1940s might also suggest that Victoriana had by this stage reacquired a certain appeal (and this theme will be more fully explored in the next chapter); on the other hand, the use of modernist settings could be understood in terms of an association between modernism and corruption. This can be identified in the 1940s. Examining the representation of modern art in popular films and fiction of that decade, Diane Waldman has documented an anti-intellectual and xenophobic strand of American popular culture through which modern art came to signify childishness, insanity, and ugliness (Waldman, 1982). Writing of earlier decades, Albrecht notes that while *L'Inhumaine* was received enthusiastically by modern architects, it failed with the public, while in other European films, such as *A nous la liberté* (1931), it is modernity that is clearly linked to the oppression of the factory system. In Hollywood the tendency was to restrict modernist design to particular locations, such as nightclubs, hotels, and ocean liners (the modern was linked to hedonistic wealth), and even this usage lasted only for a while; Albrecht states that 'by the opening of the 1939 New York World's Fair and on the eve of World War II, modern film decor had virtually disappeared from the repertoire of film set designers around the world' (104).

May also suggests complexities in the move from the Victorian to the modern, though his account places a greater emphasis on the 'progress' of history. In examining May's account, it is also important to think through the consequences of his discussion of the Victorian in an American context, and at times to question its appropriateness. In particular, it is important to be aware that the attitudes and practices that have come to be described as Victorian may not be identical with the attitudes and practices of those who were Victorian by virtue of when or where they were born. At one point in *Screening out the Past* a photograph from a film magazine of the 1920s is accompanied by a caption that reads: 'In *Photoplay*, the home has moved far beyond the functional needs of Victorianism. Now it has expanded into playland, complete with pools and jovial friends' (193–94). Two points can be made here. One, the contrast between the functional needs of Victorianism and a modern society devoted to play could itself be contrasted with another opposition, between Victorian, decorative design and a modern functionalism. That is, the derogation of the Victorian may be constructed on differing, and even contradictory foundations. Two, while Victorian society was no doubt light on swimming pools, the apparent implication that the Victorians lacked jovial friends suggests either a narrow conception of what life was like in the nineteenth century (perhaps that it was all a matter of 'spiritual frustration in dark, rambling houses'), or that 'Victorianism' is not really being used here to refer to an historical period, but rather designates a prudish and forbidding outlook not confined to any one era.

Stanley Coben, in his study of the American rebellion against Victorianism, refers to a slightly different subject matter, one that includes feminism, civil rights, and jazz, and concentrates on the 1920s. Among the statements he makes is the claim that the Ku Klux Klan 'emerged as the most powerful guardian of Victorianism during the 1920s' (1991: 136). The twentieth-century Ku Klux Klan was of course modeled on the Klan that emerged in the aftermath of the American Civil War; its name and regalia represented an attempt to claim a lineage with the nineteenth-century past, though more direct inspiration was taken from *The Birth of a Nation*, the 1915 film directed D. W. Griffith (that is, according to different perspectives, from the modern medium of the cinema, or the Victorian vision of Griffith). But the attempt to invent a tradition linking the Ku Klux Klan with the past can be traced not only in the way the organization dressed up its racism but also in Coben's comments,

which suggest that 'Victorianism' can serve as a repository for attitudes that it is reassuring to identify with an earlier time.

The understanding of Victorianism as having a particular significance within the United States itself has a history. In his discussion
of the emergence of 'Victorian' as a term of derogation, the British
historian Michael Mason concerns himself largely with a British
context and with British publications. But the example he cites of
one of the earliest references is an article on 'Victorian hypocrisy'
written by an American writer, Annie Winsor Allen, published in
1914 in an American periodical, *Atlantic Monthly* (see Mason,
1994: 9). In her article, Allen observed that in the Victorian era 'the
conversation of a group of English or American gentlemen during
most of that period was such as Frenchmen, Germans, Italians, and
Spaniards dubbed "hypocritical"' (Allen, 1914: 174), and she noted
that in the United States a reaction against this could be traced back
to a time when the Lexow Vice Committee's activities were openly
reported in the New York press in 1898. 'Victorian era' may be
taken here to be a term that encompassed Western Europe as well as
Britain and the United States, though 'Victorian hypocrisy' is seen,
or described as being seen, as particularly prevalent within the latter
two nations. Significantly, this perception is already evident when a
derogatory understanding of the Victorian first emerges into print.

One can find other, only slightly later, examples of the use of
the word 'Victorian' in an American context. 'Heaven defend us
from a return to the prudery of the Victorian regime,' pleaded the
writer of an article published in 1916 in the American periodical,
*The Dial*: 'What was all wrong in our Victorian mothers' days is all
right now,' announced the heroine in a novel (published in 1918)
written by the American writer Robert W. Chambers (both quoted
in McGovern, 1987: 95). Moving on in time a little, in the 1931
Annual Report of the Motion Picture Producers and Distributors of
America, Will Hays, President of the Motion Picture Producers and
Distributors of America, characterized contemporary American literature and theater as a 'revolt from Victorianism' (quoted in
Maltby, 1992: 574). The latter comment suggests a perception that
a revolt against Victorianism was seen to be on the ascendance in
the United States as well as Britain, though it also indicates a resistance to this pressure; the censorship of the 'Hays Code' (otherwise
known as the Production Code) could be seen as an attempt (successful or not) to reinstate threatened Victorian values, to use the

mass media as a way of reaffirming a certain version of Victorianism, and perhaps therefore of a continuation of the trend which May and Ingham link with the films of D. W. Griffith. This battle was still being fought when Joseph Breen demanded cuts in the *Dr. Jekyll and Mr. Hyde* script.

## Britain

IT WAS NOTED at the time that Hollywood tended to conceive of Britain (which mostly meant England and often meant London) as a place imbrued with the past, so much so that during World War II there were government demands that the American film industry 'tone down the typical image of a land of "castles and caste" and drop the stereotyped, monocled, "bah jove" Englishman' (comments taken from the Office of War Information 'Manual for the Motion Picture Industry,' quoted in Koppes and Black,1987: 225). Victorian Britain served a particular function within Hollywood's generic system, one that bears a certain relationship with particular films, such as *Life with Father* (1947) or *The Late George Appleby* (1946), set on the American East Coast around the turn of the century, but that was on the whole quite different from the function served in Hollywood films by the American nineteenth century, a contrast that is revealed most clearly in the case of the western. Did British Victorian settings serve the same function for Hollywood and British films? A film such as *So Evil My Love*, made in Britain for Paramount Studios, at least indicates an overlap between the two industries in this respect, while the existence of both British and American film versions of *Gaslight* (as well as of *East Lynne, Dr. Jekyll and Mr. Hyde,* and other source material written or set in the Victorian period) provides a further point of comparison, if also grounds for examining differences between the American and British treatment of the same subject.

Moving beyond film, a multi-faceted reaction against Victorianism can be identified in both the United States and Britain. Whether the British reaction operated in the way outlined by writers such as Larry May is another question. At the very least the historiography of twentieth-century reactions to the Victorians has taken different forms in Britain and the United States. When Raphael Samuel linked *Great Expectations* (1946) and *Oliver Twist* (1948) to 'a stigmatization of the Victorian' he pointed to a connection between the derogation of the Victorian, British cinema in the period when box-office attendances were at their peak, and wider popular trends. But Samuel's statement that 'these films were hugely influential in popularizing the notion of the Victorian as a time of darkness and fear' (1994: 421) suggests a relationship between the Victorian, the film industry, and its audiences that is somewhat different from that outlined by May, both in its emphasis on 'darkness and fear' rather than the ridicule stressed by May, and in the fact that if the stigmatization of the Victorian was popularized in the 1940s this would imply that in earlier decades such attitudes existed at a level other than of the popular. Other accounts of anti-Victorianism in Britain, such as those given by Michael Mason and Richard Altick (see below), have discussed this trend in relation to intellectual debate rather than popular culture.

1918 is a key date in the British history of anti-Victorianism. That year saw the publication of Lytton Strachey's *Eminent Victorians*, a book that, for Cyril Connolly, struck 'the note of ridicule which the whole war-weary generation wanted to hear' (quoted in Holroyd, 1968: 329), and which has more recently been described by Richard Altick as 'the only time on record that a single 350-page book turned an entire past society into a laughingstock in the estimation of a new one' (1995: 81). It was also in 1918 that Edmund Gosse wrote that 'for a considerable time past everybody must have noticed, especially in private conversation, a growing tendency to disparagement and even ridicule of all men and things which can be defined as "Victorian"' (276). Yet the publication of *Eminent Victorians* did not change how the Victorians were perceived on its own, and, as Mason points out (8), Gosse's 'for a considerable time past' indicates that what was being commented upon at the end of the World War I seems to have been in circulation before that war had begun.

According to Mason the very identification of an era labeled 'Victorian' did not properly emerge until the end of the nineteenth century (the key events here being the royal jubilees of 1887 and 1897); anti-Victorianism (expressed as such) was an essentially twentieth-century phenomenon. A transformation can be seen in how Edward Carpenter was, in 1916, speaking of 'that strange period of human evolution the Victorian age, which in some respects, one now thinks, marked the lowest ebb of modern civilized society,' while twenty years earlier he had referred only to historical shifts in the broadest terms (Mason: 12). As in the United States, 1913 also figures as a significant date in this history, at least according to Arthur Quiller-Couch, who identified that year as the one in which 'the fashion, since widely spread, of scorning all things "Victorian"' emerged, initially among Cambridge undergraduates (1922: 296). However, Mason suggests that the real beginnings of this trend came earlier, a suggestion supported by other accounts, such as that offered by Thomas J. Hardy, who wrote that 'it was seven years before that date [1913] that I first heard the word 'Victorian' used in a disparaging sense. A young lady of tender years—she was still at school—confided in me that her Mamma was '"a great dear and all that, but dreadfully Victorian"' (1934: 123).

A stigmatization of the Victorian appears to have emerged and became prominent within Britain during the period which May, Ingham, and others have discussed in terms of an assault on Victorianism within the United States. Allen's discussion of 'Victorian hypocrisy' lends support to the notion of this trend being an Anglo-American phenomenon. Yet accounts of British anti-Victorianism in the 1910s and 1920s tend not to emphasize the mass cultural appeal that May attributes to the rejection of Victorian values. Examining Gosse's comments on how for a considerable time past everyone must have noted a tendency to disparage and ridicule the Victorian, it is worth asking not just what he meant by 'a considerable time past' but also who he had in mind when he spoke of 'everyone.' Quiller-Couch identified Cambridge undergraduates as initiating a trend, while Compton Mackenzie described the publication, in 1903, of Samuel Butler's *Way of All Flesh* as 'the most important literary event of my time in Oxford' on account of the way in which the 'younger genera-tion' found in the novel 'a point of concentration for their ideas of the Victorian' (quoted in Mason: 9). In 1931, in a book purporting to be a symposium of 'Victorian wisdom,' it was announced that 'in England no well-educated diplomat or cultural "young-man-about-town" must fail to have published a sprightly and somewhat dis-paraging account of a great Victorian, preferably a poet, before he reaches forty' or his promise 'will henceforth be accounted as unful-filled' (Sitwell, 1931: 11). Whatever their accuracy (or flippancy), these accounts share a characterization of those challenging Victorian values as being young, male, well-educated, and presumably upper or middle class. Comparing the laughter apparently provoked by *Eminent Victorians* with that which erupted in the Cecil Spooner Theatre suggests a contrast between Bloomsbury and the Bronx.

There are further complexities and patterns that could be investigated here. One striking thing about the disparagement of the Victorians is how often it was a qualified disparagement. Even *Eminent Victorians* displays a certain respect for its subjects, a respect that was even more evident in Strachey's subsequent biography of Queen Victoria (published in 1921). Other writers, such as Arthur Machen, listed the apparent faults of the Victorians—'the Victorians couldn't write, couldn't paint, couldn't think, and couldn't properly be said to be alive at all. They lived and moved in a world of prim, feeble, old-maidish, curatical, schoolgirlish pretenses, their chief object being to avoid telling or hearing the truth about any subject whatever'—only to pronounce such notions as 'mendacious rubbish' (1926: 139). Osbert Sitwell's 'Victorianism: An English Disease' seems to be one of the few essays displaying outright hostility, while reserving that hostility for 'Victorianism'—'the survival of Victorian ideals, methods and ways of looking at things, into an age totally unsuited to them'—rather than for 'the Victorian Age' itself (1935: 77). Elsewhere, there were suggestions that the nature of antipathy toward the Victorian had changed by the 1930s. 'I think you will agree that, though the silly and superficial fashion of making fun of the greatest Victorians has to a certain extent gone the way of other silly fashions,' wrote the literary critic William Murdoch, 'there remains a deeper and more settled feeling of contempt for the Victorian spirit' (1938: 2).

Patterns and complexities can be found in establishing who made fun of, or felt contempt for, the Victorians or Victorianism, and how this was expressed. The 'young *man*-about-town' who was apparently expected to have published a disparaging account of a suitably laughable Victorian can be linked to the '*male* unit' in the Cecil Spooner Theatre, and also to a tendency to link the Victorian to the feminine in a derogatory way—as in statements such as 'What was all wrong in our Victorian *mothers*' days is all right now,' the suggestion that 'the commanding word "Victorian" has come to connote flabbly and futile, prudish and trite, grand*motherly* and sentimental' (Allen, 1914: 174), Arthur Machen's account of the 'poor Victorians' whose 'laws of their lives were dictated to them by *maiden ladies* and the vicar's *wife*' (137), or Frederick Lewis Allen's comment, in his 1931 book *Only Yesterday*, that in the 1920s 'up-to-date people thought of Victorians as old *ladies* with bustles and inhibitions' (Allen, 1987: 203).

This link, derogatory or not, between the Victorian and the feminine seems to have been especially marked in the United States. For Jane H. Hunter, '"Victorian" is a contested and complex term which in America has connotations of gender, class, and religion. "Victorians"—those who participated in a trans-Atlantic culture of literacy and uplift—were disproportionately female, and clustered in the middle and upper classes and the Northeast' (1992: 53). But, while the denigration of the Victorian could be expressed (in Britain) by Thomas J. Hardy's remembered schoolgirl as well as the undergraduates to whom Quiller-Couch and MacKenzie referred, anti-Victorianism could also be based on the image of the tyrannical father, from the patriarchs described in Edmund's Gosse's *Father and Son* (1907) and Samuel Butler's *Way of All Flesh* (1903) to the film melodramas of the 1930s in which Tod Slaughter played a villainous (and often Victorian) older male with designs upon an innocent, younger female, and later British films such as *Gaslight*, *Hatter's Castle*, and *Pink String and Sealing Wax*, which, Jeffrey Richards has argued, 'constitute a critique of Victorian patriarchy' (1998: 158).

Gender is a key aspect of the comments quoted above (if in different ways), but so also is generation. The theme of a generational divide continues from *Father and Son* through to the complaints, made by a British Parliamentary Committee of 1941, that 'standards of sexual behavior have changed greatly in the last generation and some people today conduct their lives on principles remote from those termed Victorian' (quoted in Costello, 1986: 87). While *Gaslight* (in its different versions) dramatizes the tyranny of husband over wife, films such as *Hatter's Castle* and *Pink String and Sealing Wax* (see Figure 6) supplement this scenario with an emphasis on the authoritarian rule of the father over sons and daughters. Yet in other instances the stigmatization of the Victorian could lead to its being seen as lacking adulthood rather than characterized by age. 'A child thinks of himself solely in terms of the physical self that has to be clothed, washed and fed; an attitude precisely that of the Victorians, to whom the ego was one solid entity, without spiritual complications,' wrote Anne Kavan, and not with approval, in 1946—adding that 'infantile is the operative word' (1946: 64–65). The following year E. Arnot Robertson announced that 'with certain glorious exceptions, like *Brief Encounter*, blessedly adult, truthful and contemporary, everything to do with love in the cinema is early Victorian, adolescent at that' (quoted in Ellis, 1996: 83).

Figure 6. *Pink String and Sealing Wax* (1945).

Kavan was writing in *Horizon*, Robertson in *Penguin Film Review*—publications with a high-brow or middle-brow readership. For Altick, Strachey's aim in writing *Eminent Victorians* was 'explicitly literary—to redeem the art (or, as his friend Virginia Woolf preferred, the craft) of biography from the incubus of late-Victorian hagiography' (1995: 82). For W. B. Yeats, writing in the introduction to *The Oxford Book of Modern Verse*, 'the revolt against Victorianism meant to the young poet a revolt against irrelevant descriptions of nature, the scientific and moral discursiveness of *In Memoriam* . . . the political eloquence of Swinburne, the psychological curiosity of Browning, and the poetical diction of everybody' (1936: ix). For Samuel, 'the "dark" Dickens of the 1940s was very much a creation of highbrow critics, attempting to reclaim the novels—the later novels in particular—from a sentimentalized popular taste and assimilate them to the canons of modernism' (1994: 420). Such comments lend support to a view of the battle against Victorianism being fought on the high-ground of literary culture, at most at the cross-over point where the popular medium of the cinema acquires some of the respectability of literary values, values that then may in turn spread to a broader base.

The 1946 version of *Great Expectations* is of particular interest in this context. It appears to exist as part of the British tradition of 'faithful' adaptations, and to be an example of what has come to be called 'heritage cinema.' It can be seen as epitomizing the status of British cinema as a 'literary cinema' (see MacFarlane, 1986), but in drawing upon the literary values of the time, as well as broader social and political trends—the emphasis on social change that came with the end of World War II and the arrival of a new, Labor, government—it also offered a rejection of the values of the past. The destruction, toward the end of the film, of Satis House—the mansion where Miss Havisham has entombed herself—can thus be understood as a metaphor for the destruction of Britain's Victorian heritage, the assault on Victorianism as coming from within a tradition that emphasized respect and fidelity.

However, if the dark version of Dickens to be found in the 1946 film adaptation of *Great Expectations* can be partly attributed to high-brow critics, the dark Victoriana displayed in *So Evil My Love* and other films of the 1940s had different and less prestigious sources. As noted in the previous chapter, *So Evil My Love* was one of a brief cycle of films based on novels of Victorian crimes published in the 1930s and 1940s under the name of Joseph Shearing. The Shearing novels themselves formed one part of a wider industry dealing in journalistic and fictionalized accounts of Victorian murder, and in particular in murder taking place within the apparently respectable, and often suburban, Victorian home. Such accounts can be understood as evidence of a certain kind of nostalgia—the kind of perverse nostalgia which George Orwell laid claim to in his essay, 'The Decline of the English Murder,' in which he wrote that 'our great period in murder, our Elizabethan period, so to speak, seems to have been roughly between 1850 and 1925' (1994b: 345). However, this 'nostalgia' also existed as a counter-current to the image of Victorian prudery and respectability critiqued by those who attacked Victorianism.

In *Eminent Victorians*, Strachey claimed that the apparently saintly Florence Nightingale was, in reality, possessed by a demon; he added that demons, whatever else they may be, are full of interest, and that the real Florence Nightingale was more interesting than the legendary Florence Nightingale, though also less agreeable (1986: 111). This was, in part, an attack on the woman, but it might be better interpreted as an attack on hagiography. Anti-Victorianism can be understood as an assault on an *image* of Victorian life. There is an affinity here with another view of the Victorian age, a cultural undercurrent that emphasized not Victorian respectability and prudery but rather the sensational and the melodramatic. This undercurrent can be identified within the Victorian era itself, in the melodramas and sensational novels of the time, just below the surface in a work such as *East Lynne* (in both its literary and theatrical versions), more clearly in the Gothic narratives of writers such as Robert Louis Stevenson and Bram Stoker, and blatantly in sensational journals such *The Pall Mall Gazette* and assorted crime broadsheets that created their own legends of the underside of Victorian life. It was perpetuated in the twentieth century in the continued interest in Victorian criminality; in the low-brow, 'transpontine,' melodramas that continued to be performed in the less respectable theaters in the initial decades of the century and to which the films made by Tod Slaughter in the 1930s and 1940s pay tribute. At an initially more submerged level it was perpetuated in the legend of the Victorian sexual underground that became more overt with the publication of Michael Sadleir's *Fanny by Gaslight* in 1941.

## Victorians, Vampires, and Piano Legs

> For a long time, the story goes, we supported a Victorian regime, and we continue to be dominated by it even today. Thus the image of the imperial prude is emblazoned on our restrained, mute, and hypocritical sexuality.
>
> (Foucault, 1981: 3).

FOR MICHEL FOUCAULT, writing in the section titled 'We, "Other Victorians,"' that opens his *The History of Sexuality*, the significant question raised by what he called the 'repressive hypothesis' was not, 'Why are we repressed, but, rather, Why do we say, with so much passion and so much resentment against our most recent past, against our present, and against ourselves, that we are repressed" (8–9). By way of a reply he argued that it was gratifying to define the relationship between sex and power in terms of repression because doing so gave the mere fact of speaking of sex the appearance of a deliberate transgression. Our emphasis on the repressions of the Victorians is an attempt to define them as other than ourselves.

Such moves have been identified within an academic context but also within the mass media. Charting shifts in the critical perception of the figure of the vampire in literature, Robert Mighall has contrasted these shifts with the way in which the 'Victorians' have remained 'reassuringly static, stagnated and stereotypical. Again and again criticism depicts "the tight, tidy world of upper middle class England," threatened by the "sexually 'other'" vampire; it is compelled to stage "the collision of the stodgy priggishness and determined rationalism of Victorian England with primeval irrational forces"' (1999: 286).[5] Identifying a growth of critical interest in Bram Stoker's *Dracula* in the late 1950s, Mighall linked that interest to the eroticized resurrection of the vampire inaugurated by Hammer films around the same time. Since that date the trend had been toward identification with Dracula rather than his opponents, and the 'more we identify with the vampire the more we distance ourselves from his (and our) Victorian antitheses' (1998: 241–42).

The picture of the Victorians that emerged in this chapter has been both a static and a changeable one. While the Victorian era may have been a time of radical shifts, in the twentieth century an image of Victorianism as signifying resistance to change has taken root. But if Victorianism came to mean stagnation the way it has done so has itself changed.

One account of this process has been provided by Peter Gay, in a review of Michael Mason's *The Making of Victorian Sexuality* in which he suggested that the history of twentieth-century attitudes to the Victorians had gone through three phases. In the first phase, which Gay traced back to the beginning of the century, writers attacked the prudery of their parents and grandparents, though indirectly, using sarcasm, irony, and insinuation. After World War II a second phase emerged, 'differing from the first not in its conclusions but in its drooling candor.' If the key work of the first phase was Strachey's *Eminent Victorians*, for the second it was Steven Marcus's *The Other Victorians*, described by its author as 'a series of related studies in the sexual culture—more precisely, perhaps, the sexual subculture—of Victorian England' (1969: xx), and described by Gay as a lucidly written and gravely presented caricature. For Gay, Mason's book, along with Gay's own writings, and, to a qualified extent, Foucault's *The History of Sexuality*, existed as part of a third phase, in which the assumptions of earlier accounts were challenged and corrected (Gay, 1994: 20).

Questions can be raised about the way this model, like others cited here, suggests an eventual escape from bias. What my research has also suggested is the importance of developments prior to the periods highlighted by Mighall and Gay, as well as the confirmation of Mighall's point about connections between popular representations of the Victorian past and trends within criticism, though anti-Victorianism may not have been quite the popular movement suggested in some accounts. The image of Victorian London found in Hammer films of the 1950s, 1960s, and 1970s built upon the picture constructed in the 20th Century-Fox version of *The Lodger*, the MGM version of *Dr. Jekyll and Mr. Hyde* and other films of the 1940s, and while in American cinemas of the 1940s censorship raised barriers for even the modest frankness of a film such as *Fanny by Gaslight*, the more explicit novel on which that film was based had provided a fictionalized, middlebrow account of the sexual subculture of the Victorians a decade or two before the publication of the more academic works of Marcus and others.

The 'story' of Victorian repression continues to have an appeal. The release of *The Piano* in 1993 prompted the comment, perhaps inevitable in a review of a film that (like the screen adaptations of *Gaslight*) combines desire, the nineteenth century, and piano music, that the film directed by Jane Campion 'puts us in the grip of the repressions of the nineteenth century—an era which saw polite society sheathing the ankles of piano legs with special socks in case they gave young men ideas' (Francke, 1993: 51), and that 'the Victorians were obsessed with hiding anything that could be deemed suggestive of sex or nakedness, daubing fig leaves on Adams and Eves and covering the bare legs of tables' (Bruzzi, 1993: 9). The covering of piano legs can be seen as a prime example of the extreme prudishness of the unenlightened nineteenth century. Alternatively, accounts of such behavior can be presented as evidence of a twentieth-century need to differentiate ourselves from such lack of enlightenment. According to Gay, the story of covered piano legs can be traced back to an account by Frederick Marryat, published in 1839, of a Massachusetts headmistress, who, 'if she ever existed at all, stands not as a representative figure at the center of middle-class culture, but at the most squeamish extreme in the range of permissible behavior, a target of some amused disdain even in her own time' (Gay, 1984: 341). It is perhaps another example of the Great Victorian Myth.

Faced with such stories and imagery, one can investigate their factual basis; alternatively, one can examine ways in which a derogation of the Victorian provided narratives and an iconography which could be made use of in both academic and popular discourse. In the 1940s an image of Victorian prohibition and hypocrisy informed films made in the United States and Britain, and colored debates about cinema and censorship—hence the complaint in the *Motion Picture Herald* about the 'mid-Victorian, spinsterish, attitude' of the British Board of Film Censors, and the suggestion that the British 'populace no longer exists in an atmosphere of Sweet Lavender or holds it necessary to drape the legs of the piano' (12 January 1946).

What further complicates this picture is the way in which a stigmatization of the Victorian came to be accompanied by an affection for the Victorian era and its artifacts. There were a number of ways in which images or metaphors of Victorian repression and restriction were used by filmmakers and others working within the film industries of the United States and Britain. However, by the 1940s this usage had come to be accompanied by a more nostalgic conception of the Victorian era. This nostalgia, and its relationship with the attitudes and assumptions discussed in this chapter, constitutes the subject of the chapter that follows.

# 5 THE FURNITURE IN THE ATTIC: BACK TO THE VICTORIAN

A LONDON SQUARE on a rainy, October night, in 1875. People walk by, sheltered by umbrellas, a lamplighter lights the gaslights (though it is already dark), a man and a woman peer at a newspaper article, headlined THORNTON SQUARE MURDER UNSOLVED, STRANGLER STILL AT LARGE. The door to one of the houses looking onto the square opens. An elderly man (Halliwell Hobbes) leads a young girl—Paula (played at this point in the film by Judy Ford)—down the steps and into a waiting hansom cab, watched by a whispering crowd of onlookers, who are kept back by a policeman. The elderly man returns to the house to turn out the gas and lock the door, before joining the girl in the cab, which then pulls away from the house.

The opening scene of the MGM version of *Gaslight* shows the childhood departure of Paula Alquist from Thornton Square, following the murder of her aunt. The emphasis in this scene is on the shutting up of the house and the prevention of Paula looking back. Paula is led away from the scene of the crime and supposedly away from her traumatic past. In the cab that takes her away, Paula's elderly companion puts a hand out to stop her gazing back at the scene of the crime, saying:

> No, no, Paula, don't look back. You've got to forget everything that's happened here. That's why you're going to Italy. To Senor Guardi. He was the best friend your aunt ever had, and he'll be yours too. Perhaps Senor Guardi will make you into a great singer as she was. Wouldn't you like that? You must think of the future, dear, not the past.

In speaking these lines, the actor Halliwell Hobbes was playing a more genial version of the Victorian father he had appeared as in the 1932 version of *Dr. Jekyll and Mr. Hyde*, yet his statement remains an echo of the prohibitions heard a moment before, as a policeman ordered the crowd of onlookers outside the house to 'Stand back. Stand back.' However, this drive toward the future and proscription against looking back to the past functions as an attempt to counter the opposite tendency. The house (and also Paula herself) is clearly a subject of fascination for the crowd of onlookers, while Paula clearly has a strong urge to do what she is being forbidden to do, to look back, perhaps not to leave at all. Given that the film is set in the past, this looking back can be applied also to the audience of the film, the appeal of the film being premised on the very fact of the past, specifically the secret aspects of the past, being a subject of fascination.

After this opening scene the narrative is moved forward in time (ten years) and moved away in terms in terms of geographical distance (the next scene is set in Italy). However, if Paula has grown up (from here the role is played by Ingrid Bergman) and gone abroad to escape from the past, in this second scene she appears in the company of two people who personify the different aspects of her past. One of these is her aunt's best friend (Emil Rameau as Senor Guardi); the prospect that Paula has been presented with is that of being a great singer like her aunt, that is, a move forward that would be accompanied by continuity, repetition, and resemblance (and emphasis is repeatedly placed on how much Paula looks like her aunt). The other person in this second scene is Gregory Anton (Charles Boyer), the man whom Paula then marries and who persuades her to return to Thornton Square—to the house from the past—but who turns out to be her aunt's murderer. However, in a sense Paula has never left Thornton Square, for she soon reveals that she has continued to dream of the house where her aunt was murdered. In fact it is possible to see the opening scene of Paula's leaving the house, shot as it is in a less naturalistic style than the rest of the film, as one of her dreams, part of her repeated revisiting of the trauma of her past.

Paula's return to her childhood home brings back conflicting memories. One memory is of the discovery of the dead body of her aunt. Looking back to the past is presented in *Gaslight* as an unpleasant and disturbing experience, and this sense of the past as a disturbing, fearful, dead place is conveyed also through the context in which Paula remembers her aunt's death. Paula and her husband Gregory enter the house through a door that creeks in true horror film fashion (in the previous scene Paula had referred to the place as 'a house of horror'). The drawing room of the house is gloomy, the furnishings are shrouded in white sheets, and the light from the windows is obscured by clinging vine. 'It's all dead in here. The whole place seems to smell of death,' she says. The house in Thornton Square has something of the feel of Satis House in *Great Expectations*, as well as of the decaying castle of the Gothic novel; the Victorian setting contributes to the air of lifelessness and unease.

What accentuates Paula's sadness at this return is the fact that she also remembers 'parties in this room, when it was full of flowers and light.' In part, Paula's looking back implies a nostalgia for a better world. And if, in one sense, that world has gone (nostalgia being a question of loss—flowers and light having been replaced by potted plants and light-excluding foliage), in another sense it remains perpetuated in the *mise-en-scène* of the film. Just before Paula and Gregory enter the house in Thornton Square there is a shot of the Square itself, an idealized image of a sunlit London square, complete with daffodils in springtime—an image of flowers and light. In *Gaslight*, Victorian London is presented as a place of murder and domestic cruelty but also as a place of comfort, wealth and indeed aristocracy. This emphasis becomes even more apparent in a later scene, when Paula and Gregory attend a piano recital given by 'Lord and Lady Dalroy' (Laurence Grossmith and Heather Thatcher); here they move into a world of gentility, liveried servants and spacious conservatories. Thornton Square exhibits less aristocratic trappings than Dalroy House, but its furnishings still brought connotations of wealth and elegance.

Before she returned to Thornton Square Paula had met, in Italy, a woman—Miss Thwaites (Dame May Whitty)—who happens also to be a resident of Thornton Square. As the gossipy Miss Thwaites relates the story of the murder that took place ten years ago, she tells Paula that 'all's just as it used to be, nothing has been changed, all the furniture, and everything.' Shutting up the house has functioned as an act of exclusion but it is also an act of preservation (and an incitement to curiosity).

This pattern of exclusion and preservation runs through the film as a whole. *Gaslight* concerns a series of denials, removals, concealments and losses. In the second scene Paula is told by Guardi to 'free yourself from the past.' Gregory snatches a letter out of her hand when he returns to the house with Paula; later he denies that the letter even existed. He also suggests taking away the old furniture, commenting that they should 'shut it away, so you can't even see it.' In fact the furniture is preserved by being moved up into the attic (see Figure 7). In the next scene Paula is told by Gregory that she is

Figure 7. *Gaslight* (1944).

in the habit of losing, hiding, and stealing objects (when it is actually Gregory who hides and steals objects). When a Scotland Yard detective (Joseph Cotten) is introduced into the narrative, he is soon being reprimanded by his older superior (Edmund Breon) for rummaging through the old files at Scotland Yard. All of these lost, buried, or repressed things reappear—Paula's past, the letter, the old furniture, the objects she supposedly loses, hides, or steals, the information at Scotland Yard—along with Alice Alquist's jewels and her missing glove. While the preservation of the old furniture is motivated by Gregory's belief that the jewels for which he is searching may be hidden among it, the letter that Gregory snatches from Paula has no such value for him, and in fact links him to the murder of Alice Alquist, and therefore it would seem logical for him to have destroyed it. Instead Gregory preserves this also, as if it were some treasured artifact, by shutting it up in his desk.

The house at Thornton Square functions as a museum devoted to the criminal past, to the career of Alice Alquist, and to Victoriana. It is a museum both in the sense that it exists as a storage space for the preservation (if not always for the display) of objects, and in the sense that it is sealed off from genuine change. The fact that Gregory preserves an incriminating letter may be illogical in terms of his need to conceal his past but it is in line with the film's preservationist agenda.

Having returned to London, Paula does at one point escape from the house. She goes with her husband to visit the Tower of London. The couple leaves one museum of the brutal past to go to another. Collected in this museum are artifacts that predate the Victorian era (the couple move from the Victorian Gothic to the medieval Gothic), but a link is made between the valuable artifacts stored in the Tower of London (the Crown Jewels), and the apparently valueless (but actually valuable) Victorian artifacts stored in the attic of Thornton Square (the jewels for which Gregory has been searching being, as he suspected, hidden in the attic).

The twentieth century saw a reaction against the Victorian era and what it was taken to represent. However, an examination of a range of discourses has shown that even in the period when this reaction was most evident, discussions of Victorian attitudes, art, and artifacts could fall short of outright hostility. They were also accompanied and challenged by more affectionate responses. In its different versions, *Gaslight* was both a part of the reaction against the Victorian and caught up in a Victorian revival. My purpose in this chapter is to examine some of the different models for this process of reaction and revival, moving on from this to a discussion of the evidence for the re-emergence of the Victorian in the 1930s and 1940s.

One particular focus here will be on the portraits of Queen Victoria that appeared in print, on stage and on the screen in the 1930s. A second focus will be on shifts in the status of Victorian furniture. But my intention is not simply to suggest that anti-Victorianism came to be replaced by more sympathetic responses. The Victorian era did not cease to provoke ridicule, hostility and unease during this period, and there is a particular association between the Victorian era and darkness that remains potent today and can in many ways be traced back to the 1940s. What is intriguing is how this association became mixed with more affectionate views of the era, and how this combination of unease and affection was revealed in a range of media, and the particular way in which this was revealed in the cinema. Exploring this combination, the penultimate section of this chapter will have a special concern with links between Victoriana and Surrealism, using this concern to bring out the ways in which the Victorian evoked ambivalent responses, and, in the chapter's closing section, how this ambivalence fed into the cinema.

## The Process of Historical Reconstruction

'WE CAN NOW see the Victorian period in its true light,' wrote Peter Webb in 1974 (186). 'Recent studies by Steven Marcus, Alex Comfort, Peter Fryer, and Robert Pearsall have shown a non-permissive age in which, however, pornography flourished underground, brothels catering for every extreme proliferated, and child-prostitution was commonplace. It was an age of sexual repression, in which hypocrisy seems to have characterized the sexual attitudes of the majority.'[1] In fact, as we have seen in the previous chapter, the image of Victorian hypocrisy was not new to the second half of the twentieth century, while the notion of Victorian repression and hypocrisy can be as revealing of the needs of the present as it is of the practices and attitudes of the past. For Robert Mighall, once Victorian society had come to take up mantle of a Gothic past, those repressive, hypocritical Victorians 'remained reassuringly static, stagnated, and stereotypical,' an image recycled in numerous horror films (1999: 286). Yet even this alternative view can be questioned, for it is arguable that the notion of a shifting understanding of the Victorian has been something of a constant feature of the twentieth century (the Victorians were stagnated in one sense, moveable in another).

In addition, if the idea of the passage of time facilitating a different, and more accurate, understanding of the Victorian era is not new, neither has it been restricted to the behavior and desires that the Victorians repressed. 'The present is an auspicious moment for Victorian studies,' announced David Walker Howe (1975: 352) around the same time as Webb, though in a different context (Howe speaking of 'American Victorian culture,' Webb of eroticism in Victorian art and photography):

> The Victorians themselves were so caught up in the excitement of their era and its dramatic changes that they usually glorified it in their scholarship. . . . Then came a period in the twentieth century when intellectuals were struggling against the restraints of Victorian convention, and consequently debunking was in fashion. Now, it would seem the time is ripe for a kind of

understanding that can go beyond an immediate need to cele-
brate or derogate, that can take a fresh look at the characteristics and dynamics of American Victorian culture.

Yet similar moments had been announced at earlier dates. Thus, at
the end of the 1940s it was being claimed that 'the period of reaction against the nineteenth century is over, the era of dispassionate
valuation of it has begun' (Trevelyan, 1949: 15), and even at the
beginning of the 1930s it could be argued that 'for some time now
it has seemed to us that our generation had sufficiently thrown off
the spell, evil or otherwise, of its fathers, and that having developed
an individuality of its own, distinct from the literary and political
generation that had preceded it, it was possible to see the Victorians
clearly and dispassionately' (Massingham, 1932: ix).

   Others have referred to the ending of prejudice against the
Victorians, or Victorianism, less in terms of clear and dispassionate
assessment and more in terms of positive affection, though again
there are differences as to when a change is taken to have occurred,
and the form that this change took.

   For Garrett Stewart, the closing years of the twentieth century
had seen 'an unprecedented recent proliferation' of films set at the
end of the nineteenth century, but also 'a marked difference from previous film treatments' as the place once held by 'history' was replaced
by 'a collective and more distanced nostalgia' (1995: 153). 'In Britain
today there is an extraordinary nostalgia for Victoriana. Where
Victorian artifacts were, until quite recently, disliked and destroyed,
they are now treasured and preserved,' wrote James Walvin in 1988
(163). Walvin linked that nostalgia to the appeal to 'Victorian
virtues' made by Margaret Thatcher in 1983, but a Victorian revival
has by no means been identified only in Britain. In discussing
'Victorian studies,' Howe was particularly referring to 'American
Victorian culture.' The films discussed by Stewart originated from
both Britain and the United States. It was in an American publication
that it was suggested that 'a longing for space and good workman-
ship, a nostalgia for old-fashioned style and grace, a fascination with
the decorative techniques and materials of a highly ornamental age—
all these qualities play a part in the Victorian revival of the 1980s'
(Grow and Zwech, 1984: 7). And it was in reference to a 1970 exhibition of nineteenth-century decorative arts held at New York's
Metropolitan Museum of Art that Kenneth Ames wrote that 'while

sporadic examinations of nineteenth-century furnishings had appeared before, Victorian design was still considered of dubious merit in 1970, and even today some individuals and institutions continue to act as though no noteworthy furnishings had been produced since 1840. Nonetheless Victoriana has subsequently become very popular. Articles appear regularly in *Nineteenth Century*, the magazine of the Victorian Society in America, founded in 1969, and in *Art & Antiques*, *The Magazine Antiques*, and a number of other art and collecting journals' (1983: 287).

The problem with such statements is that, just as the notion of a more dispassionate evaluation of the Victorians predates the 1970s, so also does the perception of a Victorian revival. Thus for Asa Briggs, 'it was in the 1950s, the decade when the Victorian Society was founded, that attitudes to the Victorians were beginning to change significantly' (1988: 12). Though Briggs was referring to developments in Britain, he also identified this change as a trans-Atlantic phenomenon. Still earlier dates have been specified. Looking back from the 1940s to the 1930s, fashion critic James Laver identified (1945: 109)

> a new interest in the Victorians—not the purely hostile interest of the twenties, but a sympathetic interest. The great figures of the Victorian epoch ceased to be detestable and ridiculous, and began to seem quaint. It is the inevitable milestone in the process of historical reconstruction. Victorian furniture and knick-knacks began to be collected and admired, and the early nineteen-thirties paid the eighteen-nineties the compliment of readopting their puff-sleeves.

Such models of revaluation and return necessarily involve setting up an earlier period of reaction; in order to argue that the 1970s saw a revival of Victoriana it is necessary to invoke the 1950s as a point of contrast, the same being true of the 1950s as opposed to the 1930s, the 1930s as opposed to the 1920s, and so on perhaps back to the Victorian era itself. Applied with excessive rigor this model begins to break down; Laver's argument that interest in the Victorian era in the 1920s was 'purely hostile' is contradicted by the *Bioscope* review of the film *Comin' Thro' the Rye* (1924) which announced that 'never has the atmosphere of quaintly formal yet graceful and decorative Victorian England been more vividly reproduced on the screen' (1 November 1923, quoted in Higson, 1995: 48).

Another explanation for the different dates given above is that they refer to developments markedly different in kind (films, puff-sleeves, politics, and so on) and degree. This is not to argue that these developments are unrelated, even in the case of puff-sleeves and politics. Indeed, the relationship between Victoriana on film and in other media is central to this book. However, it is true that an enthusiasm for one form of Victorianism could be accompanied by a disapproval of another form; Raphael Samuel has noted that 'Margaret Thatcher, a ruthless modernizer, though espousing "Victorian values" was not averse to using the word "Victorian" as a pejorative, and treating it as synonymous with the out-of-date' (1994: 291). In addition, to identify the existence of an attitude is one thing, to establish its extent is another.

From one perspective a Victorian revival seems to have arrived little later than the reaction against the Victorian era. In 1962, reviewing two books on Victorian furniture, Evelyn Waugh wrote:

> Enthusiasm for Victorian taste is not, as I sometimes see suggested, a modern fad. When, forty years ago, my friends at the university organized an exhibition of Victorian *objets d'art*, they were repeating on a grand scale what they had already attempted more modestly at school, and were imitating what had earlier been done in London.

Waugh went on to note that 'Arnold Bennett had a Victorian dining-room still earlier,' and that others, such as John Betjeman, Robert Byron, and Harold Acton, had taken part in this early twentieth-century Victorian revival (1983a: 597).

Support for the notion of a revival of interest in the Victorian being identifiable in the 1920s (the decade that was in many ways the high-point of anti-Victorianism) can be found in *Our Fathers*, a collection of Victorian drawings published in 1931, the introduction to which announced that even those iconoclasts such as Lytton Strachey who had made fun of the Victorians had been unable to resist a certain respect for their subject: 'Usually respect gradually became affection. Victoriana was collected in the home, family albums were paraded only half in fun, and the ancient Victorians became a subject of costume balls' (Bott, 1931: 4). Raphael Samuel, in his discussion of 'unofficial' history, also pointed to the Victoriana of the 'Bright Young Things' fancy dress parties of the 1920s, as well as to the 1928 publication of Kenneth Clark's *The*

*Gothic Revival* (1996: 21). Yet such references suggest that what Samuel described as 'an aristocratic sport' existed on a moderate scale and in a partly apologetic matter. The family albums cited in *Our Fathers* may have been 'paraded only half in fun,' but that fun half remains significant. The publication of that book (and of *Our Mothers*, which followed in 1932), was a sign of a developing shift in emphasis from derogation to appreciation, and toward a more sustained and serious interest.

'There was an element of jocularity in those early days, the wish to scandalize parents who had themselves thrown out the wax-flowers and woolwork screens which we now ardently collected,' remembered Waugh in 1962 (1983a: 597). In 1930, in his essay, 'Let Us Return to the Nineties; But not to Oscar Wilde,' he had suggested that an interest in the early Victorian period—'all those glittering bits of shell and seaweed—the colored glass paper-weights, wax fruit, Rex Whistler decorations, paper-lace Valentines'—had already been and gone (1983b: 122-3). However, the limitations of any such trend, and of his perspective, are exposed in his further comment (1983b: 124) that

> among simple minds the clothes of even a few years back excite derisive glee in theatre or cinematograph; to the more sophisticated the aesthetic and social codes of another generation are always instructive; but whereas almost any other period requires an acquaintance with Art and History far beyond the capacity of the young women who most eagerly follow the fashion, the nineties, or rather the fiction that has come to represent the nineties to the present generation, requires for its appreciation and imitation no sort of endowment of intellect or culture.

This does suggest a kind of popular (at least fashionable) interest in the Victorian, though it also assumes interest in the past to be essentially the concern of an elite.

A fashion for Victoriana becomes more identifiable in the 1930s. Laver's suggestion of a shift from twenties hostility to thirties sympathy may have been an over-simplification, but similar observations had been made in two books published in 1940. In *The Thirties*, Malcolm Muggeridge noted how 'Victorian furniture and bric-à-brac, formerly unsaleable, began to be eagerly acquired; chromium plated chairs and mathematical vases were discarded, to give place to pianos tied with bows of ribbon, and minutely carved sideboards. The Victorian Age, so confident in its own greatness and solidity, had been regarded successively with horror, sniggering amusement, and now with romantic esteem' (1971: 175). In *The Long Week-End*, Robert Graves and Alan Hodge commented that by 'the middle Thirties, neo-Victorianism was blending with Functionalism. Curtains, bedcovers, and chaircovers no longer simulated wood, metal and concrete; using their geometrics too, they grew delicately dotted, spotted, striped and flowered. Even floral wallpapers came in again and Victorian knick-knacks were rescued from street-barrows for quaint effect' (1961: 347). Echoing Waugh's conservative bias, Graves and Hodge went on to argue that fashions in dress exploited Victorian costume 'as a reminder to women that they were distinctly women, and not mere emancipated modern creatures' (350).

It is clear that such comments both identified and interpreted a trend. The understanding of a Victorian revival as representing a rejection of modern values, from modern design to female emancipation, can be traced through and beyond Margaret Thatcher's call for a restoration of the values of the Victorian era in the 1980s. Writing in 1939, Willson Discher speculated that a Victorian revival might be explainable 'by way of contrast to the strain of witnessing the psycho-analytic pretensions of up-to-date playwrights,' though he went on to say that 'no matter what your theories may be, there can be no denying the fad. Victorianism is in vogue' (1939: 152).

## Victoria the Great

DISCHER WAS SPECIFICALLY commenting on a spate of revivals of melodrama on the London stage (he may also have had in mind the staging of 'Old Time Victorian Music Hall' that Leonard Sachs had initiated in 1937: see Samuel, 1996: 21), though he identified the melodramatic tendency as taking place 'from New York and Hollywood to Preston and Darlington' (152). Graves and Hodge had also pointed to a popular trend when they wrote that 'films played a large part in the Victorian revival,' singling out three Hollywood productions released in 1934—*Little Women, The House of Rothchild,* and *The Lady of the Boulevards* (the latter being the British title of the film released in the United States as *Nana*) (351). However, the film that seemed to encapsulate a shift in attitudes was the British-made *Victoria the Great*.

The portrayal of Queen Victoria on the British stage had been forbidden by the Lord Chamberlain until 1937. A similar attitude had been taken by the British Board of Film Censors (BBFC), though the British Queen had been portrayed in a few American films during the 1930s: *Cavalcade* (1933), *The Mighty Barnum* (1934), and *The White Angel* (1936). There had also been a number of published biographies; in 1936 an American reviewer of Edith Sitwell's *Victoria of England* had commented that 'so many books have recently been written about Queen Victoria that I was inclined to put Miss Sitwell's aside at the sight of the title,' adding that 'on looking into it I found it had a character of its own, and was by no means a mere repetition of familiar facts' (*Christian Science Monitor*, 25 March).

Sitwell's biography had been preceded by Laurence Housman's *Victoria Regina*, published in 1935. Later that year Housman's book was dramatized and privately performed at the Gate Theatre in London. It was then performed publicly in a version starring Helen Hayes, which opened in New York on 26 December 1935. The play proved to be enormously popular in the United States; it was still being performed in New York on 15 May 1937 when *Vogue* reported that it had been seen by 604,000 people, while another report stated that when the play was on tour in the United States it broke records in all but two of the forty-five towns and cities visited (*New York Evening Journal*, 19 December 1936). In Britain, the centenary of Queen Victoria's ascension to the throne, and perhaps a concern to project a sympathetic image of the monarchy in the wake of the abdication of Edward VIII, led to the lifting of the Lord Chamberlain's ban on the portrayal of Queen Victoria in 1937, with the BBFC following suit. Thus *Victoria Regina* was finally allowed to open at the Lyric Theatre in London on June 21 1937 (shortly after a French version had opened in Paris). The production and release the same year of *Victoria the Great*, a film based on Housman's book, directed by Herbert Wilcox and starring Anna Neagle as Queen Victoria, was followed in 1938 by *Sixty Glorious Years*, another film directed by Herbert Wilcox in which Anna Neagle again starred as Queen Victoria.

The stage and screen productions of *Victoria Regina*, *Victoria the Great* and *Sixty Glorious Years* all attracted considerable attention, not only for their settings and costumes, but also for their reflection of shifting attitudes to the Victorian past. In Britain, the

*Daily Mail* reviewer wrote of the play that 'the costumes alone are worth seeing, whether in the crinoline episodes or in the full blaze of color and period fashions of 1897,' while for another critic 'the scenery as near as possible stole the play. . . . At one particular instant, a blue satin sofa acted everyone off the stage' (unspecified source, 27 June 1937, Theatre Museum clipping file). In the *Tatler* (14 July 1937) it was reported that 'the popularity of Mr. Laurence Housman's dramatic biography creates a legend that will overshadow the grandiloquent one in the school-books and the ironical one by Strachey and others.' In New York, it was claimed that a Fifth Avenue window display inspired by *Victoria the Great* captured 'all the charm and quaintness of that era. The confusion caused by a flowered Victorian carpet and modern Victorian wallpaper with huge baroque scrolls is controlled by the primness of the Victorian furniture, comprising a sedate sofa, upholstered in red velvet, flanked by two Gothic Victorian chests, two early Victorian chairs in black wood, and a pair of superb nineteenth-century oil lamps' (*N.Y. World Telegram*, 29 October 1937); the American release of the film inspired the reviewer for the *Daily Mirror* to write (17 October 1937) of Queen Victoria that

> [f]or a considerable portion of her own sixty year reign, she was anything but a popular sovereign and most of us have lived now though an earlier generation to which the very term 'Victorian' was anathema.
>
> Well, that is all over now. Recent biographers have been notably successful with Her Majesty as subject, Helen Hayes is touring the provinces with her 'Victoria Regina' and now comes the British film industry to give us Victoria in what, in many ways, is its finest photoplay to date.

*Victoria the Great* was a critical and box-office success in both the United States and Britain. Among the extensive publicity it received was the devotion of an entire issue of the British magazine *Film Weekly* to the film (22 December 1937). It was given approval by the educational establishment on both sides of the Atlantic. 'There are standards of conduct and she stood for them' was how the British *Teacher's World and Schoolmaster* put it (referring to Queen Victoria, discussing *Victoria the Great*, quoted in Harper, 1994: 54), while in the United States it was recommended by the Motion Picture Committee of the Department of Secondary Education of the National Education Association. The educational potential of the film was also stressed in the issue of the American *Photoplay Studies: An Organ of the Photoplay Appreciation Movement* devoted to the film (Volume III, No.8, 1937). This official approval was matched by a broader appeal. In Britain, Mass Observation did a survey on cinema-going and film preferences in Bolton in 1937; the clear favorite (among both men and women) was *Victoria the Great* (see Richards and Sheridan, 1987: 39–40).

The two 'Victoria' films directed by Wilcox can be seen as representing something of a special case, and as linked to a specific historical moment. In her survey of the British costume film, Sue Harper (53–55) relates *Victoria the Great* and *Sixty Glorious Years* to the particular historical context of the centenary of Victoria's accession and the abdication crisis, suggesting that both films can be interpreted as an attempt to allay public anxiety as well as to assert the desirability of Victorian values. As other events gradually moved the abdication of Edward VIII out of the headlines the felt need for such reassurance and reassertion may have become less pressing (Harper argues that *Sixty Glorious Years* reproduced the propaganda of it predecessor, but shifted the focus to the dangers posed by the international situation). More generally, the British (but not the American) costume film declined in significance toward the end of the 1930s, and when it returned to favor in the 1940s it was melodramas such as *Lady Hamilton* (1941) and *The Wicked Lady* (1945)—films which displayed little respect for historical accuracy—that attracted audiences, not the more stately pomp of the Victoria films (see Harper: 61).

A modified return to an officially sanctioned version of history came in 1950 with the release, and the selection for a Royal Command Performance, of *The Mudlark*. This was a screen adaptation of Theodore Bonnet's novel about a street urchin who supposedly influenced Queen Victoria to emerge from her long mourning for her husband, and thus helped restore the popularity of the monarchy—a novel which had inspired the American trade publication, *Publishers Weekly*, to write that 'the many readers who love the Victorian period in fiction will enjoy this entertaining, gently ironic novel' (16 July 1949). However, on the one hand, the fact that *The Mudlark* was a film made by an American company, 20th Century-Fox, was based on a novel written by an American, and featured an American star (Irene Dunne) playing a British queen, led to complaints of this being an attempted American annexation of the British past; on the other hand, reviews published in both the United States and Britain identified an excessive deference in the film. *Newsweek* (10 April 1950) reported that Labor M. P. Michael Foot called the film one of the greatest insults to the British Empire since Errol Flynn captured Burma single-handed; elsewhere it was suggested that 'the visiting Americans were too much on their good behavior' (*Saturday Review*, 23 December 1950), while the reviewer for the *New Yorker* thought that 'it ought to be possible to relax enough in a movie to put more meat and less wax on noble bones than has been done here' (30 December 1950). The British *Evening Dispatch* did not seem over-concerned about American cultural imperialism, but carried the less than enticing headline ROYAL FILM SINCERE, WORTHY, DULL (5 November 1950), though *Time and Tide* allowed that *The Mudlark* 'may be forgiven its dull and ponderous patches, for the treatment is tasteful, the pace is majestic rather than slow, and it is surely one Anglo-American film with an English background in which the Anglo predominates over the American' (11 November 1950).

The at best faint praise accorded to this portrait of Queen Victoria lends support to the notion that the more enthusiastic reception of *Victoria Regina*, *Victoria the Great,* and *Sixty Glorious Years* can be attributed to particular historical circumstances. What struck a chord before World War II did not necessarily have an appeal during wartime or in a postwar context. According to James Laver, the 1930s represented 'a period of transition . . . for something which never actually happened, because the war intervened and reversed the direction in which fashion seemed to be going. What that something was it is perhaps not too fanciful to call a New Victorianism' (212). The movement from derogation to celebration was not one of steady progression. Yet there is evidence to indicate that the outbreak of war was unable to halt a Victorian revival.

## New Victorian and Neo-Victorianism

AT THE BEGINNING of the 1940s a reporter for Mass Observation noted that 'since the war - possibly the trend began earlier, and is not closely related to present circumstances—both film and music hall has [sic] developed a new form of escape into Edwardian and Victorian days, particularly emphasizing the entertainment of those days.' As evidence of this trend the reporter listed the following American and British films: *It All Came True* (US), *If I Had My Way* (US), *Strike up the Band* (US), *The Villain Still Pursued Her* (US), *The Frozen Limits* (GB), *Charley's Aunt* (US), *Gaslight* (GB), *Kipps* (GB), *Dr. Ehrich's Magic Bullet* (US), *A Dispatch from Reuters* (US), *Edison the Man* (US), *My Son, My Son* (US), *We Are Not Alone* (US), and a film—presumably *The Prime Minister* (GB)—referred to as 'The Empire (?) (a film about Disraeli).' The reporter had gone on to wonder 'if this trend goes further. Is there a trend in fashions toward bustles and brimmed hats? And surely such books as *Fanny by Gaslight* have been very popular this season. Compare too *Ladies in Retirement*, the Edwardian thriller, which was one of the first plays to succeed this war.'[2] The latter two titles lead again back to the cinema; the Hollywood film version of *Ladies in Retirement* came out in 1941 (after an American stage production that *Variety* (3 April 1940) predicted to be 'headed for juicy box-office returns'), the British film version of *Fanny by Gaslight* was released in 1944. However, while 'entertainment' does feature in *Fanny by Gaslight*, so also does murder and prostitution; *Ladies in Retirement* is about a woman who murders her employer to prevent her mentally disturbed sisters being sent to an asylum. The 'New Victorianism' did not always emphasize Victorian virtues.

In the 1940s the return to the Victorian continued in different forms, in both Britain and the United States. In a book published in 1943, D. W. Brogan (writing on Britain but apparently for an American readership) referred to 'the recent boom in plays, stories, anecdotes, and even in serious studies of the role of Queen Victoria' (75). In Britain, cinema, music hall, and a nostalgia for the gaslit theaters of Victorian London came together in the 1944 film *Champagne Charlie*, a celebration of the music hall singer George Leybourne and his rivalry with 'the Great Vance'; the same year saw the publication of a book in which the American collector Ruth Lee Webb wrote that Queen Victoria's reign 'was such a long, happy one, it is little wonder that there should be a revival of interest in the Victorian style of furniture, glass, carpets, wallpapers and all sorts of decorative accessories' (4). In 1945 Alan S. Downer noted that the catalogues of American publishers were 'filled with imitations of Victorian melodrama' (9). In 1946 Anne Kavan, writing in the British publication *Horizon*, was wondering 'why these novels and novelists of the past, especially of the Victorian past, are so much in demand' (62). In the catalogue for 'Victorian Fiction: An Exhibition of Victorian Originals,' organized by Michael Sadleir and John Carter in London in 1947, it was announced that 'the public appetite for reprints of Victorian fiction is growing, but publishers' ability to satisfy it has been frustrated in recent years by the general shortage of paper and production facilities' (Sadleir: 18). The following year the literary critic Humphrey House argued that 'the evidence that a general interest in the Victorians has immensely increased during and since the war both here [in Britain] and in America is available at every turn' (1955: 78—this article was first delivered as a lecture in 1948). The evidence that he cited included articles in *Picture Post* and the *Architectural Review*, radio talks, the popularity of Anthony Trollope and George Eliot, academic history publications, and changing views of Victorian painting.

The particular context of postwar Britain, while on the one hand leading to an emphasis on the demolition of slums along with other legacies of the Victorian era, could also be cited as lending itself to what Osbert Lancaster called 'Neo-Victorianism.' For Lancaster (1953: 82), an

> avenue of escape from logically justified austerity led . . . straight back to great-aunt Harriet's front parlour. At a time when necessity, rather than choice, drew a large number of would-be home furnishers into the sale-rooms, the despised and rejected domestic equipment of the Victorian home enjoyed a new vogue. Acquired, in the first place, on the grounds of economy, so strong was the character of these pieces that like a faint touch of garlic, they completely transformed almost any interior into which they were introduced.

However, a vogue for the Victorian was also being identified in a postwar United States less constrained by austerity. In 1962 Evelyn Waugh commented that to his knowledge there had previously been a scarcity of books on Victorian furniture (1983a: 597). Yet, more than a decade before, in an American article singling out Victorian furniture as an area where there was popular demand but little published, it was noted also that Raymond and Marguerite Yates's *A Guide to Victorian Antiques, with Notes on the Early Nineteenth Century* would fill 'an important gap in the literature of antiques' (*Publishers Weekly*, 30 April 1949). The following year saw the publication (also in the United States) of Carl Dreppard's *Victorian: The Cinderella of Antiques.*

Dreppard had earlier traced the shift in attitudes to Victoriana, in an American context, in a series of books published in the 1940s. He suggested that while Victorian furniture had gone out of fashion by 1910, much of this, 'carefully and even meticulously fashioned from rosewood and walnut, was just too good to chop up for firewood. So it was either again stored, sold or given to the very poor.' The furniture remained, though it was perhaps placed out of sight—in the attic—throughout the period when the status of the Victorian was at its lowest ebb. Following this, its reputation began, slowly, to be restored. By 1942 'Victorian furniture was back in vogue with a bang,' the secondhand article attracting higher prices that it had when new, while 'New Victorian' furniture was beginning to be made—and 'when furniture is reproduced it has truly arrived as an antique' (1947: vii–ix).

A survey of forty antique shops in the United States, undertaken between 1 July and 30 August 1945 and reported on in Dreppard's *First Reader for Antique Collectors*, revealed that Victorian side chairs were on sale in 60 percent of the shops surveyed, Victorian armchairs in 40 percent, maple top Victorian side-tables in 45 percent, Victorian dining tables in 25 percent, Victorian bureaux in 30 percent, Victorian style side branches in 15 percent, Victorian large sofas in 35 percent, Victorian settees in 35 percent, Victorian beds in 35 percent, Victorian lamps in 60 percent, Victorian glass objects in 60 percent, and Victorian pottery and china ornaments in 35 percent (1947: 10–14). However, it is necessary to raise the question here of how 'Victorian' was being defined, in particular given the American context of this survey. Certainly, the term has not been limited to furniture and other artifacts produced in Britain—indeed, it appears to have been applied particularly in the United States (note also the Yates's reference to 'early Victorian *Americana*')—and was not necessarily taken as being synonymous with the period between 1837 and 1901. Elsewhere, Dreppard explained that 'Victorian' referred to artifacts made in the 'antique revival style,' and wrote that 'chronologically the Victorian style began in France with the year 1830, in England with the year 1834, and in the United States about 1842. Victoria became Queen of England in 1837. Thus she followed and neither preceded nor motivated the re-creation of the style to which we have given her name.' He also noted the existence of a looser understanding of the term prevalent prior to the 1940s, writing that 'more often than not the term "Victorian" applied to furniture was just a nice way of saying "old-stuff" or "that old junk"' (1948: 189–92).

Thus some caution is needed in linking 'Victorian' antiques too closely to the late-Victorian world of *Gaslight*. Indeed, writers often made a distinction between furniture produced before and after 1870. For Raymond and Marguerite Yates the 'era of Early Victorian Americana' had 'finally come into its own both by way of public acclaim and interest and by having achieved its one hundredth Birthday—the arbitrary rule by which the relics of bygone days reach a certain respectability whether they have earned it or not' (1949: xi-xii). However, while that statement indicates the acquisition of a certain status, the phrase 'whether they have earned it or not' suggests a lingering qualification to the acceptance of Victoriana. They went on to suggest that 'the late-Victorian era followed the year 1870 and brought with it the final corruption. A new ugliness arrived' (18). Dreppard made a similar sharp distinction between what was produced at the beginning and middle of the nineteenth century and what was produced toward the end, writing: 'Eastlake? B-r-r-r-r! Horrible! Its cousins, brothers and contemporaries? Another shudder. . . . The curtain of this chapter is drawn over this anticlimactic scene featuring a fear of the next chairs destined to be called antique. Perhaps if we are lucky that will not happen until 1960. But more likely it will not be later than 1950' (1947: 48–49). Another writer, Walter Rendell Storey, complained that Victorian and Biedermeir 'derive their present appeal from sentiment rather than appreciation of good design. Both were at their best in their first years, later degenerating into depths of tasteless atrocities' (1947: 53). However, the fact that the name 'Victorian' was being used in the context of artifacts of value suggests that this name was bringing with it more than negative connotations.

There is an indication here of the emergence, development, and limitations of interest in Victoriana. If a 1920s interest had been largely 'aristocratic,' and in the 1930s the cinema had helped to broaden this appeal—at the same time as promulgating a form of popular modernism—by the end of the 1940s Victoriana remained subject to official skepticism while having accumulated a significant following. The overall picture here is one of a continued, expert disapproval of Victorian artifacts, existing alongside a more popular appeal often defined as sentimental, a definition that can be linked to the derogatory, gendered characterization of the Victorian discussed in the previous chapter—which existed alongside appeals such as the American *House and Garden* curtain advertisement which stated that 'Charming Women love exquisitely feminine Vanderley Victorian' (May 1950: 7). The shift identified here was not a move from total rejection to universal acceptance. In the comments quoted above there is a mixture of attitudes ranging from enthusiasm and affection to distaste and revulsion. Dreppard noted both the unsanctioned appeal and the official disapproval of Victoriana, and wrote that 'most of our old-time antiquarians have not as yet accepted Victorian. Some of our mentors resent the collecting of Victorian because it is uncontrolled collection' (1950: xviii). He also spoke of 'the aura of frustration that somehow seems to cling to all things we have been calling Victorian' (1950: 11). Victorian furniture can be seen as moving toward a certain respectability in the 1940s, thought it retained less respectable connotations.

Commentators who identified a return to the Victorian in other fields often did so at least in part with a view to expressing their disapproval of this trend. House (64) went on to state that

> the Victorians are coming back all right . . . but it will be disastrous if the Victorians' stupidities, vulgarities, failures and unhappiness are minimized or explained away, or accepted as something else. For many Victorians were in many respects stupid, vulgar, unhappy or unsuccessful, and those aspects of the age remain visible in the objects, the buildings, the pictures and the literature that have been left to us.

Of the demand for novels of the Victorian past, Kavan wrote (63):

> Only the most mature human beings can bear to look our present reality in the face. . . . We run away, so to speak, backwards. This childish reaction of flight which has become so general, demonstrates strikingly the predominance of immaturity, and is at the back of the craze for all forms of Victorianism. The structure of the Victorian age could, in many of its aspects, be described as a society of children: while we, escaping into the nursery of that snug, self-confident era, are ourselves the new Victorians.

Thus the twentieth-century reaction against the Victorian came to be accompanied by successive Victorian revivals, which themselves came to be successively reacted against.

## Surrealism, Lost Forms, Hollywood

'THE MIXTURE OF banality and *haut gout*, naturalism and eeriness, which pervades the nineteenth century can arouse a certain nostalgia,' wrote the art historian, Siegfried Giedion. 'The interiors of this age, with their gloomy light, their heavy curtains and carpets, their dark wood, and their horror of the void, breathe a peculiar warmth and disquiet.' For Giedion, the nineteenth-century combination of sense and nonsense had been captured best by the Surrealists, whose works 'showed how this inextricable mixture of the banal and the eerie had penetrated our being' (1948: 389–90). The unease and even revulsion that Victoriana inspired could still be accompanied by fascination.

Giedion's perspective was modernist; his interest in the nineteenth century was primarily an interest in the ways in which the roots of modern movement were discoverable there. For Walter Benjamin, another writer investigating questions of modernity, Giedion did not go far enough. In *The Arcades Project* Benjamin wrote (1999: 458):

> 'Apart from a certain haut-gout charm,' says Giedion, ' the artistic draperies and wall-hangings of the previous century have come to seem musty.' . . . We, however, believe that the charm they exercise on us is proof that these things, too, contain material of vital importance to us—not indeed for our building practice, as is the case with the constructive possibilities inherent in iron frameworks, but rather for our understanding, for the radioscopy, if you will, of the situation of the bourgeois class at the moment it evinces the first signs of decline. In any case, material of vital importance politically; this is demonstrated by the attachment of the Surrealists to these things, as much as by their exploitation in contemporary fashion. In other words: just as Giedion teaches us we can read off the basic features of today's architecture out of buildings erected around 1850, we, in turn, would recognize today's life, today's forms, in the life and in the apparently secondary, lost forms of that epoch.

Benjamin's remarks encapsulate a number of the conflicting responses the Victorian could provoke. If he placed greater emphasis than Giedion on the power, even the radiance, of nineteenth-century furnishings, he shared with Giedion a critical perspective; he was interested in understanding the commodity fetishism of the past not on account of sentiment, but because of the insight it could give into the decline of the bourgeoisie. Yet there is a tension between this perspective and a certain nostalgia that is evident in Benjamin's reference to 'lost forms,' as well as to 'charm' and 'attachment.'[3]

The link between Surrealism and either Victoriana or Edwardiana was noted by several commentators in the 1930s and 1940s. In a review of *The Secret Life of Salvador Dali* (1944) (written for the *Saturday Book* in 1944 but not published until 1968), George Orwell noted that Dali professed 'an especial affection for the year 1900, and claims that every ornamental object of 1900 is full of mystery, poetry, eroticism, madness, perversity, etc.' Orwell identified the most persistent strain in Dali's drawings as Edwardian, arguing that they were reminiscent of the world of J. M. Barrie, Arthur Rackham, and Lord Dunsany, while Dali's deliberately perverse autobiography recalled such books as *Ruthless Rhymes for Heartless Homes*—very popular, noted Orwell, around 1912. Describing Dali's 'Edwardian leanings' as a form of pastiche, Orwell went on to note that pastiche 'usually implies a real affection for the thing parodied' (1994a: 254–55).

Others emphasized the Victorian or nineteenth-century connection. In *The Long Weekend* Graves and Hodge had highlighted the significance of the Surrealist Exhibition held in London in 1936, and argued that the attraction of Surrealism was twofold: 'its French connection with Communism and psycho-analysis, and the similarity between "objets trouvés," "collages" and "constructions" and the neo-Victorian knick-knack collecting habit' (1961: 348).

One explanation for the use and invocation of Victorian and Edwardian material by the Surrealists may be that these times had come to epitomize a certain bourgeois respectability and conservatism—perhaps evincing the first signs of decline—and thus presented an inviting target for those who wanted to reject (or distance themselves from) such values. Images of Victorian respectability lent themselves readily to ridicule. This subversive use of the products of the Victorian era can be seen in the work of Max Ernst (as was noted by Giedion: 361–63). In his collage novel, *Une semaine de* bonté (1934), in *La Femme 100 têtes* (1929), as well as in other works such as *Germinal, ma soeur* (1929), Ernst used illustrations from nineteenth-century novels and catalogues to produce a series of dark, fantastic, and disturbingly sexual images. Such works function as a further variation of the reaction against the Victorian examined in the previous chapter.

The Edwardian may have had a similar role here, though the use of the Edwardian in this context can take on more whimsical connotations, a process exemplified at a later date in the Edwardian world portrayed in the illustrations of Edward Gorey, which began appearing in the 1950s, and whose *Gashlycrumb Tinies or After the Outing* (1963) is very much in the *Ruthless Rhymes for Heartless Homes* tradition. Alternatively, it may be that the sense of unease that informed Ernst's works became dissipated over time. Compare, for instance, Ernst's collage novels with Terry Gilliam's animations for *Monty Python's Flying Circus*. The Victorian is used and played with also in the latter's work, though by now Surrealism has become light entertainment rather than dark satire. Gilliam's work is also significant here, however, for the way it demonstrates how the reconstructed Victorian of the 1940s can take on the same role as the actual Victorian artifacts used by earlier Surrealists—an animation sequence from episode two of the first *Monty Python* series (1969) features, and pokes fun at, a Victorian couple; however, the illustration used here comes not from the nineteenth century but from a still showing Anton Walbrook and Diane Wynyard in the British film version of *Gaslight*.

E. V. Lucas and George Morris's *What a Life!*, a 'collage autobiography' constructed from the catalogues of Whiteleys' department store in London, was an earlier example of what Kirk Varnedoe and Adam Gopnik refer to as 'the recognition, crucial to so many artists of the teens and twenties, that bourgeois society was producing in great volume precisely the petards on which it could be most neatly be hoisted' (1990: 258); pages from the Lucas and Morris work were later displayed at the exhibition of 'Fantastic Art, Dada and Surrealism' held at the Museum of Modern Art, New York, in 1936. This production has hardly been limited to the Victorians, but beyond the 1920s there has remained a particular association between the Victorian era and the 'abundance of paraphernalia' referred to in the opening stage directions of *Gaslight* (see below).

Where the Surrealists did claim an affinity with certain nineteenth-century writers and artists, it was with those—from Lautrémont to Lewis Carroll—who could be seen as at variance with a mainstream, Victorian realist tradition (for a later, Surreal film treatment of such material, see Jan Svankmayer's *Alice* [1988]). There was also an interest in forms of popular or apparently ephemeral culture: in melodrama and narratives of crime and sensation, the apparently, secondary lost form of the epoch. Ernst's collages evoke the nineteenth century both in their *mise-en-scène* and their melodramatic quality, at the same time as they undermine the propriety with which Victorianism was so associated.

At the beginning of the 1930s Ernst's collages were seen by another artist, Joseph Cornell, who went on to make his own collages of what he called 'the Max Ernst genre' (see Hauptman, 1999: 28 and 212). In later works, and notably in the 1930s and 1940s, Cornell continued to refer back to the late-Victorian era. However, rather than exhibiting the savage wit and irony of Ernst, Cornell's lovingly preserved and presented collages, constructions and boxes reveal an affection for their source material (see the works reproduced in McShine, 1990). In his use of old engravings, postcards, dolls, dollhouses, toys, stuffed birds, glass bells, and other artifacts, he looked back to the past, often back to the nursery. His is a nostalgic art, though works such as 'Bébé Marie'—a doll, literally boxed in and surrounded by twigs—can also convey a strong sense of unease.

There is a link here to what David Stove's has called *victorianarum*: 'that horror which even nowadays is felt, at least to a slight degree, by almost anyone who visits a display of stuffed birds under glass, for example, or of Victorian dolls and dolls' clothes' (quoted in Wilson, 1999: 145). Such horror is taken to something of an extreme in Hitchcock's 1960 film, *Psycho*, a film explicitly located in contemporary America but which discovers the Victorian Gothic within that landscape. But it can be identified also in Cornell's 'Bébé Marie,' which Jodi Hauptman's has described as 'the best example of Cornell's attraction to the dead. Outmoded even in the 1940s . . . but now, as she slowly deteriorates, she is even more frightening, suggesting crypts and (premature) burial as well as the viewer's own eventual demise' (1999: 50–51).

What is particularly interesting about Cornell in this context is the way in which his fascination with, and use of, Victoriana was mirrored by his attitude toward certain aspects of Hollywood. Cornell combined his obsession with the past with a love of cinema—Hollywood seemed to have an appeal for him similar to that exerted by the Victorian. His friend Parker Tyler shared similar tastes for Surrealism, Hollywood, and Victoriana; Deborah Solomon notes that the author of *Magic and Myth of the Movies* had a taste for Victorian clothing which 'was hand-picked from Lower East Side thrift shops to create the image of a dandy' (99).

Cornell also provides a link between the Surrealist use of objects and the uncontrolled collector to whom Dreppard referred. He was a figure on the margins even of the Surrealist movement, which was itself outside of the mainstream of contemporary culture. His work, and his own frequenting of the thrift shops of Manhattan, suggest someone who was drawn to what was considered ephemera—to objects that he treated as precious but that for the world at large lacked value.

This holds true for much of the evidence for an interest in Victoriana in the 1930s and 1940s. Even where a Victorian revival was most marked it was likely to be the subject of official disapproval, characterized as sentimental or displaying a lack of taste. At the other extreme there was an interest in and from the margins. *Bizarre*, the fetish magazine founded in 1946 by the illustrator and photographer who called himself 'John Willie,' was especially fond of late nineteenth-century fashions; early editions included features such as 'The wasp waist: figure training and deportment 1890' (Volume 4, 1946), as well as stills of Hollywood actresses in period costume (Volume 3 includes what appears to be a publicity still of Linda Darnell in *Hangover Square*, see Kroll, 1995). It is likely that this fascination with the very—literal—restrictions of the Victorian age, a fascination that was evidently not unconnected with the appeal of Hollywood, existed at an even more submerged level prior to World War II. To some extent it has gone on to work its way into the mainstream; the 1940s saw its partial emergence.

## Elegance, Wretchedness, and Age

IT WAS IN the context of this increasing but ambivalent interest that *The Lodger* and *Gaslight* appeared in 1944. Their concern with Victorian cruelty and criminality and their dependence upon images of the dark metropolis were accompanied by more affectionate, nostalgic images of the Victorian, though these images were themselves made complex by the divided nature of twentieth-century responses.

Compare the two following quotations, the first being taken from Patrick Hamilton's opening stage direction for the play which was the source of MGM's *Gaslight* (Hamilton, 1939: 7), the second from the British pressbook for the American film version of Hamilton's play (which was released in Britain under the title *The Murder in Thornton Square*):

> The scene is a living-room on the first floor of a four-storied house in a gloomy and unfashionable quarter of London, in the latter part of the last century. The room is furnished in all the heavily draped and dingy profusion of the period, and yet, amidst all this abundance of paraphernalia, an air is breathed of poverty, wretchedness and age.

> A minimum of five hundred letters a week is anticipated following the release of any film which displays antiques or some innovation in interior decoration. To prepare for the deluge of mail when the 1880 period furniture in Metro-Goldwyn-Mayer's *The Murder in Thornton Square* was first seen, a form letter was drafted explaining that the studio was not permitted to sell any of its possessions. Many of these pieces would be impossible to duplicate, and are used again and again in films of a specified period, or in rooms requiring the use of priceless antiques. But collectors among cinema-goers continue to be optimistic.

> Take a pair of cornucopia sofas, for example, owned by Metro-Goldwyn-Mayer, and the only ones of their kind in the United States. The sofas appear in a scene in *The Murder in Thornton Square* and undoubtedly whetted the appetite of antique lovers. Approximately 5 feet 6 inches in length, the sofas are created in tufted satin, fringed and festooned in typical 1880 elegance. The pieces have been so well preserved that they still retain their original covering, and are so valuable that setting a price for them would be impossible.

The reference to 'typical 1880 elegance' in the *Gaslight* pressbook indicates a sharp movement away from the 'poverty, wretchedness and age' referred to in Hamilton's stage directions. It also represents a move away from the general derogation of all things Victorian examined in the previous chapter.

One explanation for this shift might be found in the process of change and expurgation involved in Hollywood adaptation, and in

particular in Hollywood's tendency to take English settings to signify wealth and aristocracy rather than the unfashionable middle-
classes. According to Bruce Hamilton, in adapting his brother's play,
MGM 'destroyed its character, by lifting the social background from
the dingy and sinister South London atmosphere built into the play
to the level of fashionable people, opera singers, flashing jewels—
and unreality' (Hamilton, 1972: 93). However, while it is undoubtedly true that the film moved the setting up the social scale, it is also
true that this story about a jewel thief was, from the beginning, a
story of riches as well as poverty. Indeed, it derived its impact at
least in part from the contrast between surface abundance and interior wretchedness; the pressbook's emphasis on the elegance of the
settings can be seen as part of an accentuation of this contrast, and
as such as fitting in with a notion of the less attractive and darker
side of Victorian life being concealed behind an ornate and
respectable facade.

Looking at this issue from another perspective, one can say that
Patrick Hamilton's play was itself both a critique of Victorian values
and part of a wider revival of interest in Victoriana. The appeal to
this revival became accentuated in the 1940 British film version (see
Figure 8)—inspiring the Mass Observation reporter to include it
among those films providing an 'escape' into the Victorian era—and
was developed further in the 1944 American film version, with its
more ornate Victoriana.

A related contradiction can be found in the 20th Century-Fox
version of *The Lodger*. A good part of this film is set in the home
(mainly seen at night) of a couple whose reduced circumstances have
forced them to take in a lodger (who turns out to be none other than
Jack-the-Ripper himself). Somewhat at variance with this situation,
the pressbook for this film includes the following item:

> When *The Lodger* set is struck and the bric-a-brac which gives
> it atmosphere is next used, it will probably be in the air-condi-
> tioned penthouse of a Manhattan millionaire, tastes in modes
> being what they are today.
>
> For our streamlined modern era is composed so largely of
> Victorianisms both in furniture and dress, that it presents no
> problems to art directors. . . . Audubon carpets, when available,
> are as priceless an adjunct to the modern home as they were
> before the turn of the century, according to John Ewing, set

Figure 8. *Gaslight* (1940).

designer of *The Lodger*. The chandelier with pendant crystals is wired by collectors for electricity today. But modern copies of the rare smoky waterford crystal are undetectable to any but the collector's eye and are more popular than any other type today. The vogue for hand ornaments which flourished then has come back full swing after an ignominious interval when they were seen in nothing but sugar on wedding cakes. But moderns now place hand vases, hand ash trays and hands developed in antique porcelain on the plastic tables which are purely a product of the 1940s.

This suggests a further confusion of old and new, poverty and wealth, gaslight and electricity, lodging houses and air-conditioned apartments, as well as a dialectical relationship between two versions of the Victorian, the decorative and the sinister.

The influence that the emerging collectability of Victoriana had on the cinema can be seen in promotional material for films such as *Gaslight* and *The Lodger*. It is apparent in the *mise-en-scène* of the films themselves. Collecting and the preservation of the past figures also as a significant narrative element of a number of films, from *Citizen Kane* (1941) to *Kind Lady* (1951). Such characters may not be overtly concerned with the accumulation of Victoriana, and while Charles Foster Kane pays out money for classical statues, his Victorian sleigh ends up being thrown away on a bonfire (though it is, of course, none the less significant for that). Victorian could mean elegance but it could still also mean 'that old junk.'

Collections, collecting and preservation of the past often take on sinister connotations in the cinema. Kane's accumulation of objects can easily be read as a sign of excessive wealth or a psychological flaw. Gregory Anton's obsession with a set of jewels in *Gaslight* translates this into criminal territory. A museum of criminality (Scotland Yard's 'Black Museum') features in *The Lodger*. In *Moss Rose* the fact that the murderous Lady Drego keeps her son's room as it was when he was a child is the first sign that all is not right with her. In *Experiment Perilous* the Murray Hill home of Nicholas Bederaux is effectively a museum in which his wife becomes one of the exhibits alongside the assorted artworks. The fact that the imprisoned wife was played by Hedy Lamarr, one of the women idealized by Joseph Cornell (notably in his '"Enchanted Wanderer": Extracts from a Journey 'Album for Hedy Lamarr,' reproduced in MacShine: 268) provides an uncanny link between this film and those such as Cornell who strove to preserve the past.

But in other films the Victorian past is transformed into a less sinister era. In *Britannia Mews* (1948), filmed in Britain but for the Hollywood studio 20th Century-Fox, the very process of transformation examined in this chapter became an aspect of the narrative. The mews of the title (or the *Forbidden Street* as the film was known in the United States) is in the early part of the film presented as a darkly Dickensian place of poverty, drunkenness, and death. The middle-class heroine, Adelaide (Maureen O'Hara), escapes her respectable Victorian family to marry her art tutor, and to move from a well-to-do but restrictive household looking onto the mews into the squalor of the mews itself. Once there she discovers that her husband is a drunkard with little inclination for work; following his death in circumstances that are potentially incriminating to her, her life of poverty takes a turn for the worse as she becomes the victim of blackmail. However, the tone shifts in the second half of the film when she meets a second man who bears a curious resemblance to her late husband, but who is presented as a far more sympathetic and positive character. The discovery of a collection of marionettes owned by the deceased husband (played by Dana Andrews) leads to the new man (who was also played by Dana Andrews) setting up a marionette theater, the success of which leads to the neighborhood moving from the squalid to the fashionable. The film ends with the heroine announcing in a voice-over that 'my mews is now a fashionable address, famous artists and writers and artists have their studios there, and gone is the squalor of yesteryear.' From a shot of this fashionable address (see Figure 9) there is then a cut to the squalid mews of the past, over which image the heroine continues: 'But to me it will always be the place which caught the imagination of a little girl, a place of mystery, fascination . . . and heartbreak. And at the end a place of enchantment and happiness.'

In *Britannia Mews* the final word is given to the happy ending requisite in classical Hollywood cinema. What comes before indicates a shift toward the restoration of the Victorian. While *Oliver Twist*, to cite another film released in 1948, was representing Victorian London as a slum-infested city, in *Britannia Mews* we see a slum becoming gentrified. Both these images can be related to a wider context—*Oliver Twist* to a postwar rebuilding program based on Victorian housing being held in low esteem, *Britannia Mews* to the renovation of Victorian architecture, even if the latter process was only in its infancy in the 1940s.

Figure 9. *Britannia Mews* (1949).

# 6 THE BODY IN THE CANAL: DECORUM AND MELODRAMA IN THE PERIOD FILM

IN THE PREVIOUS chapters I have examined the significance of the period settings found in *Gaslight, Dr. Jekyll and Mr. Hyde,* and other films made in both Hollywood and Britain. This has involved a particular investigation into the ambivalent connotations carried by the Victorian in the first half of the twentieth century as well as a discussion of the place of gaslight in the nineteenth- and twentieth-century imagination. But my interest here is in a cycle of gaslight *melodramas*. In the present chapter I will return to the film text rather than cultural context but also to the subject of melodrama, focusing in particular on three melodramas: MGM's *Gaslight, House by the River,* and *The Suspect*. I will also be referring to a wider range of films and to wider debates about the place and meaning of melodrama within what has come to be known as classical Hollywood cinema.

The most detailed and persuasive case for Hollywood being a 'classical' cinema has been put by David Bordwell, Janet Staiger, and Kristin Thompson. At the beginning of their jointly-authored *Classical Hollywood Cinema,* David Bordwell states that 'the principles which Hollywood claims as its own rely on notions of decorum, proportion, formal harmony, respect for tradition, mimesis, self-effacing craftsmanship, and cool control of the perceiver's response—canons which critics in any medium usually call "classical"' (1985: 3–4).

Rick Altman is among those who has argued for a modification of the model of classical Hollywood cinema in which melodrama takes on a more significant role than that allowed by Bordwell. In the course of his article 'Dickens, Griffith, and Film Theory Today,' Rick Altman cites Honoré de Balzac's novel *Le père Goriot* (1834) as an example which is a 'classical' narrative rather than a melodrama, but for which 'embedded melodrama is essential to its meaning.' He concludes (1986: 333) that

> [c]lassical narrative works this way as a matter of course. . . .
> Quixote wants to be Amadis, the Consalve of Madame de La

Fayette's *Zaïde* is living in a world of Alexandrian romances, Robinson Crusoe sets out in search of an adventure romance life, Emma Bovary would recreate the world according to the version promulgated by the popular press, while Hollywood's psychologized characters live with a supporting cast drawn from Griffith.

For Altman, Bordwell, Thompson, and others pay too

> little attention to the possible contribution of melodramatic material to the classical paradigm. This repression of popular theatre has the effect of denying Hollywood cinema its fundamental connection to popular traditions and to their characteristic forms of spectacle and narrative. By eschewing the more popular serial forms and theatrical adaptations, critics abandon the opportunity to understand what is going on beneath and within the classical aspects of Hollywood narrative (337–38).

*House by the River* was promoted in its pressbook as a film which 'reveals how the floodtide affects the tormented emotions which rage behind the sedate facade of a prim Victorian mansion.' Does it also reveal a melodrama beneath its formal harmony and decorum? As the pressbook comment suggests, the notion of an underlying pressure is, in a sense, part of the surface project of the film. As the pressbook also indicates, in one way at least the melodramatic status of this and other films was overt rather than covert. '*Gaslight* will give all devotees of melodrama a first class thrill' it was claimed in the *Independent Film Journal* (13 May 1944); '*The Suspect* is sound, exciting melodrama,' wrote the reviewer for the *New York Sun* (1 February 1945); lobby cards reproduced in the film's pressbook identified *House by the River* as an 'exciting Republic melodrama.'

However, in citing such generic descriptions, it is necessary to note that other generic terms could be used to describe these films. The reviewer who emphasized the melodramatic thrills of *Gaslight* had in fact suggested that the film 'will give all lovers of *drama* a real treat and all devotees of melodrama a first class thrill,' the reviewer who described *The Suspect* as 'sound, exciting melodrama' also called the film one of 'the newest of current *dramas* about quiet men who commit murder,' while lobby cards for the *House by the River* advertised the film as both an 'exciting Republic melodrama,' and a 'suspense packed Republic *drama*' (my italics). Drama may here be an abbreviation of melodrama—in the case of the *House by the River* lobby cards, the two words appear to be used as if interchangeable (perhaps 'suspense packed Republic melodrama' would have constituted too many letters to fit on a lobby card). But, as Steve Neale suggests (1993: 75), film drama could also be contrasted with melodrama, as either 'non-comic films lacking in physical action' or as a more value-laden terms. *Gaslight*, *The Suspect*, and *House by the River* can be seen as films in which there is an appeal to melodrama, but at the same time an attempt to contain that appeal within a less melodramatic context, one that is both 'classier' and more classical.

A certain disavowal of melodrama can also be identified in reviews of the time. When Patrick Hamilton's play, the full title of which was *Gas Light: A Victorian Thriller in Three Acts*, transferred to the London West End, the critic for *The Times* wrote (1 February 1939):

> The purpose of this tale—a purpose brilliantly attained—is to play upon the nerves of the audience. In this sense it is a 'thriller,' but it would be unjust to leave it in the same category with pieces that depend on groping hands and phospherent faces or, alternatively, on gangsters and G-men.

While this review compared and contrasted the Patrick Hamilton play with Hollywood's crime or horror movies, when that play was made into a Hollywood film, *Gaslight* was praised in a *Variety* review in which it was commented (10 May 1944) that

> there are times when the screen treatment verges on a type of drama that must be linked to the period upon which the title is based, but this factor only serves to hypo the film's dramatic suspense where normally it might be construed as corny theatrics. Its sober screenplay and the performances of Miss Bergman, however, do much to dissipate whatever lack of values that element might have sustained.

Director George Cukor, the reviewer continued, was 'responsible for the film lacking the ten-twent-thirt element has been a factor in the stage play.' The reference here was to a low-brow strand of stage play prevalent earlier in the century (see Rahill, 1967: 272–83). While *The Times* distinguished the play from the sensationalized contemporary Hollywood thriller, *Variety* distinguished the film from 'corny theatrics' and the cheaper stage dramas (which here appears to mean melodrama) of the past.

In tracing the production context of Hollywood's gaslight melodramas one can identify two strands. *Gaslight, The Picture of Dorian Gray*, and *Dr. Jekyll and Mr. Hyde* were all prestige films, benefiting from the resources of MGM, the studio that epitomized Hollywood production values. *The Adventures of Sherlock Holmes, The Lodger, Hangover Square, Moss Rose*—these 20th Century-Fox productions were also 'A' features, as was Universal's *Ivy*, while even a lower budget film such as RKO's *The Spiral Staircase* carried with it a certain prestige (leading lady Dorothy McGuire was, like *Gaslight* and *Dr. Jekyll and Mr. Hyde*'s Ingrid Bergman, on loan from David Selznick. Producer Dory Schary was on his way to taking charge of production at MGM). Such films can be contrasted with the cheaper productions made earlier at Universal—*The Suspect* (though this did star name actor Charles Laughton) and *The Mystery of Marie Roget*—as well as with films made outside the Major Hollywood studios: Republic's *House by the River* or, even further down the prestige scale, the same studio's *Catman of Paris*, or 'Poverty Row' studio PRC's *Bluebeard* (reputedly shot in six days, as opposed to the fifty-four day shooting schedule of *Gaslight*). And while Hamilton's play led to an expensive, Oscar-winning MGM film, it also resulted in a relatively inexpensive British film, a film which can itself be placed in the context of a series of low-budget British titles dealing with crime in the nineteenth or early twentieth century: *The Face at the Window* (which leads back also to earlier Tod Slaughter films), *Latin Quarter, The Case of Charles Peace,* and the early Hammer variation on the Jack-the-Ripper story, *Room to Let*.[1]

But these different strands also operate *within* individual films. *Gaslight* could be seen, in its different versions, as a production that rose above its lowbrow or mass cultural antecedents. Its status as a period film can be linked to this relative prestige. However, the particular period in which these versions were set, with their conflicting connotations of value and worthlessness, complicated that status, while, as the above reviewers acknowledged, *Gaslight* retained an appeal to the emotions of the unvarnished Hollywood thriller or the cheap melodrama. *Bluebeard*, directed by 'B picture' *auteur* Edgar Ulmer for PRC, the studio that epitomized Hollywood's Poverty Row, exists at the opposite end of the Hollywood filmmaking scale to MGM's *Gaslight*. Yet if the MGM film is a prestige, Oscar-winning drama which is underpinned by a 'ten-twenty-thirty' melodrama, *Bluebeard* is a low-budget crime melodrama with artistic pretensions. While *Gaslight* makes a brief reference to Gounod's opera *Faust* (as the greatest role of the murdered aunt), in *Bluebeard* an extended sequence is devoted to a performance of that opera (a puppet performance admittedly, though also understandably, given the film's budgetary limitations). And while *Variety* compared and contrasted *Gaslight* with the lowbrow melodramas of the past, trade press reviews described *Bluebeard* as PRC's 'most ambitious production to date,' and noted that the 'incidental music, staging, costumes and photography are much above average' (*The Cinema*, 16 March 1945, and *Kine Weekly*, 22 March 1945, quoted by Jenkins: 145).

A similar combination can be identified in *House by the River*, which was made by producer Howard Welsh's Fidelity Pictures for Republic, a company that specialized in low-budget westerns, and which has been described by Richard Maurice Hurst as situated 'between Poverty Row and the Majors.' However, here also the film was an ambitious project for its studio; according to Hurst, in the postwar period Republic adopted a policy of producing a limited number of 'Premiere Pictures'—films meant to compete with the majors in the 'A' market, 'directed by top names such as John Ford and Fritz Lang [director of *House by the River*] with shooting schedules of approximately a month and million-dollar budgets' (1979: 6).

In moving on from this production context to an examination of the film itself I will begin with a relatively detailed account and analysis of the opening sequence of *House by the River*, which I will then relate to the film as a whole, then to other films including *The Spiral Staircase* and *Ivy*. In the discussion of *The Suspect* that follows I will again look at the film's opening, as well as a couple of later sequences. In the final section of the chapter the discussion will again be broadened to take in a range of films, as well as a consideration of the closing section of *Gaslight*.

## House by the River

*House by the River* opens with a succession of shots of a river seen behind the credits, a dissolve to a shot of a town situated on the river, and a cut to a shot of a house. In the garden in front of the house there is a summerhouse overlooking the river. To the side of the frame a second house can be seen. Stephen Byrne (Louis

Hayward) is working on a manuscript in the summerhouse in his garden, while Mrs. Ambrose (Ann Shoemaker) is working in the neighboring garden.

'I hate this river,' says Mrs. Ambrose when she sees the carcass of an animal drifting down the river. She then goes on to complain about the 'filth' in the river. Stephen replies that 'it's the people who should be blamed for the filth, not the river.'

Emily (Dorothy Patrick), the Byrnes' maid, approaches from the background, bringing with her a returned manuscript. 'My manuscripts are like the tide out there, they always come back,' says Stephen. This prompts Mrs. Ambrose to suggest he 'spice up' his writing—'Make them racy. That's what the public wants.' Meanwhile Emily glances at what Stephen has been writing, and then returns to the house, having been told by Stephen that she can use the upstairs bath as the one downstairs has not been mended. Stephen watches her. Once again he is interrupted by Mrs. Ambrose, who this time asks after his wife, Marjorie (Jane Wyatt). Stephen tells her that Marjorie is spending the day in the country, but will be returning for the party they are going to that evening.

Mrs. Ambrose returns to her gardening, and Stephen attempts to resume his writing. However his attention is caught by the light that goes on in the house, and it is apparent that his mind is on Emily rather than his work. After a short while he abandons his attempt to write, picks up a rose in a glass on the table, and returns to the house. Once again he glances up at the bathroom window. He goes inside.

In the gloomy hallway of the house Stephen lights a candle. He stands for a moment in front of the mirror. He puts down the rose he is still carrying and pours himself a drink, then another. When he hears the creak of the floorboards caused by Emily upstairs, he blows out the candle. Emily slowly descends the stairs, backs away in fear when she hears a sound below, and expresses relief when she discovers the cause of the sound (Stephen returning his glass to the hall table). Her unease returns when Stephen refuses to let her past. He grabs hold of her and kisses her. She struggles and screams 'Let me go!' repeatedly. Stephen, seeing Mrs. Ambrose through the window, tells Emily to 'Stop it! Do you want the whole neighborhood to hear you?,' though Mrs. Ambrose does not hear Emily's cries.

Stephen is horrified to discover that he has strangled Emily in his efforts to quiet her. Almost immediately there is a knock at the door. After repeated knocks the person at the door appears to go away, but then enters the house by the back. Stephen is relieved to discover that it is his brother, John (Lee Bowman). When Stephen then claims that there has been an 'accident,' John's initial fear is that something has happened to Marjorie. After discovering Emily's dead body he makes for the door. Asked by Stephen where he is going, he says, 'To the police. . . . This is murder.' Stephen pleads with his brother, who eventually agrees to help him to dispose of the body.

The scene ends with a fadeout.

The opening of *House by the River*—a turn-of-the-century setting, a writer sitting in a summerhouse by a river—might suggest a nostalgic view of the past. Later Marjorie will refer to the family 'inheritance' and Stephen will speak of 'girls of our class'; the entrance of Emily, signifying as it does that Stephen inhabits a world in which households employ maids, lends weight to this image of inheritance, class, and leisure. When Mrs. Ambrose advises Stephen to 'spice up' his novels, the implication appears to be that he is a genteel ('non-spicy') writer. His manuscripts come back because they are too polite.

However, the fact that his manuscript has been returned also suggests a second world in which the values of the market-place, rather than gentility, prevail. The summerhouse, the lawn and the facade of the house only constitute Stephen's immediate surroundings. Unlike *Gaslight* or *Hangover Square*, the house is not situated amidst the sedate, English setting of a London square. Next to the well-tended lawn on his side of the fence is his neighbor's garden where an ordered path gives way to a muddy vegetable patch dominated by a crude scarecrow. Both gardens border an unpicturesque river down which the carcass of an animal is floating. In addition, the two houses are on the edge of a small, and again unpicturesque, industrial town. All this implies that Stephen's world of gentility can be contrasted with an external world represented on the one hand by untamed nature (the film offers a variation on the wilderness/civilization opposition more often discussed in the context of the western—see, in particular, Kitses, 1969: 11), and on the other hand by the commercial values of the town and the culture industry (as represented by the publishers who return Stephen's manuscripts).

Stephen, comparing his manuscripts to the tides (they always come back) seems to link the river to market forces. Yet the tides/manuscript analogy also suggests the association between flood-tide and 'tormented emotions' invoked by the film's pressbook; the turbulent world beyond the garden can be linked to the apparently sedate world within the garden. In fact, Stephen's analogy is a false one, since the tides are the forces that bring back objects, while the manuscript is an object that has been brought back. The tides/manuscript analogy conceals a second analogy linking the manuscript to the rotting animal floating down the river, associating Stephen's writing with what Mrs. Ambrose calls the 'filth' of the river.

Stephen is later accused by his wife of having a 'filthy mind.' This statement, and the undertone of Stephen's analogy, suggests an alternative possibility; his manuscripts are returned because they are not polite enough. When Emily puts the manuscript that has just been returned on the summerhouse table she looks at the sealed package with curiosity. The fact that Emily (along with the film's audience) cannot see the contents of the manuscript, and is only able to glance at what Stephen has just written, gives the writing the suggestion of forbidden material, in line with this alternative, non-genteel interpretation of Stephen's work. In this opening scene Emily's curiosity (and again that of the audience) is limited to a glance, but this glance prefigures Marjorie's interest in her husband's writing and Stephen's proscription of that interest. Both Marjorie's interest and Stephen's proscription go on to become vitally important within the narrative.

The shot of Emily looking at Stephen's manuscript is followed by a shot of Emily walking back to the house, then by a shot of Stephen looking at Emily, following which Mrs. Ambrose asks 'Where is Marjorie?' Stephen's voyeuristic gaze reveals the other side of his character, while Mrs. Ambrose's comment links that voyeurism to an adulterous scenario (Stephen, Emily, and the absence of Marjorie).

At this stage Stephen is still restrained by the dictates of decorum. His behavior is a question of unrealized desire rather than melodramatic action. However, that desire now begins to disrupt the ordered world of the summerhouse. Stephen's mind is on Emily, not on his work. He is shown attempting to resume his writing, but the shots of Stephen writing are intercut with a series of shots of the house, the bathroom window, and the bathroom interior. These shots appear to be a product of his (impolite) imagination, since he would hardly be able to see the bathroom interior from where he is sitting. In fact, the remainder of the film could conceivably be interpreted as a product of Stephen's imagination, the acting out of his desires and fears. The obvious comparison here is with another Fritz Lang melodrama, *The Woman in the Window* (1944), though in that film the husband's nightmare of adultery is finally revealed as no more than a dream, while in *House by the River* the husband's 'dream' becomes and remains the film's reality.

There is a scene at a slightly later point in the film—after the murder but before Emily's body has been discovered, when Marjorie (who at this point has no knowledge of her husband's guilt) is shown sitting in her garden, talking to John about Stephen's 'peculiar' reaction to Emily's disappearance. This leads to the following interchange:

JOHN:      The mystery of her disappearance probably intrigues him.

MARJORIE: Oh probably you're right. He fancies the whole thing is a great big melodrama with himself in the leading role.

In this speech Marjorie associates melodrama with mystery, Stephen with melodrama, and melodrama with illusion. Stephen is off-screen, and melodrama is submerged under the more decorous facade presented by Marjorie and John in the garden. Yet *House by the River* has already brought melodrama onto the screen in depicting Stephen's murder of Emily, and it is Stephen who remains the scene's central subject. In this sense, Stephen is quite correct in thinking the whole thing to be great big melodrama with himself in the leading role, while John and Marjorie are in a world of illusion if they think they are not in a melodrama.

The moment in the opening scene when Stephen enters the house is when he starts to assume his melodramatic role. The word 'role' is important here because, while his actions are an expression of his desires, they also involve the adoption, followed by the rapid abandonment, of a series of different personae. When Stephen picks up the rose, lights the candle, and stands in front of the mirror, he acts as if he is preparing for a romantic role. His romantic persona is quickly discarded as he blows out the candle and frightens Emily by standing in the dark at the bottom of the stairs. This 'Gothic' guise then makes way for the violent expression of Stephen's desire. Yet even when he strangles Emily he is acting out another role. He murders Emily in order to suppress her cries of protest and so maintain the facade he presents to the outside world. Paradoxically, the part he is playing at this point is that of the respectable husband. The notion of 'Victorian hypocrisy' which the film draws upon implies both hidden immorality and surface morality. The melodrama of Stephen's attack on Emily is both a contradiction of gentility and a consequence of gentility.

What is important here is not just what is shown but the vantage point from which it is shown, and how this is combined with what is heard. After Stephen grabs hold of Emily at the bottom of the stairs there is a cut to a shot of Mrs. Ambrose seen through the window of the house. Emily's screams are audible on the soundtrack, but Mrs. Ambrose is unable to hear them, since she is outside the house. In essence, Stephen and the audience occupy the same position, just as the audience had earlier shared Stephen's voyeuristic view of Emily returning to the house. However, the next shot of Mrs. Ambrose is not from Stephen's point-of-view; she is shown from outside the house, and now neither she nor the audience can hear Emily's screams (though the audience knows that the maid is screaming).

Here there is a brief but significant shift away from Stephen's point-of-view. This is confirmed when John arrives on the scene, initially to define his brother's action as murder and a matter for the police (causing Stephen to assume the role of victim), and then to agree to help Stephen on account of his concern for Marjoric. This shift in perspective does not imply a shift away from melodrama but rather the extension of the focus from the particular acting out of Stephen's melodramatic imagination to a wider network involving the family, the law, and society. This has already been prefigured through Stephen's fear that not only will Mrs. Ambrose hear Emily's screams but that 'the whole neighborhood' will hear. It is confirmed when John defines Emily's murder as an affair involving not just Stephen and Emily but the police, the process of crime and punishment, and the relationship between Stephen, John, and Marjorie.

The scene ends with a restatement of the need for concealment. Melodrama has come to the surface, yet the melodrama existing below the surface remains central to the film's narrative. The emergence of melodrama has also brought into play different sets of melodramatic conventions. The scene opens with Mrs. Ambrose proposing a 'racy' narrative and closes with John defining events in terms of crime, investigation, and justice. In order to examine these and other discourses it is necessary to relate this opening sequence to the development of the film as a whole.

When Marjorie later speaks of Stephen fancying he is in a melodrama she is sitting on the lawn. John is standing behind her, helping her to wind up a ball of wool. The scene is again a picture of decorum, with only the distant sound of a foghorn to suggest the world of commerce beyond the garden. The melodrama within the scene is present only at a tacit level (Marjorie's use of the word notwithstanding). Any feelings the on-screen couple have for each other remain unexpressed, while at this point Stephen is playing his melodramatic role off-screen. Stephen has moved toward melodrama, while Marjorie and John restate the values of decorum.

The following scene is set in a bookshop—in other words, in the commercial world beyond the garden. Stephen is signing copies of his book, *Night Laughter* (the mystery of Emily's disappearance having given him a sudden fame). Mrs. Ambrose appears once again. Having earlier suggested that Stephen needs to 'spice up' his novels, she now tells him that

> [i]magination's not enough. Just the other day I read in a magazine that a writer must write only about the things he knows. If he puts down truthfully the things he's actually experienced, if they're exciting enough, he's bound to be very successful.

Stephen's interest in this suggestion inspires him to write *Death on the River*, a thinly disguised account of what he has 'actually experienced.' Marjorie's reference to 'a great big melodrama' implies a distinction between melodrama and experience. Mrs. Ambrose's qualification—'if they're exciting enough'—implies alternative, non-exciting varieties of experience. But in Stephen's case experience and excitement become one and the same. The melodrama of his imagination, introduced in the shots that indicate he is thinking of Emily while sitting in the summerhouse, has become the film's reality.

The next scene in which Marjorie and John are seen together opens with Marjorie looking through an album of family photographs, an album from which Stephen has removed his own picture (to use as a display for his book-signing session). As well as moving away from decorum Stephen has removed himself from the nostalgic world represented by the photograph album. Meanwhile, Marjorie's nostalgia is presented as a source of pain rather than pleasure; her attempt to recall the pleasures of the apparently more stable world of the past is counter-balanced by her own wistful expression and the gloomy *mise-en-scène* of her surroundings.

In the dialogue that follows she tells John, first, that he is 'a friend . . . more than that.' Secondly, she talks to him of the failure of her marriage to Stephen, saying 'girls have foolish ideas, and when they marry they think they've snared Prince Charming himself. And he is charming, John, very charming. But a woman sees deeper.' Thirdly, she tells him that 'we couldn't live like this if you hadn't given up your share of the inheritance.'

Stephen's 'charm,' it is suggested, exists as a mask for his pursuit of cheap pleasure. When Marjorie later accuses him of coming home 'drunk, reeking of cheap perfume,' his reply is that 'cheap perfume can be very exciting.' For Stephen, pleasure and experience mean alcohol, women, cheap perfume, and excitement—sensation rather than romance and decorum. For John and Marjorie experience is different from excitement; John's book-keeping job lacks the glamour of Stephen's literary career, while Marjorie thinks that Stephen is deluded in fancying he is in a melodrama, and she knows (now) that Prince Charming does not exist. Marjorie's disillusioning experience contrasts with Stephen's exciting experience, while her latent romantic melodrama contrasts with Stephen's 'actual' melodrama of murder and sensation.

It is clear that there are several different narrative patterns at work in *House by the River*. The plot of the film involves crime and the aftermath of crime: the murder of Emily, the disposal of her body, the recovery of her body, and the investigation into her death. It features a murder, the concealment of that murder, a detective, and an inquest. However, this pattern of crime, investigation, and justice is incomplete. In *House by the River* the results of the inquest are inconclusive. On two occasions John says that he is going to go to the police but this intention has still not been carried out by the end of the film. Although the film does feature a detective, he is not shown explaining his solution and apprehending the culprit, and Stephen's death is a consequence of his own actions and mental state rather than a direct result of police investigation. The film is less faithful to the codes of the traditional detective story than a film such as *Gaslight* (which ends with the criminal being taken away by the police).

The failure to complete the narrative of detection in *House by the River* can be attributed to the fact that in this film the sensational displaces the investigative; the detective remains on the margins, while Stephen's pursuit of excitement is placed center-stage. At the same time the film has to accommodate romance as well as crime, although that romance remains a background element, like the film's detective figure. When Marjorie refers to the failure of her marriage this negative image of romance is counter-balanced by the positive possibilities offered by John. But while Stephen is Marjorie's false Prince Charming, John is limited to being more than a friend, with the more remaining undeveloped. John is a passive rather than an active figure. At the party that they go to following Emily's murder, Stephen dances while John stands at the side. John is literally and figuratively lame; he walks with a limp and, unlike his brother, he is characterized through what he doesn't do rather than what he does (he doesn't go to the police, he doesn't tell Marjorie that he loves her, at the end of the film his brother thinks he has killed him but John doesn't die). The relationship between John and Marjorie is essentially portrayed through polite conversation. Only at the very end of the film, after the death of Stephen, do John and Marjorie embrace.

The romantic aspect of Marjorie's relationship with Stephen is defined as existing in the past, and even this past romance is defined as based on an illusion. If the relationship can be called a romance it is in the way it revolves around the pattern of initial romantic dreams followed by the fear of intimacy and/or threat, in particular the threat presented by a husband to his wife, identified by Diane Waldman as characteristic of *Gaslight* and other examples of the 'Gothic romance film' (see Waldman, 1983). However, the romantic scenes that feature in the first part of *Gaslight* are reduced, in *House by the River*, to Marjorie's reference to 'Prince Charming,' which she then immediately undermines through the move from 'Prince Charming' to the merely 'charming.'

Where the film does follow the example of *Gaslight* is in dwelling on the gloomy interior of the family home and in mixing a narrative of crime and romance with a suggestion of the supernatural. The Victorian mansion in which Stephen's murder of Emily takes place is a place of shadows, creaking floorboards, and other trappings of the horror film (just as the house in *Gaslight* is a place of doors that creak and gaslights that dim for no immediately apparent reason). Even the carcass of the animal seen floating back down the river at the beginning of *House by the River* is a pointer to Emily's later metaphorical return from the dead when her body resurfaces and is discovered floating down the river, and John's return from apparent death after Stephen thinks he has killed him—events both natural and suggestive of the supernatural—and finally to the 'ghost' of Emily Stephen sees just before his death.

The Victorian mansion is part of a small, American town. That town may be associated with commercial values, but it is also established as a place of social convention and decorum (not screaming), and of the non-melodramatic aspects of experience (John's book-keeping). It is also the site of the law, the place where the (albeit inconclusive) inquest into Emily's death is held. At the same time it is a place where murders take place (but behind closed doors), anonymous letters are sent (to John when he becomes suspected of Emily's murder), and housekeepers nurse unrealized passions for their employers (as John's housekeeper is said to do). The melodrama that is concealed behind the facade of the Victorian mansion is revealed as one aspect of a network of incompletely developed melodramatic scenarios.

At the end of the film these different discourses give way to a reassertion of the values of balance, proportion, and decorum. Marjorie reads *Death on the River*, and so discovers the truth about her husband. She is then herself discovered by Stephen, who attempts to murder her. The pattern here reflects Stephen's earlier murder of Emily. Marjorie, like Emily, tries to get past Stephen. Stephen is distracted by a noise from outside while in the process of attempting to strangle his wife, just as he was earlier distracted by the sight of Mrs. Ambrose through the window. Where the earlier distraction led to the death of Emily, on this occasion it leads to the salvation of Marjorie. Frightened by the apparent return from the dead of first John (who Stephen had thought he had killed) and then Emily (whose image appears among the billowing curtains), Stephen is himself killed when he falls down the stairs after a curtain has become tangled round his neck (see Figure 10). His final, repeated cry of 'Let me go!' is a delayed echo of Emily's last words, and the fact that he had strangled her and then claimed that she had fallen down the stairs means that his own death both compensates for, and balances, the death of Emily.

Finally, there is a cut to a shot of Marjorie and John, surrounded by the scattered pages of *Death on the River*. The couple's embrace signifies the 'happy ending' central to Hollywood cinema, though in an abbreviated form. This is followed by a shot of a river seen behind the closing credits, a repeat of the first shot over which

Figure 10. *House by the River* (1950).

the opening credits were shown. Even the very final image of the Republic Studios trademark balances the trademark shown at the very beginning of the film.

This pattern of disruption followed by reconstitution does not contradict the film's melodramatic structure. In melodrama, sensation is accompanied by compensation. *House by the River* is a melodrama of crime and punishment, in which Stephen pays (in kind) for his crime, and John pays for being a party to Stephen's criminality, while John and Marjorie are compensated for their non-criminal nature. The ending of the film conforms with Hollywood's criteria of balance, symmetry, and closure at the same time as being in line with the pattern of transgression and restitution that is characteristic of melodrama.

The question that remains here is to what extent the film's ending can cancel out the events depicted prior to the ending? Stephen's death represents a victory over the disruptive force he has embodied and the reintroduction of the values of composure represented by Marjorie. Yet the resolution remains unsatisfactory, in that the ending offers nothing to counterbalance the image of the town as a place of frustrated desires and malicious gossip, while the brevity of the closing sequence contrasts with the extended depiction of Stephen's criminality. With respect to the former, the film's lack of resolution can be attributed to the fact that the town is not the center of focus, but Stephen's crimes are central to the film's narrative.

## Ivy and Others

THERE ARE A number of ways in which *House by the River* is an atypical film. It presents an unusually stark eruption of violence and desire, and its overall tone is unnaturally dark for a Hollywood film of its time, even judged by the standards of *film noir* or other films directed by Fritz Lang. Yet there are important connections linking *House by the River* to *The Spiral Staircase* and other gaslight melodramas.

After a nighttime credit sequence, *The Spiral Staircase* opens with a nostalgic image of turn-of-the-century America (light music on the soundtrack accompanying a tracking shot down a leafy village street) and then moves, like *House by the River*, from this daylight exterior to a darker interior in which a melodrama is enacted. In *House by the River* melodrama is referred to in the course of the dialogue. In *The Spiral Staircase* a melodramatic narrative is quite literally placed within the film's overall narrative, when the heroine, Helen (Dorothy McGuire), is introduced watching *The Kiss*, an early example of film melodrama, the film within the film contrasting with its context just as Stephen's behavior contrasts with the decorum of Marjorie and John in *House by the River*.

The exaggerated gesture and sensational incident depicted in *The Kiss* (a woman is expelled from the family home, attempts to drown herself, but is rescued), indicates that this silent melodrama lacks the verisimilitude of its context. At the same time the crowded auditorium suggests that the film is, to recall Mrs. Ambrose's phrase, 'what the public wants.' Helen's rapt attention signifies her need for the excitement and romance provided by the film she watches; the melodrama she sees on the screen may not mirror the surrounding reality, but it has an emotional reality for her.

The camera then tilts upward (toward a gasolier), and there is a dissolve to a scene depicting the murder of a woman in a hotel bedroom situated above the auditorium. The upstairs murder is shown by way of a shot of the victim's outstretched and tightening hands, an image that recalls the melodramatic gestures of the actors in *The Kiss*, and it is immediately followed by a return to the close of the film being screened below.

From this point on, the melodramatic world and the world of 'actual experience' blend into each other. The placid surface of small-town, turn-of-the-century America is revealed to contain serial murder (the hotel murder is the third to have taken placed in the neighborhood), while Helen's emotional longings are given a 'real' focus in the character of Dr. Parry (Kent Smith). The film within the film proves to be a pointer to the self-consciously old-fashioned melodrama that permeates *The Spiral Staircase* as a whole. Melodrama is evident here in terms of both incident and performance. *The Spiral Staircase* concerns the threat of murder that is centered around the orphaned Helen, her romantic dreams, and ultimately her rescue. It becomes apparent that Helen is a woman who has lost her voice as well as her family, and therefore when her role is not that of a spectator she has to resort to gesture rather than words, just like the actors in *The Kiss*. In keeping with the practice of 1940s Hollywood, her inability to speak is given a psychological motivation, even to the extent of being rooted in childhood trauma, but the effect of this motivation is that she adopts the gestures of an earlier tradition of melodrama. To paraphrase Rick Altman, the part that Dorothy McGuire plays in *The Spiral Staircase* is both one of Hollywood's psychologized characters and a character drawn from silent melodrama.

*The Spiral Staircase*, unlike *House by the River*, has a narrative in which audience suspicion is diverted to one character before the guilt of a second character is established. This adds a deductive element to the viewing experience, and so suggests another set of narrative conventions, one closer to the classical detective story. However, it also accentuates the ambivalence of appearances and has the function of revealing a respectable facade concealing interior violence.

The same process can be seen at work in *Moss Rose*; a false suspect is set up before the apparently more respectable murderer is identified, in this case inhabiting the 'sedate' environment of the English country house. In both *Ivy* and *So Evil My Love* the identity of the murderer is not in doubt, at least from the point-of-view of the audience, yet the same combination of respectability and murder reappears. Both *The Lodger* and *Hangover Square* contrast the placidity of respectable London (Montague Square, Hangover Square) with the turbulence of the low-life city (Whitechapel, the Fulham Road). The latter two films open with a murder that takes place in the low-life half of the city, and both proceed to follow the murderer as he moves to the respectable half, linking these two parts together. Murder is not the central issue in *Experiment Perilous*, but here also there is an investigation into what lies behind the respectable facade of the Murray Hill home of Nick Bedereux (Paul Lukas).

The notion of an interior or embedded violence is, in a paradoxical way, part of the surface project of these films. There is a scene in *Ivy* in which a tearful Ivy Lexton (Joan Fontaine) is shown being taken in a hansom cab through a foggy, gaslit street to give evidence at the trial of Roger Gretorex (Patric Knowles), who is accused of murdering her husband (Richard Ney). The (unnamed) couple accompanying her do their best to reassure her, the dialogue running as follows:

> WOMAN: It won't be too bad, all you have to do is speak the truth.
>
> MAN: It's an ordeal, testifying against someone one knows, but if Gretorex is guilty you're only doing your duty.
>
> WOMAN: And if he isn't, be sure the court will find out the truth.
>
> MAN: And those barristers are the fellows to find it out. Dig under the surface for the truth like a surgeon.

In fact, the truth is exactly what Ivy does not want discovered, nor will the barristers discover it, since the trial ends with the conviction of Gretorex, when it was Ivy herself who murdered her husband. What is important at this point is the image of digging under the surface (and the way that this contributes to Ivy's tension), not what such an excavation actually achieves.

*Ivy* is a film in which the 'gaslight' iconography is, on the whole, less prominent than in the other films being examined here. It is not alone in featuring the trappings of modernity alongside the artifacts of the past—note, for instance, the motorcar and indeed the film show featured at the beginning of *The Spiral Staircase*. Yet *Ivy* differs in the degree to which an encroaching technology is emphasized, and in being set at a slightly later date than the other films in the cycle. The scene in which Ivy Lexton is shown on her way to court is in some respects out of key with the rest of the film, most of which takes places in sunlight rather than darkness. Indeed, the dark, gaslit street through which Ivy passes on her way to court is somewhat incongruous, since it appears to suggest that criminal trials, along with acts of murder, occur at night. In this scene the film appears to have slipped back to the milieu of *Gaslight*. The hansom cab, the newspaper account of murder, the line of voyeuristic bystanders, the gaslights, all the features of the opening scene of *Gaslight* reappear. The melodrama of *Gaslight* underlies what is in many ways the divergent material of *Ivy*.

As a whole, the films being considered here offer contrasting accentuations and draw upon a variety of narrative conventions. The undeveloped romance of *House by the River* can be compared with the extended romantic interludes of *Moss Rose*. *House by the River* begins by showing a murder being committed; the murder that takes place at the beginning of *Moss Rose* is not shown, and thus gives rise to a different narrative development. The common ground that all of the films share is in many ways a starting point from which they move toward different territory. At the same time, their narratives, structured as they are around a pattern of progress and return, work toward the retention of the melodrama they have in common, and upon which they repeatedly fall back.

This can be illustrated further through an examination of *The Suspect*, a film about a respectable businessman, Phillip Marshall (Charles Laughton), whose relationship with a younger woman, Mary (Ella Raines), is discovered by his wife (Rosalind Ivan), whom he then murders. Such an examination can also indicate other variations within the paradigm of gaslight melodrama. Here again I will start by examining the opening section of the film, relating this in particular to the discussion of *Gaslight* found at the end of the previous chapter. Secondly, I will develop the question of 'embedded melodrama' raised in the discussion of *House by the River*, focusing in particular on two speeches that are given within the film, and looking at the relationship between what is said at these points and the narrative development of the film as a whole.

## The Suspect

*The Suspect* opens with a nighttime credit sequence. Behind the credits the elongated shadow of a man falling on a cobbled street can be seen, and, to the left of the frame, the shadowy figure of the man himself. This is followed by a daylight street scene, with accompanying light music. Philip (in fact the shadowy man seen behind the credits) returns home, stopping to talk to the next-door neighbor, Mrs. Simmons (Molly Lamont), commenting on the 'lovely spring weather,' and admiring her garden.

Almost immediately this nostalgic image of the past begins to crack. As Philip says 'My wife hasn't got much time to look after the garden,' a hansom cab draws up in front of the house, and Philip goes inside to discover who has asked for the cab. It becomes apparent that the charming exterior of the house conceals an interior marked by domestic discord. The cab is for Philip's son John (Dean Harrens), who is leaving home, driven out by his mother's 'rages.' The scene ends with Philip moving out of the marital bedroom into John's old room, ignoring his wife's protests, and replying to her comment that 'I'd like to know what's going on in your head,' with 'It's much better that you shouldn't, Cora. It might frighten you.' A latent, interior violence is set up in terms of both the psychological (what's going on in Philip's head) and the domestic (what's going to go on in the house).

Like *Gaslight*, *The Suspect* opens with a departure by hansom cab. In *Gaslight* that departure takes place at night, in autumn, after a crime has been committed. The newspaper caption (THORNTON SQUARE MURDER UNSOLVED, STRANGLER STILL AT LARGE) that establishes the time and place at the beginning of *Gaslight* signifies danger and disturbance, and this sense of disturbance is reinforced by the music. The house is seen in daylight and spring, but only after this nighttime, autumnal scene. The consequence of this is that the first image underlies the second. In *The Suspect* this image of 'flowers and light' has been moved to the beginning of the film. While the narrative of *Gaslight* is preceded by murder, in *The Suspect* the opening scene precedes the crime.

This means that, for the purposes of the story, the house in *The Suspect* is not immediately associated with mystery, murder, and melodrama. It is true that there is a difference between the light and charming exterior of the house and its darker interior, but initially it appears that what is concealed behind the exterior is ordinary domestic discord. A title establishes the time and place: 'It was an unpretentious street, but it had a pretentious name. That was the fashion in the London of 1902. They called it Laburnum Terrace.' At this point the tone is deflationary rather than disturbing, emphasizing the pretensions of 1902 rather than the dangers of the 1870s (a still from the film accompanying the review in *The Sketch*, 16 May 1945, was captioned 'Time 1900: in gaslit suburbia'). John is moving out, not to escape from the memories of the past, but because his mother had been on at him to mend the kitchen sink, and had eventually destroyed the extra work he had taken home with him with a view to gaining promotion, and perhaps getting the job in Canada that is on offer.

A comparison with *Gaslight* also reveals a shift in terms of date and class. In the second scene Philip is shown in his place of work, 'Frazer & Nicholson, Purveyors of Tobacco to His Royal Highness King Edward VII,' and Mary (whom Philip will marry after he has murdered his first wife) is introduced seeking work. In arguing her case, Mary announces that she is able to use 'the new typewriting machine,' to which Philip replies that 'we have never felt the need for such contraptions at Frazer and Nicholson's.' It is significant that the period of *The Suspect* is early twentieth century rather than the late nineteenth century of *Gaslight*. It is clear that this Edwardian world is still a world bound by tradition, but it is also a world of emerging new technologies, typewriters as well as gaslights and hansom cabs, even potentially a world of independent working women. In addition, the world that is portrayed is middle-class rather than upper-class. There are not even any servants to do the domestic chores in the Marshall household, as there are in *Gaslight*, *House by the River,* and other gaslight melodramas. Philip Marshall does not have a genteel occupation such as musician or writer. He is a shopkeeper (albeit a gentlemanly shopkeeper).

One character, Mr. Simmons (Henry Daniell), the husband of the woman seen working in her garden, disparages shopkeepers as 'horse-leeches, sucking the blood of their betters.' There is a notion of class here, but it is not supported by the trappings displayed in *Gaslight* (Mr. Simmons claims an upper class background, but there is nothing to confirm this) and it is presented in a fundamentally unsympathetic light. Philip, John, and Mary all work for a living, while Mrs. Simmons works in her garden. These characters are all presented sympathetically. Even the detective who later endeavors to prove that Philip is guilty of murder is portrayed in a fundamentally favorable light when he protests that he is only doing his job. It is Mr. Simmons who lives off other people. Philip may be identified with traditional values, but he is also identified with work and the values of self-improvement.

John's departure at the beginning of *The Suspect* is a career move. While Paula's departure at the beginning of *Gaslight* is also presented as a potential career move, a means of becoming a great singer, this potential is complicated by the fact that it would involve her becoming like her aunt (it is both a move to the future and a return to the past). The second scene of *Gaslight* shows Paula abandoning career for romance. In contrast, John's departure in *The Suspect* is essentially an uncomplicated event. He does not look back, figuratively or actually. His career goal is clearly established in the first scene and on the way to being realized at the end of the film (he is on the boat to Canada).

John is a secondary figure, but as a character with a clear, realizable goal he provides a pointer to the film's self-help ideology, given expression when Philip tells Mr. Simmons that 'a man makes his own opportunities.' He also provides a pointer to the narrative of the film as a whole. The narrative of the traditional crime story is based around identifying a guilty party by means of a series of clues—through the interpretations of the traces of a crime committed some time in the past. As noted in the previous chapter, such traces feature to a significant degree in *Gaslight*, functioning not only as a means of identifying the criminal but also in terms of a wider emphasis on the preservation of the artifacts of the past. In *The Suspect* Philip leaves no traces of his crime. In part this is to shift the emphasis to a different kind of crime story, one which is concerned with the psychology of the criminal (and the cat-and-mouse play between the law and the criminal) rather than the process of deduction. But it is also in line with the film's forward-looking narrative drive.

Insofar as the opening scene of the film does establish a connection between the house and murder, it is thus through anticipation rather than retrospection. Inside the house Philip goes up the stairs, avoiding a broken step as he does so. When he comes down the stairs he warns his son about the step. When he goes up the stairs again he again avoids the step, but he doesn't warn his wife, who stumbles. Cora's stumble prefigures the fact that Philip later explains her death as a result of her tripping on the broken step. The very ordinary domestic details of the house contain the potential for crime rather than the traces of a pre-existing criminality. At this point the audience is invited to look forward to what is going to happen rather than to look back to what has already happened.

Even the film's opening credits would seem to point to future rather than past events. The shadows on the wallpaper identifiable in the opening credits of *Gaslight* appear to represent the murder of Alice Alquist, that is, the event that precedes the narrative, and to which there is a repeated reference back. In *The Suspect* the shadow across a cobbled street seen behind the opening credits appears to be an image from the very end of the film, when Philip is seen walking down a cobbled street at night. While *Gaslight* is structured around looking back, *The Suspect* can be seen as beginning with its ending. It is structured around looking forward.

Philip's murder of Cora complicates this, however. The murder leaves no physical traces, and in a sense it frees him from the past (allowing him to marry a younger woman, and to plan to emigrate to Canada along with his wife and son). Yet, as in *Gaslight*, the murder, when it does take place, functions for the remainder of the film as a past event determining the actions of the characters.

'I thought when we'd had the whole house done over you'd forget. But it's no use, is it,' says Mary to Philip toward the end of the film. It is significant that Mary refers to 'the whole house.' In *Gaslight* the furniture is moved up to the attic, but the house in *The Suspect* contains no blocked off fourth floor for preserving the artifacts of the past. Yet this more extensive refurbishment is still characterized as inadequate. The artifacts of the past may have been removed, but the past has not been forgotten. Indeed, have the artifacts of the past been removed at all? For the verbal statement made by Mary appears to be contradicted by the visual information provided by the *mise-en-scène*. The sofa situated under a painting that appears in the film's first scene (see Figure 11) can still be identified under the same painting (though moved slightly to the side), in the scene in which Mary and Philip resolve to go to Canada. If anything, the difference between the two scenes is that the house has become more cluttered and resonant of the past and criminality. In terms of the diegesis the furniture has come quite literally to conceal death and criminality; underneath the sofa in the later scene is the dead body of Mr. Simmons, Philip's second murder victim.

Figure 11. *The Suspect* (1945).

Unlike Belle Adair in *Moss Rose*, in *The Suspect* Philip does not reach Canada (the New World). At the end of the film he remains in London to face the consequences of his criminality. Mary's comment that 'it's no use' is thus an accurate indicator of the film's fatalistic narrative structure. While there is no question of forgetting in the first scene, forgetting becomes impossible after Cora's murder. John and Mary may be able to leave for the New World, but Philip remains restricted to the Old World, as does the narrative of the film. The London of *The Suspect* displays more signs of modernity than the London of *Gaslight*, but it remains a location that signifies the past, as opposed to Canada, which signifies the future. Philip cannot escape from London because his sense of 'English' decency compels him to give himself up to the police. London ultimately remains an enclosed world, a limitation to social mobility, and this sense of a closed circle is only reinforced if one links the opening credits (a man's shadow on a cobbled street) to the film's ending (the same man, seen from a different angle, walking down a cobbled street at night).

In *House by the River* Marjorie is mistaken if she believes that her husband is intrigued by the mystery of Emily's disappearance.

Stephen knows that Emily has been murdered and her body thrown in the river, and therefore her disappearance is not a mystery to him. Nor is it a mystery to the audience that has been witness to the murder. In one review of *The Suspect* it was noted that 'there is no mystery attached to the killing of Mrs. Marshall nor to that of a second murder committed by Marshall to keep the first from cropping out' (*New York Daily News*, 1 February 1945). However, as already noted, the word 'mystery' has wider implications. It could be associated with period settings, hence Darryl Zanuck's comment (in reference to *Hangover Square*) on 'the flavor of mystery that goes with the period' (see chapter three). It has also been used to refer to a literary genre rather than to a specific problem presented to characters within a narrative.

In some accounts of the crime genre the mystery novel is categorized as a specific form of crime fiction. Tzvetan Todorov, for instance, distinguishes between two forms of crime narrative, the mystery and the adventure story. He argues that in the adventure story the emphasis is on the story that is present, the crime either becoming a pretext for a series of adventures or being replaced by a search or quest. The mystery, on the other hand, consists of two superimposed stories: the story of a crime and the story of an investigation. According to Todorov, in the purest form of the mystery, the classical detective story, the first story is the significant one but is actually absent, while the story that is present recounts how the first story came to be known: 'The investigation consists in returning to the same events over and over, checking and correcting the slightest details, until at the very end the truth breaks out with regard to this initial history. In the second case there is no mystery, no backward turn' (1971: 135–36).

Many of the films I have been examining here feature a crime or crimes but lack a central mystery that the audience needs to solve, yet many of the same films make use of the trappings of the classical detective story; they feature a crime, a police investigation, and an eventual acknowledgment of guilt by the criminal. They feature a 'backward turn.' In this sense they are 'mysteries.' Stephen's murder of Emily occurs on-screen in *House by the River*, but Philip Marshall's murder of his wife in *The Suspect* takes place in the gap between scenes. In this way *The Suspect*, unlike *House by the River*, does conform to the codes of the classical detective story as described by Todorov. It is concerned with a crime that is absent.

*The Suspect* is also a film that is marked by understatement. Charles Laughton had become known for his exaggerated style of performance but this style was toned down for his performance of the role of Philip. It was presumably this lack of physical action and this relatively muted performance style that led another reviewer to find the film to be 'without the damaging tinge of melodrama' (*Independent*, 6 January 1945).

However, following through the notion of the absent story being the significant story opens up a different possibility: that the 'damaging tinge' of melodrama evident on the surface of *House by the River* can be traced in *The Suspect* at a submerged level. Given that the character Laughton plays is a murderer, his relatively restrained acting style suggests a move away from a great big melodrama but also the same combination of exterior decorum and interior violence that can be found in other gaslight melodramas. In addition, the network of different narrative discourses that can be traced within *House by the River* can also be traced within *The Suspect*.

These points can be demonstrated by examining two short speeches that are delivered in the course of *The Suspect*. The first is taken from the second scene in the film, when Philip Marshall raises what he refers to as 'a very serious' matter with Merridew (Raymond Severn), a young office boy employed under him. The 'serious' matter referred to concerns a penny missing from the stamp box. When Merridew promises to put the money back Philip replies:

> That's what all embezzlers plan to do. . . . It's the first step that counts. After that it becomes too easy. Sixpence tomorrow, half a crown the day after, and then a five pound note. I know you always mean to pay it back, but I'm afraid you'll finish paying it back in the Portland Quarries.

The second speech occurs toward the middle of the film, when Mary is asked by one of the women she works with about her 'young man' (who is, in fact, the middle-aged Philip). She gives two accounts. Initially she says that he is

> tall and slender and poetic. The most subdued eyes. Not the least bit of swank about him, you'd never dream he came from one of our best families. . . . Of course his family won't have a thing to do with me, but he doesn't care a button. He has a vast income of his own. . . .

She then admits that none of this is true, describing him as

> not in the least bit romantic . . . and I don't care because I'm not
> either . . . and he works in a shop, the same as I do, and he has
> a son . . . and he's kind and thoughtful, and always looking after
> one. . . .

On both these occasions a distinction is set up between a world that is illusory and even absurd and the 'actual experience' of the characters in the film. The 'road to ruin' melodrama that Philip outlines is undercut by his mock-serious manner and the fact that what he is talking about is a penny taken by a boy to buy a sugar-bun; the scene does not represent genuine threat, but rather has the function of showing Philip at work and emphasizing his good nature and good humor. Having overheard Philip's lecturing of Merridew, Mary later compliments him for being gentle with the boy. In a similar way the old-fashioned, melodramatic world sketched by Mary is self-evidently absurd. The audience of the film knows from the beginning that Mary's initial description is imaginary, and therefore this scene has the function of emphasizing her down-to-earth, unromantic perspective on life.

Both scenes have another function, however. Even as Mary and Philip distance themselves from melodrama their remarks point to the underlying presence of melodrama within the narrative. That melodrama is present in *The Suspect* through a narrative of romance and denial on the one hand and a narrative of crime and punishment on the other hand.

Even while Mary is deluding her audience she appears to be mistaken herself, since the prosaic description she gives of Philip is later offset by the revelation of his criminality. In addition, Mary's knowledge that Philip has a son is accompanied by her ignorance of the fact that he also has a wife, and her initial statement that her lover's family won't have a thing to do with her is closer to the truth than she thinks, in that Philip's wife does her best to destroy the Philip-Mary relationship. Again, despite Mary's claim that she is not in the least bit romantic, that relationship could hardly be described as anything other than a romance. Finally, if she first paints a picture of old-fashioned romance, and then distances herself from that picture, it is important to reiterate that *The Suspect* is a period film, set in London at the beginning of the century. For a mid-1940s audience the world that Mary inhabits could itself be characterized as old-fashioned and romantic. Her statement that she works in a shop is true, but it is also true that she works in a shop supplying fashionable clothes to wealthy customers. If Mary appears to be saying that the world she inhabits is an unromantic world of shopworkers rather than a romantic world of handsome aristocrats (dull experience rather than exciting fantasy), a closer examination reveals that the two worlds have a number of features in common.

In a similar way Philip's mock-serious lecturing of Merridew functions as an indicator of the crime-and-punishment melodrama that underpins the film as a whole, for Merridew's minor transgression is followed by Philip's major crime (the murder of his wife), which in turn leads to his being blackmailed by Mr. Simmons (whom he then murders), and finally to his returning to face the murderer's equivalent of the hard labor of the Portland Quarries (execution).

In *House by the River* the character of Marjorie has the function of distancing the narrative from melodrama. A similar, more sustained attempt at distancing is made in *The Suspect*. While violence and desire are brought to the foreground in both *House by the River* and *The Spiral Staircase*, such melodramatic material remains in the background in *The Suspect*, obscured by Philip's sense of decorum and Mary's apparent realism. The gloomy house bordering a river into which Stephen throws Emily's body in *House by the River* can be contrasted with the ordinary respectability of the house in which Philip commits his off-screen murders in *The Suspect*. In *House by the River* we only see the rear exterior of the house; in *The Suspect* we only see the front.

Allusion is made to the rear of the Marshall house. It transpires that at the back of the house there is a canal, and though this canal is never seen, at the end of the film we learn that it is into this canal that Philip throws the body of his second victim. The same narrative of submerged but emergent melodrama is present here as in *House by the River*, though in *The Suspect* it is present at a less visible level. In Altman's discussion of 'embedded melodrama' he argues that 'not all melodrama is alike. . . . In some soils an underground stream will seep to the surface, in others it forms a spring, in others it erupts' (1986: 354). Here he appears to be suggesting two varieties of difference within melodrama. On the one hand he points to different melodramatic forms and conventions. On the other hand he points to a difference between the covert and the overt, between embedded melodrama and eruptive melodrama. The difference between the hidden canal in *The Suspect* and 'the floodtide' in *House by the River* is broadly equivalent to Altman's distinction between a melodrama that seeps to the surface and a melodrama that erupts.

## Critque and Closure

WHAT HAPPENS IN these films? In *The Suspect* Philip Marshall murders first his wife, then his wife-beating neighbor. In *House by the River* Stephen Byrne, having murdered the family maid, attempts to murder his wife and his brother. In *Gaslight* Gregory Anton attempts to drive his wife insane, having earlier murdered her aunt. In *Experiment Perilous* Nick Bedereux also attempts to drive his wife insane (having earlier murdered one of her admirers), and almost kills her and their son. Ivy Lexton murders her husband in *Ivy*, while in *So Evil My Love* Henry Courtney plans to have his wife Susan committed to a sanatorium; Henry is subsequently murdered, Susan is accused of the murder, though the actual culprit is her apparently respectable companion, Olivia.

Other films that portray marriage and the family in terms of confinement, sometimes madness, and murder, include a series of melodramas made in Britain: the British National version of *Gaslight* (in the British film the character equivalent to Gregory Anton murders his own aunt before setting out to undermine his wife's sanity), *Pink String and Sealing Wax*, *Hatter's Castle*, and *The Mark of Cain*.

In *Hangover Square*, *The Lodger*, and *The Man in the Attic*, on the other hand, the madness and murder find expression away from home, while in *Kind Lady* criminal intentions are attributed to those who invade the home. In *Moss Rose* and *The Spiral Staircase* it is the family rather than marriage that is corrupt, though the idea of marriage inspires a certain fear, exemplified in a sequence in *The Spiral Staircase* in which a dream about a wedding ceremony develops into a nightmare. *Moss Rose* concerns a mother so obsessed with her son that she murders the women he becomes involved with, while *The Spiral Staircase* is about a man who attempts to shift the blame for the murders he commits onto his half-brother, and who is eventually killed by his step-mother.

Nor do all of the films offer a challenge to patriarchal attitudes. *The Lodger* is remarkable for the amount of sympathy it reserves for the figure of Jack-the-Ripper, and this is even more the case with its remake *The Man in the Attic*. *Bluebeard* is similar in this respect. In

*The Suspect* the wife-beating husband is balanced by the figure of Cora Marshall, who verbally abuses her husband. In addition, if the majority of the films do appear to offer a critique of either patriarchy or the family it can be objected that such a critique is weakened by the films being set in the past—elsewhere.

There are several other films made around this time which use similar period settings, and in which the family is presented as a place of security. In films such as *A Tree Grows in Brooklyn* (1945) and *I Remember Mama* (1948), the family may be threatened but it is not itself a threat. The use of period settings may have been a means of diffusing the issues they address by placing them at a distance, but the effect of the nostalgic associations of such settings was also to give an extra charge to the melodramatic disruptions evident within the films.

How, then, is this disruption resolved? Returning to the MGM version of *Gaslight*, how, and how successfully, is the mystery and melodrama set up at the beginning, resolved, and ultimately contained within the bounds of classical Hollywood cinema?

'Don't you see the way everything fits in?' the Scotland Yard detective asks Paula toward the close of *Gaslight*. The things that fit in are the different elements of the previously unsolved case of the murder of Alice Alquist, the disappearance of her jewels, and the previously unexplained activities of Paula's husband. The detective can also be taken to be referring to the space within the house; it is at this point that the blocked off and until then unseen fourth floor becomes an element of the on-screen space and linked to the rest of the film. The overall structure of balance and symmetry is evident here, as it is evident in Hollywood cinema as a whole.

In *Gaslight* this joining of different spaces and different narrative strands also heralds the completion of the film itself. Having moved through spring and summer, the final section of the film is a return to the autumn of the first scene, and this seasonal movement is paralleled by a movement from night through day to night again. The lighting of the gaslights at the beginning of the film is then balanced by the prospect of dawn at the end.

The preservation of the past also has a function in terms of the film's narrative. For in leaving the past behind her in the opening scene, Paula left unresolved the mystery (who killed Alice Alquist?) and the melodrama (the 'strangler still at large') announced in the opening scene. *Gaslight* adheres to the conventions of the mystery story and the psychological melodrama in having a heroine who must return to the past in order to supply the elements that would remain missing from the narrative if a straightforward linear progression were pursued.

Does it adhere also to the conventions of Gothic fiction? It has been argued (Baldick and Mighall, 2000: 220) that in the Gothic novel

> [m]odern values are confirmed and modern virtues rewarded in the denouement, when the heroine escapes finally from the clutches of the Inquisition and is allowed to marry the suitor of her choice as she takes up residence in a tastefully designed villa, allowing the feudal castle to fall into ruins.

*Gaslight* does leave Paula free to marry the suitor of her choice. Patrick Hamilton's play ended with the heroine ready to leave the twentieth-century equivalent of the feudal castle (now translated into a Victorian house) and find a new life with her cousins in Devon; this family had been erased from the picture for the MGM film, but the closing note of looking to the future was, if anything, accentuated. However, even emphasis on modern values in the Gothic novel was accompanied by a fascination with the past, while in *Gaslight* that emphasis is complicated further by an ambivalence about modernity, by the fact that authority (patriarchy, Scotland Yard) is presented as threatening and archaic but also reassuring, while the furnishings of the past are both sinister and appealing.

The ending of *Gaslight* provides a resolution to the problems set up in the first scene. Yet the fact that the first scene sets up a pattern of overt progression over repetition, preservation, and return has ambiguous narrative implications. The second scene is underpinned by the mystery and melodrama unresolved within the first scene. In terms of strict chronology there is a movement from A to B to C, and so on, but this move can also be seen as one from A to B(A) to C(A), where A is the information that subtends and troubles the second scene, and indeed the film as a whole, even when it is not directly addressed. The past functions as a point of departure, allowing a movement toward the future, but this progression is accompanied by a lack of change and by a sense of retrospection.

To what extent is this pattern of progression overlaid over retrospection specific to *Gaslight*? What variations to the pattern are provided by other films of the period? In *Gaslight*, shutting the furniture up in the attic means that the artifacts of the past remain unchanged, if unseen. Under different narrative conventions another effect could be played out. Thus a variation on the preservation of the past evident in *Gaslight* can be identified in *The Picture of Dorian Gray*, in which the portrait shut up in the attic is not preserved but registers the degeneration that is not visible on the face of its subject. In *Gaslight* Paula has divided memories of the past: 'flowers and light' on the one hand, discovering the dead body of her aunt on the other hand. A different narrative pattern is set up in *Hangover Square*, structured as it is around an absence of memory; the film concerns George Harvey Bone, who commits murder during recurrent memory lapses. Here memory is associated with violence to the almost complete exclusion of the lighter, more nostalgic associations evident in *Gaslight*. *Hangover Square* is a film that excludes 'natural' light; it contains only a single, short, wintry, daylight exterior sequence. The repressed past that returns at the end of this film, in the form of a series of brief, disruptive flash-backs, results in George's final mental collapse and death. Memory, its loss and its return, is presented as literally fatal.

The return of the past in *Hangover Square* is a return to violence. There is a shift away from the nostalgia evident in *Gaslight*, a shift that can be illustrated by comparing the musical recitals featured in both films. The scene in *Gaslight* in which Paula and Gregory attend a piano recital takes place in the brightly lit conservatory of Dalroy House, where Paula and Gregory sit listening to classical music, surrounded by elegantly-dressed women in light-colored evening gowns. In *Hangover Square* George performs his concerto in a location that is again marked as aristocratic (it takes place at the home of his patron, Sir Henry Chapman), but where the lighting is distinctly low-key, the audience is composed mainly of dark-suited, stern-faced patricians, and the music tests the bounds of the classical.

This points to variations between these films, but it is important also to stress the complications within these scenes. It is particularly, it is important to note the relationship between setting and narrative in the piano recital scene in *Gaslight*. This scene witnesses another of Gregory's moves to displace his own kleptomania onto Paula, in this instance by making it seem that she has stolen his watch. The elegance of the occasion is used to accentuate Paula's humiliation and the disruptive effect of the eruption of melodrama into a composed environment. Paula's attempt to control her tears, and Gregory's admonition to 'please control yourself,' only add to her distress. The value of the surrounding Victoriana adds to the effect of surface luxuriance and therefore adds to the force of the disruption. This close relationship between the different aspects of the past (the elegant and the threatening), and between a forward-looking narrative and a repetitive return to the past, is a distinctive feature of *Gaslight* and the other gaslight melodramas.

These films offer a series of variations on a set of common themes. The period setting and narrative structure of *Gaslight* allow a network of diverse and even contradictory associations to cluster around the notion of the past. In other films a similar *mise-en-scène* and differing arrangements of common narrative elements led to other associations and emphases. These different films are all informed by the attitudes I discussed in chapters four and five. They emerge in a culture still cluttered with Victorian furniture, and their approach to the past displays the ambivalent feelings that was evoked by that clutter, profusion, and paraphernalia.

At the end of *Gaslight,* the Scotland Yard detective is also trying to persuade Paula to see that her marriage is dysfunctional and that her husband doesn't fit in. The solution he is offering involves identifying Gregory Anton as actually Sergius Bauer, that is, as a criminal and an outsider, who is to be taken away at the end of the film. It also involves a clarification of the fact that Gregory and Paula are not actually husband and wife (Sergius Bauer having been already married to a woman in Prague). In this sense the separation of Gregory from Paula becomes part of the identification of a false union rather than an act of divorce. The sympathetic detective then counterbalances the unsympathetic Gregory/Sergius and helps type the latter as an individual deviant male rather than as a representative of men in general. The detective is speaking as a representative of Scotland Yard and as a potential partner. His position serves to equate Paula's interests with the law. His status as a non-threatening male alternative to Gregory, along with Gregory's bigamy, dilutes any feminist critique evident in the earlier implicit equation of marriage with misogyny.

In *Gaslight* the opening credits, shown over an image of a gaslight on the wall, are accompanied by a medley of music that blends into the eerie soundtrack of the opening scene. The closing credits are shown over the same image, now accompanied by a conventional musical flourish. In this sense the movement from opening to closure represents a completion of the circle, a resolution of the film's disparate elements, and an excision of the threat suggested at the beginning. The excitement of melodrama is contained within the bounds of classical Hollywood cinema.

Yet unresolved elements remain. The shadows on the wallpaper that can be identified in the opening credits of *Gaslight*, and which appear to represent the murder of Alice Alquist, are retained in the film's final image. The detective-Paula relationship remains undeveloped at the end of the film. In fact, it can be argued that an untroubled relationship with an alternative man has to remain undeveloped given the outcome of the Paula-Gregory 'romance,' the earlier relationship having placed a question mark over the portrayal of any other romantic relationship. As Diane Waldman points out, when the alternative romance is developed in *Experiment Perilous* 'the narrative comes dangerously (if unintentionally) close to suggesting that the pattern [of male tyranny] will be repeated' (1983: 37). As in *House by the River*, the ending cannot cancel out the actions, relationships, and desires depicted in the previous sequences.

In *Gaslight* and the other gaslight melodramas there is a tension between the demands of classical narrative and the excitement of melodrama. An attempt is made to contain melodrama, to place it at a distance, even to define it as illusory. There is also a tension between the period settings of the films and their melodramatic narratives, between a *mise-en-scène* that signifies stasis (the sedate facade of the house) and a melodrama signifying motion, emotion, and action (the floodtide beyond the house and the raging emotions that lead to murder within the house). As Altman says, in examining the classical paradigm it is important to pay attention to the contribution made by melodrama. His notion of 'embedded melodrama' is relevant to Hollywood films in general, to the way in which different generic conventions can be discovered within individual films, to the fact that Hollywood drew upon more than one melodramatic tradition, and to the point that the containment of those traditions did not signify their effacement. It is particularly relevant to the Hollywood films I have been examining here, which work through a combination of period detail and a resort to (varying degrees of) the overtly melodramatic, within the confines of Hollywood filmmaking.

The decorum of the period film could work against the excitement of melodrama and the goal-directed action of Hollywood narrative.

While a reviewer of *House by the River* announced that 'the story starts with a bang, dispensing with such details as period, setting, etc.' (*Los Angeles Times*, 24 March 1950), another complained that the director of *Moss Rose* 'evidently thought that by showing in detail every action of his characters, from buttoning up a coat to opening a letter, he would succeed in achieving an appropriately sinister pace' (*New Yorker*, 12 July 1947). Where they lacked more than a sinister pace, films such as *Moss Rose* lacked what is generally taken as a basic characteristic of the Hollywood film but also what was taken as a characteristic of Hollywood melodrama. A sense of value and preservation is displayed in the films' use of a Victoriana that was at least beginning to acquire the status of the antique when these films were produced. It was still accepted that *Moss Rose* was a melodrama, yet such a self-consciously 'old-fashioned' melodrama could itself gravitate toward the status of the period piece.

If there is a tension within these films between *mise-en-scène* and melodrama there is a tension also within the *mise-en-scène* of the gaslight melodrama. As I hopefully demonstrated in chapter two, the image of the gaslight itself has a complex set of associations. It could suggest the advances of modern technology, it came to take on nostalgic connotations, yet it also became suggestive of a past associated with darkness, deception, and murder. The gaslights in *Gaslight* exist as an element of the film's display of Victoriana, but they also signified theatrical effect: light, shadow, and the heightening of suspense.

The preservation of the past in the gaslight melodrama as a whole is imbrued with sinister connotations. An ambiguity about the meaning of the Victorian era and its artifacts can be identified within the films examined in this chapter and within their wider cultural arena. An elaborate *mise-en-scène* signified wealth and nostalgia but also possessiveness, claustrophobia, and a return to a past that had been repressed. The rejection of Victorianism upon which the darker characterizations of the gaslight era drew had itself been based on a notion of a surface respectability concealing crimes of sex and violence. The rediscovery of the appeal and value of Victoriana did not wipe out those darker associations. To some extent it gave them greater prominence, while one effect of the revaluation of the artifacts of the past was to accentuate the perceived gap between their period charm and the pandemonium they concealed. In its turn the effect of this disjunction between exterior and interior was to accentuate the disruptive effect of the emergence of melodrama.

# 7 MELODRAMA AND THE CONSTRUCTION OF THE PAST

WARNER: Why, Don, did you have so much fog?
ME:   You may recall that at the time there was a strike on. The only way I could keep on shooting was hiding the modern buildings with heavy fog.

DON SIEGEL'S ACCOUNT of the making of his directorial debut, *The Verdict* (Siegel, 1993: 103), suggests that, at one level, the gaslights and other period trappings of these and other films may have functioned as 'so much fog,' obscuring a contemporary reality of modern buildings, film industry practices, and the industrial action prevalent in mid-1940s Hollywood. Yet the passage of time from an era when a reviewer could write that 'there's no world of today save the world of London by gaslight' (Helen Fletcher on *The Suspect, Time & Tide,* 12 May 1945) has brought a situation in which such films have themselves come to be obscured or overlooked. Making up for that neglect has brought some fascinating films back into the limelight (if that is the appropriate word); it is to be hoped that it has also illuminated the relationship between Hollywood, Britain, and the culture of the time.

My identification of a cycle of gaslight melodramas, produced by the American and British film industries between the late 1930s and early 1950s, has not been intended to suggest a planned schedule of production, nor would I deny that grouping these films together is partly a critical construction. It remains important to stress that at the time of their release such films were understood as a related phenomenon by both filmmakers and audiences. If this leaves the gaslight melodrama as a less than totally clear-cut phenomenon, it is necessary to emphasize that film cycles in general have not existed as neat and discrete groups of titles. Cycles of films were an essential part of the process of production in Hollywood and other film industries. They represented an attempt to standardize innovation and success. They were also central to promotion and exhibition. The cycle of Hollywood gaslight melodramas was a result of the use made within the industry of existing generic patterns and other available resources. It was an attempt by different studios to fit sometimes incongruous material into existing popular formulas. But it was also constructed outside the studio, from the need for publicity departments, film reviewers, and critics to link films together and fit them into established or emergent patterns of filmmaking. It was a process rather than a fixed entity. A similar process can be seen in the identification of *film noir* and the Gothic romance film, though close examination reveals that these cycles have been constructed at a greater distance from their moment of production.

As well as being dependent on reviews and publicity material, the identification of this specific cycle has been premised on the belief that these films are important because of the particular use they make of their period settings. Different arguments have been made about the appeal of the past, from a concern that going 'back to Victoria' signified an escape from the realities of the present (see Kavan, 1946), to a belief that, because they were supervised to a lesser degree, films set in the past were paradoxically able to be 'about' the present in ways denied to more obviously contemporary films (see Williams, 1988: 24). Cinema's reconstruction of the past has been characterized as a means of processing contemporary concerns (Sorlin, 1980). In the particular context of British cinema and film studies, the so-called 'heritage film' has been seen as projecting 'an elite, conservative vision of the national past' (Higson, 1996: 233), while such a stance has itself been accused of elitism, as existing in a tradition of dismissals of versions of history characterized as inauthentic, trivial, feminine (Cook, 1996). My own research has not led me to select any one of these explanations to the exclusion of the others. Period settings have been used in the cinema for a complex set of reasons, and to divergent effect. If this sounds like an inexact and therefore disappointing conclusion, my argument is that the turn-of-the-century settings used in the gaslight melodramas are, in fact, especially interesting on account of this complexity, since such settings carried with them both appealing and disturbing connotations, and a particularly acute juxtaposition of these divergent connotations is evident in the 1940s. It is the relationship between these different views of the past that is significant, not just the fact that there were differing views.

The paradoxical picture revealed by my research into notions of the Victorian is that films (and other texts) produced in the twentieth century and formulated as a critique of Victorian values were themselves part of a Victorian revival, while the conservation, revaluation and reproduction of Victorian artifacts could be used to accentuate the era's darker associations. There were historical limitations to how this material was understood, but my overall argument has been that the importance of the period settings of the gaslight melodramas rested not in those settings having a single meaning but in the way in which the period represented has been an area of shifting and contested meaning.

The American crime films of the 1940s which seem immediately relevant to their time may be those films *noir* which made use of contemporary urban locations and a lighting style which emphasized their technological modernity. But critics who have studied this trend have tended to overlook the films which do not conform to a particular image of what constitutes *film noir* (those mean streets imperfectly lit by flashing neon signs and bordered by down-at-heel bars and cheap hotels). In the 1940s generic distinctions were indeed understood as separating two forms of crime narrative, on the one side a hard-boiled, contemporary, 'American' style, on the other an 'English' mystery tradition identified with the past. This distinction is essential to the understanding of the gaslight melodramas, though it has been revealing to discover the extent to which the distinction concealed common features and concerns. In addition, and in a curious way, by returning to the past, the gaslight melodramas were drawing upon a Victoriana that was part of the social reality of the 1940s; they were making use of a furniture that for their audiences was at least as 'real' as that found in the streets, bars, and lodgings of *film noir*.

Within film studies, the valuation of the 'undervalued' has become something of a standard rhetorical device. I don't want to overstate the case regarding the neglect of the gaslight melodrama; some of the films I have been discussing, *Gaslight* in particular, have received their fair share of attention in recent years. But in discussions of the studio era there has been a tendency to concentrate on particular, now familiar titles, or to discuss other films only from familiar perspectives (*House by the River* as a Fritz Lang film, for instance). In addition, the films I have been examining are of interest partly because of the fact that they deal with material often held in low esteem. Walter Benjamin suggested that the charm exercised by nineteenth-century artifacts was proof of their vital and political importance, for it was possible to recognize today's life and form in the apparently secondary, lost forms of that epoch (1999: 458). The material examined in this book exists as evidence of that charm, and if that material is not now lost but recycled on afternoon television, its apparently secondary status should not allow us to overlook its importance.

In identifying a cycle of gaslight melodramas I am also stressing the value of understanding such films as melodramas. This emphasis is based on a conception of Hollywood melodrama that diverges from the understanding to be found in many preceding studies of the subject. According to Geoffrey Nowell-Smith, 'the term melodrama is used by film scholars to designate two types of film in particular—those (particularly in the very early period) which show a clear historical descent from nineteenth-century theatrical melodrama, and the sagas of love and family life (often overlapping with so-called 'women's pictures') that had such a powerful presence in Hollywood in the 1930s, 1940s, and 1950s' (1996: 194). As he goes on to say, these uses are not strictly compatible, though there is still a value in exploring the relationship between the different uses. A few film scholars have lately suggested that, far from understanding melodrama as a 'female' genre, the term was used by within Hollywood to refer to supposedly 'male' genres, to 'the adventure film, the thriller, the horror film, the war film, and the western' (see Neale, 1993: 76). In a review of the Lon Chaney film *The Unholy Three* (1925) (*Life*, 27 August 1925, quoted in Neale: 25) it was stated that

> [m]elodrama, on the screen, is identified almost entirely with fast physical action: cowboys or sheikhs or cavalrymen riding madly across the country, men hanging by their teeth from the ledges of skyscrapers, railroad wrecks, duels, heroines floating on cakes of ice toward waterfalls, and every known form of automobile chase.

Discussions of later Hollywood films have tended to be based on a more domestic, less action-based understanding of melodrama; Nowell-Smith had himself earlier contrasted the active hero of the western with the 'passive or impotent hero or heroine of the melodrama' (1987: 115). The particular films I have been looking at are of interest for the way in which they tend to use a domestic setting while still appealing to the sort of melodramatic excitement (if often at a submerged level) documented by the reviewer of the Lon Chaney film. This is to acknowledge that they represent a specific conjunction of disparate elements. Yet the majority of these films were also mainstream products of the American film industry, and their individual characteristics point to wider patterns of generic complication and cross-gender appeal within melodrama and film-making trends of the time.

My examination of particular gaslight melodramas made in Hollywood has revealed a network of different melodramatic narratives existing in partial alliance and partial tension within an overall structure of balance and symmetry. It has also revealed a tension between the films' period trappings and the excitement of their melodramatic narratives. These tensions are both specific and general. They are linked to the differing connotations that Victorian, turn-of-the-century and gaslight settings brought with them, though such tensions are not exclusive to this particular cycle. They have a wider relevance to the Hollywood studio system, which can be understood in terms of its classical codes, its embedded melodrama, and the interaction between the two. Melodrama may have had a different history in the United States and Britain (see, for instance, Christine Gledhill's discussion of 'the easier assimilation of the melodramatic within a realist ethos in American culture'—1992: 165), but a mutual dependence linked the film industries of these two nations in the 1940s, and in both industries one can find evidence of the integration, transformation and attempt to contain the melodramatic identifiable in Hollywood films from *Gaslight* to *House by the River* and beyond.

Melodrama, however much it may have simplified or offered palliative solutions, remained and remains a resonant and important form of expression. The dimming gaslight in *Gaslight* (in its different versions) has a more complicated relationship to technological change than the victim who in nineteenth-century melodrama found her or himself tied to the railway tracks (see Grimstead, 1971: 84)[1] in that it brought to the screen the technology of another era (and, for its American audiences, of another country). Yet, in its own way gaslight represented, and has continued to represent, a telling symbol for the fears of a society marked by transformation and exploitation. The gaslight settings featured in this and other examples of the cycle brought with them a variety of different connotations, but in their most melodramatic moments these films gave expression to fears and desires located in contemporary experience.

In *Gaslight Melodrama* I have examined a cycle of films, though the book has not simply been concerned with a particular film cycle. The approach here has been a contextual one; I have emphasized historical and cultural context, and have been concerned to see films as part of a wider set of cultural discourses, ranging from biographies of 'eminent Victorians' to artifacts found in the thrift shops of Manhattan. As such, this study can itself be located in its own time, in that my work is part of a more general movement within film studies away from an exclusive emphasis on textual analysis and toward a concern with film's historical base. My own interest in history is not based simply on how it can give a clearer insight into past events. My aim has been to combine textual analysis with archival research with a view to establishing a clearer and more accurate picture of an aspect of the past. But I have also been concerned with the construction of history and genealogy.

In my discussion of twentieth-century attitudes to the Victorian I examined the ways in which different historical narratives have served particular needs beyond factual accuracy. In my investigation of the source material of the gaslight melodramas of the 1940s I considered ways in which the traditions that such films drew upon can be seen as invented traditions. Finally, as stated at the beginning of this chapter, my identification of a cycle of gaslight melodramas is accompanied by an acknowledgment that such a cycle represents a critical construction as well as being a production and promotional trend of the time.

# Notes

## 1. INTRODUCTION: *GASLIGHT*, GASLIGHT, AND GASLIGHT MELODRAMA

1. For another discussion of the relationship of this scene to *Gaslight* see Cavell, 1989: 367–68.
2. On the popular understanding of 'to gaslight' as meaning to make some-one appear insane, and how this relates to women's experience of watch-ing the Bergman/Boyer film, see also Walsh, 1984: 177 and 192.
3. Neal Graham pressbook collection, Doheny Library, University of Southern California (USC). Later references to pressbooks are either to those (*Hour of 13, House by the River, The Lodger, The Picture of Dorian Gray,* and *The Verdict*) held in this collection, or the British Film Institute Library pressbook collection (*Fanny by Gaslight,* the British pressbook for the American *Gaslight,* and *Moss Rose*).

## 2. INDUSTRIAL LIGHT AND MAGIC: IMAGES OF GASLIGHT FROM THE NINETEENTH TO THE TWENTIETH CENTURY.

1. 'Mr. Zanuck's suggested revisions for the Revised Temporary Script of Oct 16, 1946,' Memo from Molly Mandaville to Ray Klune, 20th Century-Fox Produced Scripts Collection, 610. Box FX-PRS-787, Theater Arts Library, UCLA.
2. See the 'Gaslight' website at http: //www.mtroyal.ab.ca/programs/arts/english/gaslight.
3. On the 'softness' of gaslight see also Bergman, 1977: 261, where David Belasco's technical adviser is quoted as saying that 'the light for the old gas foot-lights was soft and diffuse, quite different from the glare the modern incandescent lamp produces.' On the relationship between theater and cine-ma see also the chapter titled 'Dissolves by Gaslight,' in Fell, 1986: 12–36.
4. On the role of gaslight in early cinema, Richard Maltby states that 'although cinema uses electricity, it is a mistake to think of it as an electric medium. In its earliest forms it made no use of electrical power; it was hand driven or "cranked" rather than powered by an electric motor, and illuminated by gas, not electric light' (1995: 145).
5. Jules Furthman script, dated 21 August–24 October 1944, 20th Century-Fox Produced Scripts Collection, 610. Box FX-PRS-787, Theater Arts Library, UCLA.

### 3.  GOTHIC SOURCES/LONDON DISCOURSES: THE DARK METROPOLIS ON PAGE AND SCREEN

1.  Note on 'Treatment' by Ernest Pascal, dated 22 October 1938, 20th Century-Fox Screenplay Collection, USC.
2   'Campaign Suggestions on *Ivy*,' Correspondence File, Universal Studios Collection, USC.
3.  The first two quotes are taken from 'Mr. X Rough Dialogue Script' dated 8 January 1951 and 'Untitled Screenplay based on *The Mysterious Mr. X*' dated 11 January 1951. These and other scripts are from the MGM Collection, USC.
4   Opening section of 'Notes on Conference with Mr. Zanuck,' 26 June 1944, 20th Century-Fox Screenplay Collection, USC. Several scripts for the film can be found in the Barré Lyndon Collection, Academy of Motion Pictures, Arts and Sciences (AMPAS). For another account of this process see Mank, 1994: 324-350.
5.  Letter from the Vice-President of the PCA to Harold Auten (President of Eagle-Lion), 2 October 1945, *Man of Evil* PCA File, AMPAS. See Barefoot, 2000, for a more detailed account of the film's American censorship problems.
6.  The first quotation is from a letter from Carl E. Milliken to Arthur Kelly, 21 September 1944. The letter from Breen is dated 1 May 1945. Both are taken from the *Man of Evil* PCA file, AMPAS.

### 4.  LADY ISABEL, DR. JEKYLL, AND OTHER VICTORIANS: TWENTIETH-CENTURY RECEPTION, REACTION, AND RECONSTRUCTION

1.  It has to be said that Lean's *Great Expectations* is actually set before the Victorian era, though a perception of Dickens as a Victorian novelist may have meant that a filmed version of a Dickens novel was understood as a reflection upon the Victorian.
2.  'Comments on the Present Script,' 23 December 1940, MGM Collection, USC.
3.  Memo to Victor Saville, 20 December 1940, MGM Collection, USC.
4.  Joseph Breen to L. B. Mayer, 12 November 1940, *Dr. Jekyll and Mr. Hyde* PCA file, AMPAS.
5.  The writers who Mighall is quoting are Burton Hatlen and Gail B. Griffin.

### 5.  THE FURNITURE IN THE ATTIC: BACK TO THE VICTORIAN

1.  The studies to which Webb refers are: Steven Marcus, *The Other Victorians: A Study of Sexuality and Pornography in Mid-Nineteenth-Century Britain* (1966), Alex Comfort, *The Anxiety Makers* (1967), Peter Fryer, *The Birth Controllers* (1965), the same author's introduction to

*Prostitution* by William Acton (1968), and Ronald Pearsall, *The Worm in the Bud: The World of Victorian Sexuality* (1971).

2. 'Victorianism in films and music hall,' Mass Observation File Report 485, 7 November 1940, Mass Observation Archive, University of Sussex. Sue Harper (whose writings alerted me to this passage) identifies the reporter as Len England, and interprets the passage as suggesting a 'lack of consonance between costume texts and contemporary dress' (1994: 131). However, this is based on a slight mistranscription of the original report, which she quotes as: 'Is there a trend toward bustles and brimmed hats? And *yet* surely such books as *Fanny by Gaslight* have been very popular this season' (my italics). The addition of the word 'yet' changes the sense from a speculation as to whether there might be a consonance between dress and reading habits to a denial of any such link.

3. See also the section in Benjamin's *One-Way Street* titled 'Manorially furnished Ten-Room apartment' (1979: 48–49), where he states that the 'furniture style of the second half of the nineteenth century has received its only adequate description, and analysis, in a certain type of detective novel at the dynamic center of which stands the horror of apartments. . . . This character of the bourgeois apartment, tremulously awaiting the nameless murderer like a lascivious old lady her gallant, has been penetrated by a number of authors who, as writers of 'detective stories'—and perhaps also because in their works part of the bourgeois pandemonium is exhibited—have been denied the reputation they deserve.' For another discussion of this passage in relation to a Hollywood gaslight melodrama see Tom Gunning on *House by the River* (2000: 370).

## 6. THE BODY IN THE CANAL: DECORUM AND MELODRAMA IN THE PERIOD FILM

1. To give some idea of these variations in budgets and shooting schedules: production and distribution costs for MGM's *Gaslight* were $2,458,275, according to the Plaintiff's trial brief, *Loew's Incorporated and Patrick Hamilton v. Columbia Broadcasting System et al.* [n.d.], MGM Legal Files, Folder 71, AMPAS; a 54 day shooting schedule for this film was specified in August 1943 edition of *MGM News*, *Gaslight* Production File, AMPAS (this figure does not include time spent on retakes); production costs for British International's *Gaslight* were £39,000, according to Jeffrey Richards (1986: 70); *Moss Rose* cost $2,020,000 to make, *Hangover Square* $1,155,000, and *The Lodger* $870,000—my source here is Solomon, 1988: 242-3 and 220; production costs for *Ivy* are identified as $1,673,082 and for *The Suspect* as $582,736 in the films' Production files, USC; the six day shooting schedule for *Bluebeard* is mentioned in Jenkins, 1982: 145.

### 7. MELODRAMA AND THE CONSTRUCTION OF THE PAST

1.  In Augustin Daly's *Under the Gaslight* it is a man who is tied to the railway tracks. It is only later that the victim becomes a woman.

# Gaslight Filmography

THE FILMOGRAPHY INCLUDES films that combine crime narratives with turn-of-the-century settings; beyond this core, it has been extended to include titles which contributed to the cycle of gaslight melodramas. It is limited to films made in Britain or the United States, released between 1939 and 1954, and set in the Victorian or Edwardian era (though not necessarily in Britain). Films are listed in the order of their original release, and under the title by which they were known in their country of origin; alternative American titles of British films are also given, as well as British titles of American films. Other details given are country of production, production company, producer, director, literary or theatrical source, scriptwriters, director of photography, art director where known, principal cast members, as well as the time and place in which the film is set.

Abbreviations

d   Director
p   Producer
s   Source
sc  Scenario or script
ph  Director of Photography
ad  Art Direction
c   Principal cast
GB  Great Britain
US  United States

## 1939:

*The Face at the Window*, GB, Pennant/Ambassador. p/d: George King. s: play by F. Brooke Warren. sc: A. R. Rawlinson, R. Faye. ph: Hone Glendinning. ad: Philip Bawcombe. c: Tod Slaughter, Marjorie Taylor, John Warwick. Paris 1880.

*Hound of the Baskervilles*, US, 20th Century-Fox. p: Gene Markey. d: Sidney Lanfield. s: Sir Arthur Conan Doyle novel. sc: Ernest Pascal. ph: Peverell Marley. ad: Thomas Little. c: Basil Rathbone, Nigel Bruce, Richard Greene, Lionel Atwill. Late-Victorian London and Dartmoor.

## 1940:

*The Adventures of Sherlock Holmes*, US, 20th Century-Fox. GB title *Sherlock Holmes*. p: Gene Markey. d: Alfred Werker. s: William Gillette play based on characters created by Sir Arthur Conan Doyle. sc: Edwin Blum, William Drake.

ph: Leon Shamroy. ad: Richard Day, Hans Peters. c: Basil Rathbone, Nigel Bruce, George Zucco, Ida Lupino. Late-Victorian London.

*Crimes at the Dark House*, GB, Pennant. p: George King. d: George King. s: Wilkie Collins novel, *The Woman in White*. sc: Edward Dryhurst, Frederick Hayward, H. F. Maltby. ph: Hone Glendinning. ad: Bernard Robinson. c: Tod Slaughter, Hilary Eaves, Sylvia Marriot. England and Australia, 1850.

*Gaslight*, GB, British National. US title *Angel Street*. p: John Corfield. d: Thorold Dickinson. s: Patrick Hamilton play. sc: A. R. Rawlingson, Bridget Boland. ph: Bernard Knowles. ad: Duncan Sutherland. c: Anton Walbrook, Diana Wynyard, Frank Pettingell. London 1885 (initial sequence 1865).

## 1941:

*Dr. Jekyll and Mr. Hyde*, US, MGM. p: Victor Saville, Victor Fleming. d: Victor Fleming. s: Robert Louis Stevenson novel, *The Strange Case of Dr. Jekyll and Mr. Hyde*. sc: John Lee Mahin. ph: Joseph Ruttenberg. ad: Cedric Gibbons, Daniel B. Cathcart, Edwin B. Willis. c: Spencer Tracy, Ingrid Bergman, Lana Turner, Donald Crisp. Late-Victorian London.

*Hatter's Castle*, GB, Paramount British. p: Isadore Goldsmith. d: Lance Comfort. s: A. J. Cronin novel. sc: Paul Merzback, R. Bernaur, Rodney Ackland. ph: Max Greene. ad: James Carter. c: Robert Newton, Deborah Kerr, James Mason. Glasgow, 1879–90s.

*Ladies in Retirement*, US, Columbia. p: Lester Cowan. d: Charles Vidor. s: Reginald Denham and Edward Percy play. sc: Reginald Denham and Edward Percy. ph: George Barnes. ad: Lionel Banks. c: Ida Lupino, Louis Hayward, Isobel Elsom, Elsa Lanchester, Edith Barrett. The Kent Marshes in the late-Victorian era.

## 1942:

*The Mystery of Marie Roget*, US, Universal. p: Paul Malvern. d: Phil Rosen. s: Edgar Allan Poe story. sc: Michel Jacoby. ph: Elwood Bredell. ad: Jack Otterson, Richard H. Riedel. c: Maria Montez, Patric Knowles, Maria Ouspenskaya. Paris 1889.

## 1944:

*Bluebeard*, US, PRC. p: Leon Fromkess. d: Edgar Ulmer. sc: Pierre Gendron. ph: Jockey Feindel [according to the credits, though according to Ulmer Eugene Schufftan was actually director of photography, see Jenkins, 1982: 145]. ad: Paul Palmentola. c: John Carradine, Jean Parker, Nils Asther. Paris 1885.

*Experiment Perilous* US, RKO. p: Warren Duff. d: Jacques Tourneur. s: Margaret Carpenter novel. sc: Warren Duff. ph: Tony Gaudio. ad: Albert

D'Agostino, Jack Okey. c: George Brent, Hedy Lamarr, George Lukas. 1900s New York, plus sequences set in nineteenth Europe and New England.

*Fanny by Gaslight*, GB, Gainsborough. US title *Man of Evil*. p: Ted Black. d: Anthony Asquith. s: Michael Sadleir novel. sc: Doreen Montgomery, Aimée Stuart. ph: Arthur Crabtree. ad: John Bryan. c: Phyllis Calvert, Stewart Granger, James Mason. London (and additional scenes set in France) in the latter part of the nineteenth century.

*Gaslight*, US, MGM. GB title *The Murder in Thornton Square*. p: Arthur Hornblow, Jr. d: George Cukor. s: Patrick Hamilton's play. sc: John Van Druten, Walter Reisch, John L. Balderston. ph: Joseph Ruttenberg. ad: Cedric Gibbons, William Ferrari, Edwin B. Willis, Paul Huldchinsky. c: Ingrid Bergman, Charles Boyer, Joseph Cotten. London (and additional scenes set in Italy) in the 1870s and 1880s.

*The Lodger*, US, 20th Century-Fox. p: Robert Bassler. d: John Brahm. s: Marie Belloc Lowndes novel. sc: Barré Lyndon. ph: Lucien Ballard. ad: James Basevi, John Ewing. c: Laird Cregar, Merle Oberon, George Sanders. London 1888.

## 1945:

*Hangover Square*, US, 20th Century-Fox. p: Robert Bassler. d: John Brahm. s: Patrick Hamilton novel. sc: Barré Lyndon. ph: Joseph LaShelle. ad: Lyle Wheeler, Maurice Ransford. c: Laird Cregar, Linda Darnell, George Sanders. London, 1903.

*Latin Quarter* GB, British National. US title *Frenzy*. p: Louis H. Jackson, Derrick de Marney. d: Vernon Sewell. s: Pierre Mills and Charles Vylars play, *L'Angoisse*. sc: Vernon Sewell. c: Derrick de Marney, Joan Greenwood. Paris 1890s.

*The Picture of Dorian Gray*, US, MGM. p: Pandro S. Berman. d: Albert Lewin. s: Oscar Wilde novel. sc: Albert Lewin. ph: Harry Stradling. ad: Cedric Gibbons and Hans Peters. c: Hurd Hatfield, George Sanders. Late-Victorian London, plus a sequence set in the Home Counties.

*Pink String and Sealing Wax*, GB, Ealing. p: Michael Balcon. d: Robert Hamer. s: Roland Pertwee play. sc: Diana Morgan, Robert Hamer. ph: Richard S. Pavey. ad: Duncan Sutherland. c: Googie Withers, Mervyn Johns, Gordon Jackson. 1880s Brighton.

*A Place of One's Own*, GB, Gainsborough. p: R.J. Minney. d: Bernard Knowles. s: Osbert Sitwell novel. sc: Brock Williams, Osbert Sitwell. ph: Stephen Dade. c: James Mason, Barbara Mullen, Margaret Lockwood. 1900s England.

*The Suspect*, US, Universal. p: Islin Auster. d: Robert Siodmak. s: James Ronald novel, *This Way Out*. sc: Bertram Millhauser. ph: Paul Ivano. ad: John B.

Goodman, Martin Obzina. c: Charles Laughton, Ella Raines, Henry Daniells, Rosalind Ivan. 1900s London.

## 1946:

*Catman of Paris*, US, Republic. p: Marek M. Libkov. d: Lesley Selander. sc: Sherman L. Lowe. ad: Gano Chittendon. c: Carl Esmond, Adele Mara, Douglass Dumbrille. Turn-of-the-century Paris.

*The Spiral Staircase*, US, RKO. p: Dore Schary. d: Robert Siodmak. s: Ethel Lina White novel, *Some Must Watch*. sc: Mel Dinelli. ph: Nicholas Musuraca. ad: Albert S. D'Agostino, Jack Okey. c: Dorothy McGuire, George Brent, Ethel Barrymore. New England, early 1900s.

*Temptation*, US, Universal. p: Edward Small. d: Irving Pichel. s: Robert Hitchens novel, *Bella Donna*. sc: Robert Thoeren. ph: Lucien Ballard. ad: Bernard Hetzbrun. c: Merle Oberon, George Brent, Charles Korvin. Cairo and London, 1900.

*The Verdict*, US, Warner Bros. p: William Jacobs. d: Don Siegel. s: Israel Zangwill novel, *The Big Bow Mystery*. sc: Peter Milne. ph: Ernest Haller. ad: Ted Smith. c: Sidney Greenstreet, Peter Lorre, George Coulouris. 1890s London, plus a sequence set in France.

## 1947:

*Ivy*, US, Universal-International. p: William Cameron Menzies. d: Sam Wood. s: Marie Belloc Lowndes novel, *The Story of Ivy*. sc: Charles Bennett. ph: Russell Metty. ad: Richard H. Reidel. c: Joan Fontaine, Herbert Marshall. Edwardian London, with sequences set in the English south coast and the Mediterranean.

*A Man about the House*, GB, British Lion. p: Ted Black. d: Leslie Arliss. s: John Perry play, based on Francis Brett Young novel. sc: Leslie Arliss, J.B. Williams. ph: Georges Perinal. c: Margaret Johnston, Dulcie Gray, Kieron Moore. Italy, 1908.

*Moss Rose*, US, 20th Century-Fox. p: Gene Markey. d: Gregory Ratoff. s: Joseph Shearing novel. sc: Jules Furthman, Tom Reed. ph: Joe MacDonald. ad: Richard Day, Mark Lee-Kirk. c: Peggy Cummins, Victor Mature, Ethel Barrymore, Vincent Price. Edwardian London, Devon, and brief Canadian sequences.

*Uncle Silas*, GB, Two Cities. US title *The Inheritance*. p: Josef Somlo. d: Charles Frank. s: Sheridan Le Fanu novel. sc: Ben Travers. ph: Robert Krasker. ad: Ralph Brinton. c: Jean Simmons, Derrick De Marney, Katrina Paxinou, Derek Bond, Esmond Knight. England 1890.

**1948:**

*Blanche Fury*, GB, Cineguild. p: Anthony Havelock-Allan. d: Marc Allégret. s: Joseph Shearing novel. sc: Audrey Erskine Windrop, Hugh Mills, Cecil McGivern. ph: Guy Green, Geoffrey Unsworth. ad: John Bryan. c: Valerie Hobson, Stewart Granger, Walter Fitzgerald, Michael Gough. Staffordshire in the 1860s.

*The Mark of Cain*, GB, Two Cities. p: W. P. Lipscomb. d: Brian Desmond Hurst. s: Joseph Shearing novel, *Airing in a Closed Carriage*. sc: W. P. Lipscomb, Francis Crowdy, Christina Brand. ph: Erwin Hillier. ad: Vetchinsky. c: Sally Gray, Eric Portman, Patrick Holt. Turn-of-the-century Manchester, plus sequences set in London and France.

*So Evil My Love*, GB, Paramount. p: Hal B. Wallis. d: Lewis Allen. s: Joseph Shearing novel, *For Her to See*. sc: Leonard Spielelglass, Ronald Millar. ph: Max Greene. ad: Thomas H. Morahan. c: Ann Todd, Ray Milland, Geraldine Fitzgerald, Raymond Huntley. 1880s London, with brief sequence in Paris, Liverpool and aboard ship.

*The Woman in White*, US, Warner Bros. p: Henry Blanke. d: Peter Godfrey. s: Wilkie Collins novel. sc: Stephen Morehouse Avery. ph: Carl Guthrie. c: Gig Young, Eleanor Parker, Sidney Greenstreet, Alexis Smith, John Abbott. England in the 1850s.

**1949:**

*Britannia Mews*, GB, 20th Century-Fox. US title *Forbidden Street*. p: William Perlberg. d: Jean Negulesco. s: Margery Sharp novel. sc: Ring Lardner, Jr. ph: Georges Perinal. ad: Andre Andrejew. c: Maureen O'Hara, Dana Andrews. Late-Victorian London, with a brief sequnce in the Home Counties.

*The Case of Charles Peace*. GB, Argyle. p: John Argyle. d: Norman Lee. s: Doris Davidson, Norman Lee. ad: George Paterson. c: Michael Martin Harvey, Chilli Boucher, Valentine Dyall. England in the 1870s.

**1950:**

*House by the River*, US, Republic. p: Howard Welsch. d: Fritz Lang. s: A. P. Herbert novel. sc: Mel Dinelli. ph: Edward Cronager. ad: Boris Leven. c: Louis Hayward, Lee Bowman, Jane Wyatt. Small American town, 1890s.

*Madeleine*, GB, Pinewood-Cineguild. p: Stanley Haynes. d: David Lean. sc: Stanley Haynes, Nicholas Phipps. ph: Guy Green. ad: John Bryan. c: Ann Todd, Leslie Banks. Glasgow and the Scottish coast, 1857, with brief contemporary introduction.

*Room to Let*, GB, Exclusive Films. p: Anthony Hinds. d: Godfrey Grayson. s: Margery Allingham radio play. sc: John Gilling. ph: Cedric Williams. ad: Denis

Wreford. c: Jimmy Hanley, Valentine Dyall. London 1904 framed by contemporary sequences.

*So Long at the Fair*, GB, Ealing. p: Betty Box. d: Anthony Darnborough, Terence Fisher. s: Anthony Thorne novel. sc: Hugh Mills, Anthony Thorne. ph: Reginald Wyer. ad: George Provis. c: Jean Simmons, Dirk Bogarde. Paris 1889.

### 1951:

*The Late Edwina Black*, GB, IFD/Elvey Gartside. US title *Obsessed*. p: Ernest Gartside. d: Maurice Elvey. s: William Dinner and William Morum play. sc: Charles Frank, David Evans. ph: Stephen Dade. ad: George Provis. c: Geraldine Fitzgerald, David Farrer. Rural England, 1890.

*Kind Lady*, US, MGM. p: Armand Deutsch. d: John Sturges. s: Edward Chodorov play based on a story by Hugh Walpole. sc: Jerry Davis, Edward Chodorov, Charles Bennett. ph: Joseph Ruttenberg. ad: William Ferrari, Cedric Gibbons. c: Maurice Evans, Ethel Barrymore. Turn-of-the-century London.

### 1952:

*Hour of Thirteen*, GB, MGM. p: Hayes Goetz. d: Harold French. s: Philip MacDonald novel, *X vs. Rex*. sc: Leon Gordon, Howard Emmett Rogers. ph: Guy Green. ad: Alfred Junge. c: Peter Lawford, Dawn Adams, Roland Culver. Late-Victorian London.

### 1954:

*The Man in the Attic*, US, 20th Century-Fox. p. Robert L. Jacks. d: Hugo Fregonese. s: Marie Belloc Lowndes novel, *The Lodger*. sc: Robert Presnell, Jr., Barré Lyndon. ph: Leo Tover. ad: Lyle Wheeler, Leland Fuller. c: Jack Palance, Constance Smith. London 1888.

# Bibliography

This bibliography is divided as follows:

1. Research Libraries and Special Collections
2. Principal Trade Journals
3. Collections of Film Reviews
4. Other Works Cited


## 1. RESEACH LIBRARIES AND SPECIAL COLLECTIONS

Academy of Motion Pictures, Arts and Sciences, Los Angeles
  Barré Lyndon Collection
  Hal B. Wallis Collection
  MGM Legal Department Records
  Production Code Administration Case Files
  Production Files
BFI National Library, London
  British Board of Film Censors Scenario Reports
  Clipping Files
  Pressbook Collection
  Script Collection
  Thorold Dickinson Collection
British Library, London
  Humanities and Social Sciences
  Newspaper Library
Department of Special Collections, Theater Arts Library, University of California at Los Angeles
  RKO Production Files
  RKO Script Collection
  20th Century-Fox Legal Department Collection
  20th Century-Fox Produced Scripts Collection
Doheny Library, University of Southern California, Los Angeles
  Albert Lewin Collection
  John Brahm Collection
  Neal Graham Pressbook Collection
  MGM Collection
  20th Century-Fox Screenplay Collection
  Universal Studios Collection
  Warner Bros. Archive

Library of Congress, Washington, D.C.
        Humanities and Sciences Division
        Motion Picture, Broadcasting and Recorded Sound Division
Museum of Modern Art, New York
        Clipping Files
National Archives at College Park, Maryland
        Records of the Office of War Information
New York Public Library, Lincoln Center for the Performing Arts
        Clipping Files
        Billy Rose Theater Collection
Mass Observation Archive, University of Sussex, Brighton
Theatre Museum, London
        Clipping Files

## 2.   PRINCIPAL TRADE AND REVIEW JOURNALS

*Film Daily*
*Hollywood Reporter*
*Kinematograph Weekly* (also known as *Kine Weekly*)
*Motion Picture Herald*
*New York Motion Picture Critics Reviews*
*Publishers Weekly*
*Today's Cinema* (also known as *The Cinema*)
*Variety*

## 3.   PRINCIPAL COLLECTIONS OF FILM REVIEWS

*New York Times Film Reviews* (1970). Vol. 3, 1938–48. New York: Times
    Books.
*New York Times Film Reviews* (1970). Vol. 4, 1949–58. New York: Times
    Books.
Slide, Anthony (ed.) (1982) *Selected Film Criticism: 1931–40*. Metuchen,
    London: Scarecrow Press.
Slide, Anthony (ed.) (1983) *Selected Film Criticism: 1941–50*. Metuchen,
    London: Scarecrow Press.
*Variety Film Reviews* (1983), Vol. 6, 1938–42. New York, London: Garland.
*Variety Film Reviews* (1983), Vol. 7, 1943–48. New York, London: Garland.
*Variety Film Reviews* (1983), Vol. 8, 1949–53. New York, London: Garland.

## 4.   OTHER WORKS CITED

Albrecht, Donald (1986) *Designing Dreams: Modern Architecture in the
    Movies*. New York: Harper & Row, .
Allen, Annie Winsor (1914) 'Victorian Hypocrisy' in *Atlantic Monthly*, 114,
    174–88.

Allen, Frederick Lewis (1987) 'The Revolution in Manners and Morals' [1931], in John Ingham (ed.) *Assault on Victorianism: The Rise of Popular Culture in America 1890–1945.* Toronto: Canadian Scholars' Press, 187–210.

Altick, Richard D. (1995) 'Eminent Victorianism: What Lytton Strachey Hath Wrought,' in *The American Scholar*, 64 (1), 81–89.

Altman, Rick (1986) 'Dickens, Griffith, and Film Theory Today,' in *South Atlantic Quarterly*, 88 (2), 321–59.

Ames, Kenneth. (1983) 'American Decorative Arts/Household Furnishings,' in *American Quarterly*, 35(3), 280–303.

Anonymous (1855) 'The Charities and the Poor of London,' in *The Quarterly Review*, 97, 407–50.

Auden, W. H. (1980) 'The Guilty Vicarage' [1948], in Robert W. Winks (ed.) *Detective Fiction: A Collection of Essays*. Englewood Cliffs, N.J.; Prentice-Hall, 15–24.

Barefoot, Guy (1994) '*East Lynne* to *Gas Light*: Hollywood, Melodrama, and Twentieth-Century Notions of the Victorian' in Jacky Bratton, Jim Cook, Christine Gledhill (eds.) *Melodrama: Stage Picture Screen*. London: BFI Publishing, 65–81.

—— (2000) '*Fanny by Gaslight, Man of Evil*, and the Production Code,' in *Journal of Popular British Cinema*, 3, 125–28.

Barty-King, Hugh (1984) *New Flame: How Gas Changed the Commercial, Domestic, and Industrial Life of Britain Between 1813 and 1984*. Tavistock, Devon: Graphmitre.

Baudelaire, Charles (1995) 'The Painter of Modern Life' [1845], in *The Painter of Modern Life and Other Essays*, tr. Jonathan Mayne. London: Phaidon Press, 1–41.

Baxter, Peter (1975) 'On the History and Ideology of Film Lighting,' in *Screen*, 16 (3), 83–106.

Behlmer, Rudy (ed.) (1993) *Memo from Darryl F. Zanuck*. New York: Grove Press.

—— (ed.) (1989) *Memo from David O. Selznick*. Hollywood: Samuel French.

Benjamin, Walter (1999) *The Arcades Project*, tr. Howard Eiland and Kevin McLaughlin. Cambridge, Mass. and London: Harvard University Press.

—— (1997) *Charles Baudelaire: A Lyric Poet in the Era of High Capitalism*, tr. Harry Zohn. London: Verso.

—— (1979) *One Way Street* [1928], tr. E. Jephcott and Kingsley Shorter. London: Verso.

Bergman, Gösta (1977) *Lighting in the Theatre*. Stockholm: Almqvist & Wiksell.

Biggs, Margaret (1951) 'Foreword' to Margaret Flower *Victorian Jewellery*. New York: Duell, Sloan, and Pearce.

Booth, Michael (1991) *Theatre in the Victorian Age*. Cambridge: Cambridge University Press.

—— (1981) *Victorian Spectacular Theatre 1850–1910*. London: Routledge & Kegan Paul.

Bordwell, David, Janet Staiger, and Kristin Thompson (1985) *The Classical Hollywood Cinema: Film Style and Mode of Production to 1960*. London: Routledge.

Bordwell, David, and Kristin Thompson (1997) *Film Art*, 5th edition. New York: McGraw-Hill.

Bott, Alan (1931) *Our Fathers (1870–1900): Manners and Customs of the Ancient Victorians: A Survey in Pictures and Text of Their History, Morals, Wars, Sports, Inventions, and Politics*. London: William Heinemann

—— (ed.) (1932) *Our Mothers: A Cavalcade in Pictures, Quotation, and Description of Late-Victorian Women 1870–1900*. London: Victor Gollantz.

Bratton, Jackie, Jim Cook, and Christine Gledhill (1994) 'Introduction,' in Jackie Bratton, Jim Cook, and Christine Gledhill (eds.) *Melodrama: Stage Picture Screen*. London: BFI Publishing, 1–8.

Briggs, Asa. (1990) *Victorian Things*. Harmondsworth: Penguin.

Britton, Andrew (1977) '*Meet Me in St. Louis*: Smith, or the Ambiguities,' in *Australian Journal of Film Theory*, 3, 7–25.

Brooks, Peter (1985) *The Melodramatic Imagination: Balzac, Henry James, Melodrama, and the Mode of Excess*. New York: Columbia University Press.

Bruzzi, Stella (1993) 'Bodyscape' in *Sight and Sound*, NS, 3 (10), 6–10.

Burt, Daniel S. (1981) 'G. W. M. Reynolds: A Victorian Gothic,' in Gerould Daniel (ed.) *Melodrama*, Vol.7. New York: New York Literary Forum.

Butler, Samuel (1993) *Way of all Flesh* [1903]. Oxford: Oxford University Press.

Cavell, Stanley (1989) 'Naughty Orators: Negation of Voice in *Gaslight*,' in Sanford Budrich and Wolfgang Iser (eds.) *Languages of the Unsayable: The Play of Negativity in Literature and Literary Theory*. New York: Columbia University Press, 340–77.

Chandler, D. (1936) *Outline of History of Lighting by Gas, etc*. London: Chancery Lane Printing Works.

——, and Douglas A. Lacey (1949) *The Rise of the Gas Industry in Britain*. London: British Gas Council.

Chandler, Raymond (1980) 'The Simple Art of Murder' [1944], in *Pearls are a Nuisance*. London: Pan, 173–90.

Coben, Stanley (1975) 'The Assault on Victorianism in the Twentieth Century,' in *American Quarterly*, 27 (5), 604–25.

—— (1991) *Rebellion Against Victorianism: The Impact for Cultural Change in 1920s America*. New York: Oxford University Press.

Collins, Philip (1987) 'Dickens and the City' in William Sharpe and Leonard Wallock (eds.) *Visions of the Modern City: Essays in History, Art, and Literature*. Baltimore: John Hopkins University Press, 101–21.

Collins, Wilkie (1986) 'The Use of Gas in Theatres; or, The Air and the Audience: Considerations on the Atmospheric Influences of Theatres' [1885], Steve Farmer (ed.), in *Wilkie Collins Society Journal*, 6, 19–26.

Cook, Pam (1996) '"Neither Here nor There": National Identity in Gainsborough Costume Drama' in Andrew Higson (ed.) *Dissolving Views: Key Writings on British Cinema*. London: Cassell, 51–65.

Costello, John (1986) *Love, Sex, and War: Changing Values 1939–1945*. London: Pan.

Cummins, Maria Susanna (1854) *The Lamplighter*. London: Nelson.

Custen, George F. (1997) *Twentieth Century's Fox: Darryl F. Zanuck and the Culture of Hollywood*. New York: Basic Books.

De Haas, Arlene (1931) *East Lynne . . . Suggested by Mrs. Henry Wood's Famous Novel, with Scenes from the Fox Movietone Starring Ann Harding and Clive Brook*. New York: Grosset and Dunlap.

Dickens, Charles (1997) 'Night Walks' [1860] in *Selected Journalism, 1850–1870*, David Pascoe (ed.). Harmondsworth: Penguin, 73–80.

———— (1995) *Sketches by Boz: Illustrative of Every-day Life and Every-day People* [1839]. Harmondsworth: Penguin.

Disher, M. Willson (1939) 'Melodrama and the Modern Mind,' in *Theatre World*, 30 (4), 152.

Doane, Mary Ann (1988) *The Desire to Desire: The Woman's Film of the 1940s*. Basingstoke: Macmillan.

Doré, Gustave, and Blanchard Jerrold (1971) *London* [1872]. Newton Abbot: David & Charles.

Dorpat, Theo (1996) *Gaslighting: the Double Whammy, Interrogation, and Other Methods of Covert Control in Psychotherapy and Psychoanalysis*. Northvale, N.J.: Jason Aronson.

Douglas, Ann (1979) *The Feminization of American Culture*. New York: Alfred A. Knopf.

Downer, Alan S. (1945) 'A Preface to Melodrama: I. The Less Eminent Victorians,' in *Players Magazine*, 21 (4), 9–10.

Dreiser, Theodore (1998) *Sister Carrie* [1900]. Oxford: Oxford University Press.

Dreppard, Carl W. (1947) *First Reader for Antique Collectors*. Garden City, N.Y.: Doubleday.

———— (1948) *Handbook of Antique Chairs*. Garden City, N.Y.: Doubleday.

———— (1950) *Victorian: Cinderella of Antiques*. Garden City, N.Y.: Doubleday.

Drummond, William (1966) *Gaslight: Presented on the Stage as "Angel Street" by Patrick Hamilton*. New York: Paperback Library.

Eisner, Lotte H. (1976) *Fritz Lang*, tr. Gertrud Mander. London: Secker & Warburg.

Eliot, T. S. (1974) *Collected Poems 1909–1962*. London: Faber & Faber.

Ellis, John (1996) 'The Quality Film Adventure: British Critics and the Cinema, 1942–48,' in Andrew Higson (ed.) *Dissolving Views: Key Writing on British Cinema*, London: Cassell, 66–93.

Elsaesser, Thomas (1987) 'Tales of Sound and Fury: Observations on the Family Melodrama,' in Christine Gledhill (ed.) *Home is Where the Heart Is*. London: BFI Publishing, 43–69.

Ernst, Max (1976) *Une semaine de bonté: A Surrealist Novel in Collage* [1934]. New York: Dover.

Fell, John L. (1986) *Film and the Narrative Tradition*. Berkeley: California University Press.

Finler, Joel W. (1992) *The Hollywood Story: Everything You Ever Wanted to Know about the American Movie Business*. London: Mandarin.

Fishman, William J. (1988) *East End 1888: A Year in a London Borough among the Labouring Poor*. London: Duckworth.

Fletcher, John (1995) 'Primal Scenes and the Female Gothic: *Rebecca* and *Gaslight*,' in *Screen*, 36 (4), 341–70.

Ford, George H. (1981) 'Light in Darkness: Gas, Oil, and Tallow in Dickens's *Bleak House*,' in Samuel I. Mintz, Alice Chandler, and Christopher Mulvey (eds.) *From Smollett to James: Studies in the Novel and Other Essays Presented to Edgar Johnson*. Charlottesville: University Press of Virginia, 183–210.

Foucault, Michel (1981) *The History of Sexuality, Vol. 1*, tr. Robert Hurley. Harmondsworth: Penguin.

Francke, Lizzie (1993) 'The Piano,' in *Sight and Sound*, NS, 3 (11) (1993), 50–51.

Frank, Frederick S. (1998) 'Gothic Gold: The Sadleir-Black Gothic Collection,' in *Studies in Eighteenth–Century Culture*, 26, 287–312.

Gay, Peter (1984) *The Bourgeois Experience: Victoria to Freud. Vol. 1: The Education of the Senses*. Oxford: Oxford University Press.

——— (1994) 'They Weren't Thinking of England' [review of *The Making of Victorian Sexuality* by Michael Mason], in *Times Literary Supplement*, 4736, 22.

Giedion, Siegfried (1969) *Mechanization Takes Command: A Contribution to Anonymous History* [1948]. New York: Norton.

Gledhill, Christine (1992) 'Between Melodrama and Realism: Anthony Asquith's *Underground* and King Vidor's *The Crowd*,' in Jane Gaines (ed.) *Classical Hollywood Narrative: The Paradigm Wars*. Durham, N.C.: Duke University Press, 129–67.

——— (1987) 'The Melodramatic Field: An Investigation,' in Christine Gledhill (ed.) *Home is Where the Heart Is: Studies in Melodrama and the Woman's Film*. London: BFI Publishing, 5–39.

Gloag, John (1947) *The English Tradition in Design*. London: Adam & Charles Black.

Gorey, Edward (1998) *Gashlycrumb Tinies or After the Outing* [1963]. London: Bloomsbury.

Gosse, Edmund (1918) 'The Agony of the Victorian Age,' in *Edinburgh Review*, 228, 276–95.

——— (1907) *Father and Son*. London: Heinemann.

Graves, Robert, and Alan Hodge (1961) *The Long Weekend: A Social History of Great Britain, 1918–1939* [1940]. London: Four Square Books.

Gray, Donald (1977) 'Picturesque London,' in *Indiana University Bookman*, 12, 41–62.

Grimstead, David (1971) 'Melodrama as Echo of the Historically Voiceless,' in Tamara K. Haraven (ed.) *Anonymous Americans*. Englewood Cliffs, N. J.: Prentice-Hall, 80–98.

Grow, Laurence, and Dina Van Zwech (1984) *American Victorian: A Style and Source Book*. New York: Harper & Row.

Gunning, Tom (2000) *The Films of Fritz Lang: Allegories of Vision and Modernity*. London: BFI Publishing.

Gussow, Mel (1971) *Don't Say Yes Until I Finish Talking: A Biography of Darryl F. Zanuck*. London: W.H. Allen.

Hamilton, Bruce (1972) *The Light Went Out*. London: Constable.

Hamilton, Patrick (1939) *Gas Light: A Victorian Thriller in Three Acts*. London: Constable.

——— (1974) *Hangover Square: A Story of Darkest Earl's Court* [1941]. Harmondsworth: Penguin.

Hardy, Thomas J. (1934) 'Those Victorians,' in *Books on the Shelf*. London: Phillip Allen.

Haralovich, Mary Beth (1979) 'Sherlock Holmes: Genre and Industrial Practice,' in *Journal of the University Film Association*, 31 (2), 53–57.

Harper, Sue (1994) *Picturing the Past: The Rise and Fall of the British Costume Film*. London: BFI Publishing.

Harrison, Brian (1973) 'Pubs,' in H. J. Dyos and Michael Wolff (eds.) *The Victorian City*, Vol. I. London: Routledge & Kegan Paul, 161–90.

Hauptman, Jodi (1999) *Joseph Cornell: Stargazing in the Cinema*. New Haven and London: Yale University Press.

Haycraft, Howard (1941) *Murder for Pleasure: The Life and Times of the Detective Story*. New York: Appleton-Century.

Haydock, Ron (1978) *Deerstalker: Holmes and Watson on Screen*. Metuchen, N.J.: Scarecrow Press.

Heilman, Robert (1958) 'Charlotte Brontë's New Gothic,' in R. C. Rathburn and M. Steinmann (eds.) *From Jane Austen to Joseph Conrad*. Minneapolis: University of Minnesota Press, 118–32.

Higham, Charles, and Joel Greenberg (1968) *Hollywood in the Forties*. London: A. Zwemmer.

Higson, Andrew (1996) 'The Heritage Film and British Cinema,' in Andrew Higson (ed.) *Dissolving Views: Key Writings on British Cinema*. London: Cassell, 232–48.

Hobsbawm, Eric (1992) 'Introduction: Inventing Traditions,' in Eric Hobsbawm and Terence Ranger (eds.) *The Invention of Tradition*. Cambridge: Cambridge University Press, 1–14.

Hoggart, Richard (1958) *The Uses of Literacy: Aspects of Working Class Life with Special Reference to Publications and Entertainments*. Harmondsworth: Penguin.

Hollinger, Karen (1993) 'The Female Oedipal Drama of *Rebecca* from Novel to Film,' in *Quarterly Review of Film and Video*, 14 (4), 17–30.

Holroyd, Michael (1968) *Lytton Strachey: A Critical Biography. Vol. II. The Years of Achievement (1910–1932)*. London: Heinemann.

House, Humphrey (1955) 'Are the Victorians Coming Back?,' in *All in Due Time: The Collected Essays and Broadcast Talks of Humphrey House*. London: Hart-Davis, 75–93.

Howe, David Walker (1975) 'American Victorianism as a Culture,' in *American Quarterly*, 27 (5), 507–32.

Hunter, Jane H. (1992) 'Inscribing the Self in the Heart of the Family: Diaries and Girlhood in Late-Victorian America' in *American Quarterly*, 44 (1), 51–81.

Hurst, Richard Maurice (1979) *Republic Studios: Between Poverty Row and the Majors*. Metuchen, N.J.: Scarecrow Press.

Ingham, John (ed.) (1987) *Assault on Victorianism: The Rise of Popular Culture in America 1890–1945*. Toronto: Canadian Scholars' Press.

Jackson, Rosemary (1981) *Fantasy: The Literature of Subversion*. London: Methuen.

James, Henry (1974) 'Miss Braddon' [1865] in Norman Page (ed.) *Wilkie Collins: The Critical Heritage*. London: Routledge, 122–24.

James, Louis (1974) *Fiction for the Working Man 1830–50: A Study of the Literature Produced for the Working Classes in Early Victorian Urban England*. Harmondsworth: Penguin.

——— (1980) 'Was Jerrold's Black Ey'd Susan more popular than Wordsworth's Lucy?,' in David Bradby, Louis James, and Bernard Sharratt (eds.) *Performance and Politics in Popular Drama*. Cambridge: Cambridge University Press, 3–16.

James, P. D. (1997) *A Certain Justice*. London: Faber & Faber.

Jansen, Joh (1992) 'City Lights as Seen by Painters,' in *International Lighting Review*. 43 (3), 118–22.

——— (1974) 'Lighting Effects in Painting,' special issue of *International Lighting Review*. 25 (4).

Jenkins, Steve (1982) '*Bluebeard*,' in *Monthly Film Bulletin*, 94 (577), 144–45.

Jones, Nigel (1991) *Through a Glass Darkly: The Life of Patrick Hamilton*. London: Scribner.

Kaplan, E. Ann (1992) *Motherhood and Representation: The Mother in Popular Culture and Melodrama*. London: Routledge.

Kavan, Anne (1946) 'Back to Victoria,' in *Horizon*, 13, 61–66.

Keogh, J. G. (1984) 'The Crowd in No Man's Land: Gas-Light and Poe's Symbolic Effects,' in *Antigonish Review*. 58, 19–31.

Kitses, Jim (1969) *Horizons West: Anthony Mann, Budd Boetticher, Sam Peckinpah: Studies of Authorship within the Western*. London: Thames & Hudson.

Koppes, Clayton R., and Gregory D. Black (1987) 'What to Show the World: The Office of War Information and Hollywood, 1942–1945,' in *Journal of American History*, 64 (1), 87–105.

Kroll, Eric (ed.) (1995) *The Complete Reprint of John Willie's Bizarre*, 2 Vols. Köln: Taschen.

Lancaster, Osbert (1953) *Homes, Sweet Homes*, revised edition. London: John Murray.

Laver, James (1945) *Taste and Fashion: From the French Revolution to the Present Day*, revised edition. London: Harrap.

Lee, Ruth Webb (1944) *Victorian Glass: Specialties of the Nineteenth Century*. Northboro, Mass.: published by the author.

Leonard, William T. (1981) *Theatre: Stage to Screen to Television*, 2 Vols. Metuchen: Scarecrow Press.

Lichton, Frances (1950) *Decorative Art of Victoria's Era*. New York: Charles Scribners.

Lowndes, M. Belloc (1947) *The Lodger* [1913]. London: Pan.

McArthur, Colin (1997) 'Chinese Boxes and Russian Dolls: Tracking the Elusive Cinematic City,' in David B. Clarke (ed.) *The Cinematic City*. London: Routledge, 19–45.

McCarthy, Todd (1997) *Howard Hawks: The Grey Fox of Hollywood*. New York: Grove Press.

MacFarlane, Brian (1986) 'A Literary Cinema? British Films and British Novels,' in Charles Barr (ed.) *All Our Yesterdays: 90 Years of British Cinema*. London: British Film Institute, 120–42.

MacGovern, James R. (1987) 'The American Woman: Pre-World War I Freedom in Manners and Morals,' in John Ingham (ed.) *Assault on Victorianism: The Rise of Popular Culture in America 1890–1945*. Toronto: Canadian Scholars' Press, 94–113.

Machen, Arthur (1926) 'The Poor Victorians,' in *Dog and Duck: A London Calendar Et Caetera*. London: Jonathan Cape, 137–45.

MacKenzie, Compton (1933) *Literature in My Time*. London: Rich & Cowan.

McShine, Kynaston (ed.) (1990) *Joseph Cornell*. New York: Museum of Modern Art.

Maltby, Richard (1995) *Hollywood: An Introduction*. Oxford: Blackwell.

—— (1992) 'To Prevent the Prevalent Type of Book: Censorship and Adaptation in Hollywood, 1924–1934,' in *American Quarterly*, 44 (4), 554–83.

Mank, Gregory William (1994) *Hollywood Cauldron: Thirteen Horror Films from the Genre's Golden Age*. Jefferson, N.C.: McFarland.

Marcus, Steven (1969) *The Other Victorians: A Study of Sexuality and Pornography in Mid-Nineteenth-Century Britain*. London: Corgi.

Marsh, Ngaio (1947) *The Final Curtain*. London: Collins.

Mason, Michael (1994) *The Making of Victorian Sexuality*. Oxford: Oxford University Press.

Massingham, H. J., and Hugh (eds.) (1932) *The Great Victorians*. London: Nicholson & Watson.

Mast, Gerald (1982) *Howard Hawks: Storyteller*. New York: Oxford University Press.

May, Larry (1983) *Screening out the Past: The Birth of Mass Culture and the Motion Picture Industry*. Chicago: University of Chicago Press.

Mayhew, Henry (1851) *London Labor and London Poor*. Vol. 1. London: Griffen Bohn.

Meisel, Martin (1994) 'Scattered Chiaroscuro: Melodrama as a Matter of Seeing' in Jacky Bratton, Jim Cook, and Christine Gledhill (eds.) *Melodrama: Stage Picture Screen*. London: BFI Publishing, 65–81.

Mighall, Robert (1999) *A Geography of Victorian Gothic Fiction: Mapping History's Nightmares*. Oxford: Oxford University Press.

—— (1998) '*Vampires and Victorians: Count Dracula and the Return of the Repressive Hypothesis*,' in Garry Day (ed.) *Varieties of Victorianism: The Uses of a Past*. Macmillan 236–49.

Modleski, Tania (1984) *Loving with a Vengeance: Mass Produced Fantasies for Women*. New York: Methuen.

Moretti, Franco (1998) *Atlas of the European Novel 1800–1900*. London: Verso.

Muggeridge, Malcolm (1971) *The Thirties, 1930–1940, in Great Britain* [1940]. London: Fontana.

Murdock, Walter (1938) *The Victorian Era: Its Strength and Weakness*. Sydney: Angus & Robertson.

Myers, Denys Peter (1990) *Gaslighting in America: A Pictorial Survey, 1815–1910*. New York: Dover.

Narremore, James (1998) *More Than Night: Film Noir and Its Contexts*. Berkeley: California University Press.

Neale, Steve (1993) 'Melo Talk: On the Meaning and Use of the Term "Melodrama" in the American Trade Press,' in *Velvet Light Trap*. 32, 66–89.

——— (1999) 'Recent Work on Melodrama and the Woman's Film,' in Pam Cook and Mieke Bernick (eds.) *The Cinema Book*, 2nd edition. London: BFI Publishing, 164–66.

Nowell-Smith, Geoffrey (1996) 'The Heyday of the Silents,' in Geoffrey Nowell-Smith (ed.) *The Oxford History of World Cinema*. Oxford: Oxford University Press, 192–204

——— (1987) 'Minnelli and Melodrama,' in Christine Gledhill (ed.) *Home is Where the Heart Is: Studies in Melodrama and the Woman's Film*. London: BFI Publishing, 70–74.

O'Dea, William T. (1958) *The Social History of Lighting*. London: Routledge.

Orwell, George (1994a) 'Benefit of Clergy: Some Notes on Salvador Dali' [1944] in *The Penguin Essays of George Orwell*. Harmondsworth: Penguin, 248–56.

——— (1994b) 'Decline of the English Murder' [1946] in *The Penguin Essays of George Orwell*. Harmondsworth: Penguin, 345–48.

Ottoson, Robert (1981) *A Reference Guide to the American Film Noir: 1940–1958*. New York: Garland.

Place, J. A., and L. S. Peterson (1976) 'Some Visual Motifs of *Film Noir*,' in Bill Nichols (ed.) *Movies and Methods*. Berkeley: University of California Press, 325–38.

Poe, Edgar Allan (1986) 'The Philosophy of Furniture' [1840], in *The Fall of the House of Usher and Other Writings: Poems, Tales, Essays, and Reviews*. Harmondsworth: Penguin, 414–20.

——— (1908) 'The Man of the Crowd' [1840] in *Tales of Mystery and Imagination*. London: Dent, 101–9.

Prawer, S. S. (1980) *Caligari's Children: The Film as Tale of Terror*. Oxford: Oxford University Press.

Quiller-Couch, Arthur (1922) 'The Victorian Age' in *Studies in Literature*. Cambridge: Cambridge University Press, 283–305.

Radcliffe, Ann (1980) *The Mysteries of Udolpho* [1794]. Oxford: Oxford University Press.

Radway, Janice (1981) 'The Utopian Impulse: Popular Literature, Gothic Romances and Feminist Protest,' in *American Quarterly*, 33 (2), 140–62.

Rahill, Frank (1967) *The World of Melodrama*. Philadelphia: Pennsylvania State University Press.

Reff, Theodore (1987) 'Manet and the Paris of Haussman and Baudelaire,' in William Sharpe and Leonard Walloch (eds.) *Visions of the Modern City: Essays in History, Art and Literature*. Baltimore: John Hopkins University Press, 135–67.

Rich, Adrienne (1980) 'Women and Honor: Some Notes on Lying,' in *On Lies, Secrets, and Silence, Selected Prose 1966–1978*. London: Virago, 185–94.

Richards, Jeffrey (1986) *Thorold Dickinson: The Man and His Films*. London: Croom Helm.

—— (1998) 'Tod Slaughter and the Cinema of Excess,' in Jeffrey Richards (ed.) *The Unknown 1930s: An Alternative History of the British Cinema, 1929–1939*. London: I. B. Tauris, 138–59.

——, and Dorothy Sheridan (eds.) (1987) *Mass-Observation at the Movies*. London: Routledge & Kegan Paul.

Roe, F. Gordon (1952) *Victorian Furniture*. London: Phoenix House.

Russ, Joanna (1973) 'Somebody's Trying to Kill Me and I Think It's My Husband: The Modern Gothic,' in *Journal of Popular Culture*, 6 (2), 666–91.

Rybcznyski, Witold (1988) *Home: A Short History of an Idea*. London: Heinemann.

Sadleir, Michael (1981) *Fanny by Gaslight* [1940]. Harmondsworth: Penguin.

—— (1947a) *Forlorn Street*. London: Constable.

—— (1947b) *Victorian Fiction: An Exhibition of Original Editions at 7 Albemarle Street, London, January to February 1947, arranged by John Carter with the Collaboration of Michael Sadleir*. Cambridge: Cambridge University Press.

—— (1951) *Nineteenth-Century Fiction: A Bibliographical Record, Based on His Own Collection*, Vol.1. London: Constable.

—— (1944) '"All Horrid?" Jane Austen and the Gothic Romance' in *Things Past*. London: Constable, 167–200.

Sala, George Augustus (1859) *Gaslight and Daylight*. London: Chapman & Hall.

Samuel, Raphael (1989) 'Introduction: Exciting to be English,' in Raphael Samuel (ed.) *Patriotism*. London: Routledge, xviii–lxvii.

—— (1994) *Theatres of Memory, Vol. 1: Past and Present in Contemporary Culture*. London: Verso.

Schatz, Thomas (1999) *Boom and Bust: American Cinema in the 1940s*. Berkeley: University of California Press.

—— (1981) *Hollywood Genres, Formulas, Filmmaking, and the Studio System*. New York: Random House.

Schirelbasch, W. (1988) *Disenchanted Night: The Industrialization of Light in the Nineteenth Century*. Berkeley: University of California Press.

Shearing, Joseph (1948) *For Her to See*. New York: Pocket Books [edition published under the title *So Evil My Love*].

Showalter, Elaine (1976) 'Desperate Remedies: Sensation Novels of the 1860s,' in *The Victorian Newsletter*, 49, 1–5.

Siegel, Don (1993) *A Siegel Film, An Autobiography*. London: Faber & Faber.

Silver, Alain, and Elizabeth Ward (eds.) (1980) *Film Noir*. London: Secker & Warburg.

Sitwell, Osbert (1931) 'Foreword' in Margaret Barton and Osbert Sitwell (eds.) *Victoriana: A Symposium of Victorian Wisdom*. London: Duckworth, v–vi.

——— (1935) 'Victorianism: An English Disease' in *Penny Foolish: A Book of Tirades and Panegyrics*. London: Macmillan, 76–79.

Smith, Edgar W. (ed.) (1944) *Profile by Gaslight: An Irregular Reader About the Private Life of Sherlock Holmes*. New York: Simon & Schuster.

Smith, Murray (1988) '*Film Noir*, the Female Gothic, and *Deception*,' in *Wide Angle*, 10 (1), 62–75.

Solomon, Aubrey (1988) *Twentieth Century-Fox: A Corporate and Financial History*. Metuchen, N.J.: Scarecrow.

Solomon, Deborah (1997) *Utopia Parkway: The Life and Work of Joseph Cornell*. London: Jonathan Cape.

Sorlin, Pierre (1980) *The Film in History: Restaging the Past*. Oxford: Blackwell.

Spencer, Kathleen (1987) 'Victorian Urban Gothic: The First Modern Fantastic Literature,' in George E. Slusser and Eric S. Rabkin (eds.) *Intersections, Fantasy and Science Fiction*. Carbondale: South Illinois University Press, 87–96.

Stevenson, Robert Louis (1946) *A Child's Garden of Verses* [1885]. London: Collins.

——— (1899) 'A Plea for Gas Lamps' in *Virginibus Puerisque*. London: Chatto & Windus, 271–78.

——— (1979) *The Strange Case of Dr. Jekyll and Mr. Hyde and Other Stories* [1886]. Harmondsworth: Penguin.

Stewart, Garrett (1995) 'Film's Victorian Retrofit,' in *Victorian Studies*, 38 (2), 153–98.

Stokes, Roy (1980) *Michael Sadleir: 1888–1957*. Metuchen, N.J.: Scarecrow.

Storey, Walter Rendell (1947) *Furnishing in Style*. New York: American Studio Books.

——— (1937) *Period Influence in Interior Decoration*. New York: Harper & Bros.

Strachey, Lytton (1986) *Eminent Victorians* [1918]. Harmondsworth: Penguin.

——— (1971) *Queen Victoria* [1921]. Harmondsworth: Penguin.

Thomas, Trefor (1996) 'Introduction' to G. W. M. Reynolds *The Mysteries of London*. Keele: Keele University Press, vii–xxiv.

Todorov, Tzvetan (1977) *The Poetics of Prose*, tr. Richard Howard. Oxford: Oxford University Press.

Trevelyan, G. M. (1949) 'Introducing the Ideas and Beliefs of the Victorians,' in *Ideas and Beliefs of the Victorians: An Historical Revaluation of the Victorian Age*. London, 1949: Sylvan Press, 15–19.

Tristan, Flora (1982) *The London Journal of Flora Tristan* [1840–1842], tr. Jean Hawkes. London: Virago.

Vardac, Nicholas (1949) *Stage to Screen: Theatrical Origins of Early Film, David Garrick to D. W. Griffith*. New York: Da Capo.

Vardedoe, Kirk, and Adam Gopnik (1990) *High and Low, Modern Art and Popular Culture*. New York: Museum of Modern Art.

Vicinus, Martha (1977a) 'Dark London,' in *Indiana University Bookman*, 12, 63–92.

—— (1977b) 'Introduction,' in *Indiana University Bookman*, 12, 1–4.

Viviani, Christian (1987) 'Who is Without Sin?: The Maternal Melodrama in American Film, 1930–39,' in Christine Gledhill (ed.) *Home is Where the Heart Is: Studies in Melodrama and the Woman's Film*. London: BFI Publishing, 83–99.

Waldman, Diane (1990) 'Architectural Metaphor in the Gothic Romance Film,' in *Iris*, 12, 55–69.

—— (1983) '"At Last I Can Tell It To Someone!": Feminine Point of View and Subjectivity in the Gothic Romance Film of the 1940s,' in *Cinema Journal*, 23 (2), 29–40.

—— (1982) 'The Childish, the Insane, and the Ugly: The Representation of Modern Art in Popular Films and Fiction of the Forties,' in *Wide Angle*, 5 (2), 52–65.

Walsh, Andrea (1984) *Women's Film and Female Experience, 1940–50*. New York: Praeger.

Walvin, James (1988) *Victorian Values*. London: Cardinal.

Waugh, Evelyn (1983a) 'Collectors' Pieces' [review of *Victorian Furniture* by R. W. Symonds and B. B. Whineray, and *19th Century Furniture* by Elizabeth Aslin, 1962], in *The Essays, Articles, and Reviews of Evelyn Waugh*, ed. Donat Gallagher. London: Methuen, 597–601

—— (1983b) 'Let Us Return to the Nineties; But not to Oscar Wilde' [1930], in *The Essays, Articles, and Reviews of Evelyn Waugh*, ed. Donat Gallagher. London: Methuen, 122–25.

Webb, Peter (1983) 'Sexual Attitudes in Victorian Art and Literature,' in *The Erotic Arts*, revised edition. London: Phaidon, 186–202.

West, Rebecca (1984) *The Fountain Overflows* [1957]. London: Virago.

Wilde, Oscar (1997) *Complete Poetry*, Isobel Murray (ed.) Oxford: Oxford University Press.

Willemen, Paul (1972–73) 'Towards an Analysis of the Sirkian System,' in *Screen*, 13 (4), 128–34.

Williams, Linda (1988) 'Feminist Film Theory: *Mildred Pierce* and the Second World War,' in E. Dierdre Pribram (ed.) *Female Spectators*. London: Verso, 12–30.

Williams, Raymond (1973) *The Country and the City*. London: Chatto & Windus.

Wilson, Shelagh (1999) 'Monsters and Monstrosities: Grotesque Taste and Victorian Design,' in Colin Trodd, Paul Barlow and David Amigani (eds.), *Victorian Culture and the Idea of the Grotesque*. Aldershot: Ashgate, 143–62.

Wood, Ellen (1984) *East Lynne* [1861]. London: J. M. Dent.

Worthington, William E. (1986) *Beyond the City Lights: American Domestic Gas Lighting Systems; An Exhibition at the National Museum of American History, October 17, 1985-April 20 1986*. Washington, D.C.: Smithsonian Institute.

Yates, Raymond F., and W. Marguerite (1949) *A Guide to Victorian Antiques, with Notes on the Early Nineteenth Century.* New York: Harper & Bros.

Yeats, W. B. (1936) 'Introduction,' in *Oxford Book of Modern Verse*, chosen by W. B. Yeats. Oxford: Clarendon Press, v-xlii.

Zola, Émile (1962) *Therese Raquin* [1868], tr. Leonard Tancock. Harmondsworth: Penguin.

# INDEX